SURFING

—— THE ——

EDGE OF CHAOS

Also by Richard Pascale

The Art of Japanese Management (coauthor)

Managing on the Edge: How the Smartest Companies Use Conflict to Stay Ahead

SURFING

—— THE ——

EDGE OF CHAOS

The Laws of Nature and the New Laws of Business

RICHARD T. PASCALE

MARK MILLEMANN and LINDA GIOJA

THREE RIVERS PRESS

NEW YORK

Published by Three Rivers Press, New York, New York. Member of the Crown Publishing Group.

Random House, Inc. New York, Toronto, London, Sydney, Auckland
www.randomhouse.com

Three Rivers Press and the Tugboat design are registered trademarks of Random House, Inc.

Originally published in hardcover by Crown Business in 2000.

Printed in the United States of America

Library of Congress Cataloging-in-Publication Data

Pascale, Richard T.
  Surfing the edge of chaos : the laws of nature and the new laws of business / Richard Pascale, Mark Millemann, and Linda Gioja.—1st ed.
  Includes bibliographical references.
  1. Management science. I. Millemann, Mark. II. Gioja, Linda. III. Title.
  T56.P355   2000
  658—dc21   00-031746

ISBN 0-609-80883-4

10 9 8 7 6 5 4 3

First Paperback Edition

Dedicated to Ann Carol, Pat, and Jeffry
for the foundation of love
and the structure of support

CONTENTS

SURFING
—— THE ——
EDGE OF CHAOS

CHAPTER 1

MANAGEMENT AND THE SCIENTIFIC RENAISSANCE

There is a new scientific renaissance in the making. It will usher in new industries, alter how businesses compete, and change how companies are managed. This book explores the managerial implications of this new renaissance.

Scientific discovery shapes managerial thinking. Principles identified more than two hundred years ago, during an earlier scientific renaissance, have had wide influence on how managers think today. Derivative ideas from Newton's laws of motion and his early work on gas thermodynamics were literally lifted, equation by equation, and applied to the emerging field of economics.[1] When they were extended into the realm of enterprise, these applications shaped the practice of management and today's deep-seated beliefs about change.

We are entering another scientific renaissance. The magnets for the inquiry are called *complex adaptive systems*. Also known as "complexity science," this work grapples with the mysteries of life itself, and is propelled forward by the confluence of three streams of

1

inquiry: (1) breakthrough discoveries in the life sciences (e.g., biology, medicine, and ecology); (2) insights of the social sciences (e.g., sociology, psychology, and economics); and (3) new developments in the hard sciences (e.g., physics, mathematics, and information technology). The resulting work has revealed exciting insights into life and has opened up new avenues for management.[2]

Efforts to understand life are as old as humanity itself. For uncounted millennia, they centered on the selective breeding of animals and plants to improve yields and reduce susceptibility to disease. By the time the first scientific renaissance ended in the 1880s, geneticist Gregor Mendel had unlocked the secrets of heredity.[3] Selective breeding, formerly an art, fell within the grasp of science.

A second milestone of great consequence was the discovery, in 1953, of the double helix of DNA by James Watson and Francis Crick.[4] By the end of the twentieth century, the vast new frontier they had opened was closing in on both understanding, and possibly altering, the biochemistry of life.

For several decades after Watson and Crick's discoveries, efforts to decipher DNA sequences and other facets of living systems were thwarted by their enormous complexity. But powerful computers and arcane technology for observing microscopic organisms and genetic dynamics permitted considerable progress. A trickle of breakthroughs began. Among them was the capacity to identify particular genes that made a plant or animal resistant to disease or amplified desirable features. By the 1990s, Genenech, Amgen, Immunex, Monsanto, and a host of other firms were developing biotechnology to the point where patented pharmaceuticals and seeds had become commercial realities. These nascent capabilities are accompanied, in turn, by new challenges—business, ethical, and social.

Living Systems and Organizational Change

Many subterranean streams have combined to form the current flow of interest in living systems. Most attention is galvanized by the extraordinary economic potential of biotechnology or the social consequences of vanishing rain forests and global warming. However, another tributary will prove as important as all the rest: Understanding the mysteries of life will alter how we think about organizations, management, and social change.

Businesses, it turns out, can learn a great deal from nature. Besides providing an account of pathbreaking applications of living systems theory to management, this book reveals how cornerstone principles of the life sciences have been translated into practice and have considerably improved the odds of success in achieving discontinuous change.

The New "Life" Cycle

The industrial revolution was fueled by the earlier scientific renaissance. It was predicated on the machine model of take → make → break: taking raw materials, converting them into products, and eventually "breaking"—in two meanings of the word—both breaking environmental and social balance through high-impact extraction and production techniques, and by fostering a spiral of obsolescence in which the products are used and discarded. Clear-cut forests, rusting machinery, and the heaping detritus of salvage yards are the fossil remains of this era.

The emerging life science model unfolds like a species in a new ecological niche: innovate → proliferate → aggregate. Nature favors adaptation and fleet-footedness. Most species compete when they must, but organisms strive, when possible, to reproduce more rapidly than their rivals and to dominate by sheer strength of numbers. Economists call this "increasing returns." Discovering a new niche and proliferating rapidly fosters ubiquity. One witnesses it in commerce when Microsoft Windows, or a brand franchise such as Amazon.com, or the QWERTY sequence of a keyboard becomes the *lingua franca* for an industry or technology. Major families may join forces to create self-reinforcing arrangements. In nature, in the benevolent exchange between insects and plants, nectar is swapped for pollination services. In business, the merger of AOL with Time Warner is an effort to establish supremacy through aggregation in the e-business and communications industries.

Of Colonies and Companies

Rapid rates of change, an explosion of new insights from the life sciences, and the insufficiency of the machine model have created a critical mass for a revolution in management thinking. The fallout of the scientific renaissance has fostered uncertainty and soul-searching.[5] Executives ask: How do we make practical sense of all this? How do we get the change and performance we need? Clues, it turns out, are to be found in the world of the termite.

Come with us to a remarkable structure: the twelve-foot-high mound of the African termite, home to millions of inhabitants.[6]

The mound is an architectural marvel. Naturalist Richard Conniff has described its perfect arches, spiral staircases, nurseries, storage facilities, and living quarters that vary with the status of individual termites. Tunnels radiate out from the mound more than 160 feet in any direction. These structures enable the termites to forage for grass, wood, and water within an 80,000-square-foot area without being exposed to predators.[7]

Within the mound, a ventilation system—operated by opening and closing vents—creates a motion similar to respiration. Oxygen is "inhaled" into the twelve-foot tower of mud, and carbon dioxide is "exhaled." The system also holds the internal temperature steady (plus or minus one degree Fahrenheit) even though the external climate ranges from freezing winters to 100-degree-plus summers. Humidity is constant at 90 percent.[8]

This organizational wonder—which evolved over 100 million years or so—is a tribute to an elaborate social structure. Every inhabitant obeys a series of genetically programmed *rules,* such as: "Position yourself between the termite in front and the one behind, and pass on whatever comes your way." As a whole, members of the mound constitute a sophisticated society that makes it possible to meet the ever changing needs of the colony.[9]

Entomologists have known about the workings of the termite for centuries. In the past two decades, though, a group of leading scientists has offered a different, intriguing perspective. They see the mound as a stunning example of a *complex adaptive system*.

A complex adaptive system is formally defined as a system of independent agents that can act in parallel, develop "models" as to how things work in their environment, and, most importantly, refine those models through learning and adaptation.[10] The human immune system is a complex adaptive system. So is a rain forest, a termite colony, and a business.

Over the past several years, substantial literature has introduced the new science of *complexity*. This is a broad-based inquiry into the common properties of all living things—beehives and bond traders, ant colonies and enterprises, ecologies and economies, you and me. In aggregate, the coverage on this topic to date has achieved two significant things:

1. It has evoked wonder and excitement about the living world around us—how life surges and declines; how nature competes, cooperates, and thrives on change.
2. It has whetted some managerial appetites for a new approach that might help to unshackle the potential of people and organizations and has begun to challenge the machine model as a suitable management platform for the information age.

We aim to take a step beyond. This book describes a new management model based on the nature of nature, but it also does what no other book has done before. It distills, from the science of complexity, four bedrock principles that are inherently and powerfully applicable to the living system called a business.

In brief, these principles are:

1. *Equilibrium is* a precursor to *death*. When a living system is in a state of equilibrium, it is less responsive to changes occurring around it. This places it at maximum risk.
2. In the face of threat, or when galvanized by a compelling opportunity, living things move toward the *edge of chaos*. This condition evokes higher levels of mutation and experimentation, and fresh new solutions are more likely to be found.
3. When this excitation takes place, the components of living systems *self-organize* and new forms and repertoires *emerge* from the turmoil.
4. Living systems cannot be *directed* along a linear path. Unforeseen consequences are inevitable. The challenge is to *disturb* them in a manner that approximates the desired outcome.

If properly employed, these principles allow enterprises to thrive and revitalize themselves. In contrast, the machine-age principles, although familiar and enduring, often quietly facilitate the stagnation and decline of traditional enterprises that are faced with discontinuous change.

The choice is that simple and that stark.

Complexity and *chaos* are frequently used interchangeably, even though they have almost nothing in common. The world is not chaotic; it is complex.

Humans tend to regard as chaotic that which they cannot control. This creates confusion over what is meant by the term *chaos*. From a scientific point of view, chaos is that unlikely occurrence in which patterns cannot be found nor interrelationships understood.[11] A swarm of bees or the ants that overrun a picnic blanket may seem chaotic but they are actually only behaving as a complex adaptive systems. E-commerce and the upending of traditional business platforms may feel "chaotic," but, technically, these innovations are complex.

Living Systems Pioneers

Let us be clear. "Living systems" isn't a metaphor for how human institutions operate. It's the way it is.[12] Pioneering efforts by the companies described herein have demonstrated that ideas can produce a concrete bottom-line impact and profound transformational change. Indeed, some of the largest and most successful organizational transformations during recent years have been modeled on the principles of living systems. This book was largely inspired by business leaders who not only embraced those principles as their guidelines for change, but also, through trial and error, found ways to translate them into concrete management practices.

Surfing the Edge of Chaos bridges theory and practice through six in-depth examples of living systems: British Petroleum, Hewlett-Packard, Monsanto, Royal Dutch/Shell, Sears, and the U.S. Army. We have observed leaders who explicitly or implicitly regarded their organizations as living systems and employed the four principles described above as a superior management platform in revitalizing their enterprises. We have seen executives consciously put these insights into practical use and create demonstrable successes that most probably could not have been achieved otherwise. Most business books have examples, but few take the long view and trace the ups and downs. We discuss both the successes and the failures.

There is no mystery—no secret formula, no magic potion—about the way the living systems model works. The examples identify insights about complex adaptive systems as they operate in the natural world and translate them to the world of business. Sensible lessons are gathered from observing the pitfalls and triumphs experienced by companies that have adopted the new model.

Our personal advisory relationships with the CEOs and other senior leaders in most of the six organizations provide intimate accounts of what transpired, not anecdotal or journalistic treatments. These accounts point toward practical design principles and processes and toward tools that can be used to unleash the potential of an organization. A fresh and unorthodox brand of leadership is necessary to initiate and shepherd an adaptive journey. Finally, we identify core disciplines that enable an organization to *sustain* its vitality once it has been reawakened.

Those are our promises for this book.

We do not propose that the four principles stated earlier form a new silver bullet. The practices that stem from them are not foolproof; indeed, they are not always superior to traditional approaches. As we shall see shortly, a lot depends on the challenge faced and the magnitude of change sought.

"Concrete" Examples

In Mexico, Cemex, the world's third largest (and only global) cement company, dispatches its fleet of cement mixers based on the same simple rules that govern how ants scavenge a colony's territory with ruthless efficiency. Cemex recognizes what homeowners know only too well: Construction projects *never* proceed on schedule. Schedule a cement delivery in advance and you can bank on the site's being ready earlier (high-cost workers then hang around awaiting the delivery with nothing to do) or not being ready as planned (the cement then starts to harden in the truck).

Suppliers and customers alike have unhappily accepted this state of affairs for years. Logically speaking, how could it be otherwise when the construction site's state of readiness is dependent on so many unpredictable elements? But Cemex defies that logic. It promises to provide cement *where* you want it and *when* you want it, on two hours' notice. Cemex sells promises—not just cement—and uses them as compelling marketplace differentiators. And Cemex delivers.

How is it possible?

Cemex loads its fleets of cement trucks each morning and dispatches them with no preordained destination. The trick lies in how they make their rounds. Like ants scavenging a territory, they are guided to their destination by simple rules. Ants use chemical messages (called pheromones) to convey these instructions; Cemex uses an algorithm based on *greed* (deliver as much cement as rapidly as possible to as many customers as possible) and *repulsion* (avoid duplication of effort by staying as far away from other cement trucks as possible). It's scary to have a fleet loaded with, of all products, wet cement, which could harden before it is delivered. Yet the ant model works with remarkable efficiency. Cemex has obliterated competition in the eight nations where it operates (including the western and southwestern regions of the United States). Cemex's decision to emulate a living system delivers an incremental return of $388 million per year to the bottom line.[13]

A fluke? Not hardly. In 1998, British Telcom introduced a similar system to dispatch its service fleet of 80,000 vehicles. Savings in the first year: £250 million.[14] The U.S. Army employed the ant pheromone model to direct its drone ground surveillance coverage in Bosnia and Serbia (and to redirect drones when one was shot down). Coverage efficiency increased from 60 percent (using the old mainframe-based optimization model) to 87 percent (feeding the ant algorithm into a battle-hardened personal computer).[15]

Cemex has adopted one of the simplest applications of complexity science. Our corporate examples extend considerably beyond this realm. At Monsanto (now merged with Upjohn to form Pharmacia), CEO Robert Shapiro embraced the framework of living systems as the centerpiece of his efforts to reinvent a lackluster manufacturer of low-margin petrochemicals as a leading life-sciences enterprise.

As subtext to this story, Shapiro, a longtime McKinsey client, had to mind-wrestle with the partners of the formidable consulting firm. Instead of the top-down strategic reinvention that McKinsey was advocating, Shapiro persuaded the members of the consulting team to play the role of stewards and facilitators.

Over 10,000 Monsanto employees became involved in 300 cross-business and cross-functional teams. Within that context, workers freed of top-side direction identified new business opportunities.

The campaign to implement these initiatives generated tensions that moved the company toward the edge of chaos. Self-organizing groups sparked dozens of breakthrough innovations and a staggering reduction in costs. Share price soared from $15 to $49. Along the way, Shapiro radically changed Monsanto's strategy and culture.[16]

Monsanto's transformation from an undifferentiated also-ran to a front-runner in genetically engineered crops impacted the world community in unforeseen ways. Opposition to bioengineering mounted, changing the companies' future.[17] Monsanto was confronted with another kind of disruptive change—one that was played out in the spotlight of media attention and shifting world opinion.

Management: Past and Future Tense

We have noted that contemporary business practices can trace their managerial heritage to the scientific work of Newton (irreducible and mathematical laws explaining the mechanics of nature) and Dalton (dividing complex molecules into individual atoms, and observing the interaction of molecules under pressure as the precursor to thermodynamics). As *The Wall Street Journal*'s Thomas Petzinger explains:[18]

> [From the 1680s onward], Isaac Newton was the new Moses, presenting a few simple equations—the laws of nature—which never failed in predicting the tides, the orbit or movement of any object that could be seen or felt. Output was exactly proportional to input. Everything was equal to the sum of its parts. Newton's mechanics seemed so perfect, so universal, that they became the organizing principles of all post-feudal society, including armies, churches, and economic institutions of every kind. . . . The very equations of economics, including many we use today, were built explicitly on the principles of mechanics and thermodynamics, right down to the terms and symbols. The economy was said to "have momentum," was "well oiled" or "gaining steam."
>
> As a model for everything, Newtonianism, it turned out, had limitations. It worked only within the narrow range of Newton's instruments.

The "laws of nature" fell to pieces in space, as Einstein's relativity physics showed, and at the subatomic level, as quantum physics showed. Scientists realized that however useful in solving smooth, mechanical problems, Newton's calculus was meaningless in understanding the vast preponderance of nature: the motion of currents, the growth of plants, the rise and fall of civilizations.

Einstein's insight into relativity—overturning, as it did, the orderly world of classical physics—exerted broad influence over many other disciplines. Early in the twentieth century, relativism was mirrored in art (Picasso and Pollack), poetry (T. S. Eliot), music (Stravinsky), literature (James Joyce), and interpretative religion. Object and observer became inseparable. Structure was connected to process, the medium to the message, doing to being. The rational and analytical were inseparable from the emotional and intuitive.[19]

Except in management. The reason is plain enough: If it ain't broke, don't fix it. For the greater part of the century, particularly from the 1950s onward, dazzling new technologies (electronics, engineered materials, computers, and bioengineering, to name a few) opened vast frontiers of commerce in which traditional management models flourished. Factor in fifty-five years without destructive global conflict and the result was the emergence of industrial economies with vast wealth, spending power, and consumer appetites. A good part of the twentieth century, excluding the Great Depression and the war years, may be regarded as an era of low-hanging fruit. In short, management didn't change because it didn't have to. True to Woody Allen's quip that 90 percent of life is just showing up, our large and lumbering corporations thrived because they showed up; their lack of agility was not a significant drawback, given their advantages of scale and the cornucopia of economic opportunity spread before them.

Then some unlikely startups, borne on the wings of new business models, proceeded to spoil the party. The newcomers—companies like Amazon.com, Southwest Airlines, Home Depot, and Nokia—ran rings around traditional companies mired in their comfortable equilibrium.

Gradually, a new consensus began to form within the ranks of management experts. It recognized that companies with talent and the instincts to innovate and collaborate can commercialize ideas and seize the high ground before slower, well-established rivals even spot the new hill. It held that by inspiring frontline workers to operate as independent agents, pursuing their own solutions with little central control, formidable business enterprises and social movements can emerge.

But beware: While this new agile species exploits some elements of complexity, a halfway understanding of what has transpired is likely to create more hazards than heroes. In other words, if you are hoping to skim this book to glean a few new tricks from the examples and resettle into the easy chair of the old mindset, think twice. It would be akin to trading in a reliable workhorse like the World War II propeller-driven Spitfire for an F–18, but continuing to use inaccurate maps and a defective navigational system. You will just get to the wrong destination faster.

Corporations around the world now write checks for more than $50 billion a year in fees for "change consulting."[20] And that tab represents only a third of the overall change cost if severance costs, write-offs, and information technology purchases are included. Yet, consultants, academic surveys, and reports from the "changed" companies themselves indicate that a full 70 percent of those efforts fail.[21] The reason? We call it *social engineering,* a contemporary variant of the machine model's cause-and-effect thinking. *Social* is coupled with *engineering* to denote that most managers today, in contrast to their nineteenth-century counterparts, recognize that people need to be brought on board. But they still go about it in a preordained fashion. Trouble arises because the "soft" stuff is really the *hard* stuff, and no one can really "engineer" it.

We will use *social engineering* repeatedly as a billboard phrase to highlight this managerial tradition. Its central premises are:

- *Leaders as Head, Organization as Body.* Intelligence is centralized near those at the top of the organization—or those who advise them.
- *The Premise of Predictable Change.* Implementation plans are scripted on the assumption of a reasonable degree of predictability and control during the time span of the change effort.
- *An Assumption of Cascading Intention.* Once a course of action is determined, initiative flows from the top down. When a program is defined, it is *communicated* and *rolled out* through the ranks. Often, this includes a veneer of participation to engender buy-in.

That these familiar tenets of social engineering are not compatible with the way living systems work is probably self-evident. But, as we noted earlier, the traditional approach does have its place. The tools associated with social engineering work well when the solution is known in advance and an established repertoire exists to implement it. These conditions apply in many situations, and it is not our intent to minimize them. However, even in such straightforward applications, if employee ownership of an initiative, for example, SAP, is a prerequisite for success, regarding each person as on intelligent "node" in a living system and involving them as such, improves implementation. We don't reject all the *tools* of social engineering in all cases, but advocate the end of it as a *context.* Tools for control do not equal social engineering. What we are advocating is appropriate use of tools of the old paradigm, incorporated in a new management repertoire. Social engineering as a context is obsolete—Period.

But that is not the focus of this book. Harder to handle are those nonroutine challenges where discontinuous change is sought. These challenges often demand a leap in capability, and solutions are unproven or unknown. In these instances, nimbleness and agility are essential, and tapping the full potential of the organization as a living system becomes imperative. This is not a "maybe" or a "sort of." It's a deal breaker. Facing such an adaptive challenge, we must throw out the old notion about how a business should be led, organized, and run. We must abandon familiar organizational principles and processes and adopt strange and unfamiliar ones. The lessons of living systems provide the best map for this new territory: a mental framework for seeing order in the disorder; powerful distinctions that accelerate change; mental hooks to rely on as we scale the cliffs of the worn-out business model to reach the business model of the future. Behaving like a gardener, not thinking like a mechanic, becomes the mantra of choice.

As a general rule, adults are much more likely to act their way into a new way of thinking than to think their way into a new way of acting. Many new—and some established—enterprises, such as those discussed herein, illustrate that rule. Despite many missteps along the way, they have evolved organizations and management approaches that smack more of a beehive than a bureaucracy. And as they have enacted this new reality, they have come to think differently.

Beyond Dilbert

Is complexity science the dawning of a new age or simply grist for "Dilbert"? Will old-line "social engineers" bolt a few showcase features of living science onto the traditional machinery, in much the same way as they compromised Total Quality Management and Self-Managed Teams? Overcoming these propensities is the quest of this book. To be sure, the old order persists. But, to quote Petzinger:

> [The] new order is poised to overtake it—haltingly in some places, unevenly in others—but inexorably in every corner of the economy and society at large. How can we be so sure the Newtonian model is giving way to the natural one? Two reasons: for one, the marketplace leaves companies no choice. In an era when change arrives without warning and threatens to eradicate entire companies and industries overnight, organizations can survive only by engaging the eyes, ears, minds and emotions of all individuals and by encouraging them to act on their knowledge and beliefs. Second, and far more importantly, the new living systems model will thrive and persist because it bears more closely to what we are as humans.[22]

To repeat, living systems isn't a metaphor. It is the way it is.

This book is an effort to ensure that a dilution of these ideas doesn't happen. The lessons of complexity are simply too important to be lost or frittered away. We have seen how they can transmute the most leaden of organizations into the gold of a flexible, fast-reacting, innovative enterprise. We believe the story of those achievements must be told, in depth, and their significance must be made clear.

In other words, we have seen the future and have wrapped it between the covers of this book.

PART ONE

CHAPTER 2

EQUILIBRIUM IS DEATH

Yellowstone, the first national park in the United States, has long been regarded as a national treasure. Its 2.2 million acres (3,450 square miles) of diverse terrain and wildlife reconnects us to the vast wilderness that once was North America.

But during the 1970s and 1980s, when the park's popularity brought in excess of 10 million visitors a year, the National Park Service faced a quandary: Should it continue to maintain Yellowstone as a kind of natural theme park and maximize visitor throughput? Or should priority be given to the park's ecosystem? The latter choice would impose restrictions on public access and favor the best interests of nature in shaping park utilization decisions.

Under pressure, the Park Service adopted the theme-park approach and endeavored to optimize use of the park's assets by virtually programming a "wilderness experience." But complex adaptive systems have a perverse nature that defies human efforts to tame them. In 1988, the park's ecosystem demonstrated this with a vengeance when lightning ignited the largest fire in recorded North American history. Fires are common in forests. But the size and intensity of the Yellowstone conflagration were fueled by the unforeseen consequences of the programmed policies. Here's why.

For more than a century, the Park Service had maintained equilibrium in the forest by quickly extinguishing fires, denying the natural rhythm of fire and regrowth whereby forests cleanse and renew themselves.

In theory, the Park Service allowed fires to burn if they did not threaten people at campsites or hotels. In fact, because fires can so easily get out of control (and always attract bad press), they were extinguished as quickly as possible.

As a result, a thicker-than-normal layer of deadfall and debris had built up on the forest floor. The 1988 lightning strikes created multiple fires. A prolonged drought during the preceding months and ill-timed winds then conspired to incinerate the forest with intensity and velocity that are rarely witnessed in North America. The conflagration destroyed large trees and charred the living components of topsoil that would otherwise have survived. Yellowstone still bears the scars.[1]

What applies to forests applies to the business world as well. Prolonged equilibrium is a precursor of disaster, whether it happens unwittingly or, as in Yellowstone, by intent. In this chapter, we explore both accidental and deliberate sources of equilibrium. We show the dread impact of equilibrium on companies like Sears and International Business Machines Corporation (IBM).

All things in the universe—animate and inanimate—lose energy over time. Steel rusts, as painters of San Francisco's Golden Gate Bridge will testify. If the rusted steel is left unattended, it will turn into ferrous oxide dust. Living things, if not refueled by food or sunlight, perish and decay. "Ashes to ashes, dust to dust" is a poetic way of stating the Second Law of Thermodynamics.

The Law of Requisite Variety, an obscure but important law of cybernetics, states that the survival of any system depends on its capacity to *cultivate* (not just tolerate) variety in its internal structure.[2] Failure to do so will result in an inability to cope successfully with variety when it is introduced from an external source. For example, fish in a bowl can swim, breed, obtain food with minimal effort, and remain safe from predators. But, as aquarium owners know, such fish are excruciatingly sensitive to the slightest perturbations. Fish in the sea have to work much harder to sustain themselves, and they are subject to many threats. But because they cope with more variation, they are more robust when faced with change.

The lesson of Yellowstone and the imperatives of the Law of Requisite Variety make us uneasy. Equilibrium is associated with balance— a good thing, surely. Disequilibrium is balance gone haywire.

Balance, or equilibrium, occurs in nature when the components of a biosystem are in sync. At the individual level, equilibrium occurs when an organism matches the requirements of its environment while meeting its own needs with the available resources. But when a fire in Yellowstone (or e-commerce in retailing) abruptly alters the stable environment, that which has remained latent (debris on the forest floor, or unmet consumer needs) can suddenly become manifest. Coping mechanisms that have atrophied during long periods of equilibrium usually prove inadequate for the new challenge. Survival favors heightened adrenaline levels, wariness, and experimentation. Alfred North Whitehead got it right. "Without adventure [which we might define as disequilibrium caused by breaks with convention], civilization is in full decay."[3]

A qualification is warranted here. The extent to which prolonged equilibrium is a precursor of disaster must be assessed in the context of scale and time. At certain scales (i.e., small) and in some time frames (i.e., short), equilibrium can be a desirable condition. But over long intervals of time and on very large scales, equilibrium becomes hazardous. Why? Because the environment in which an organism (or organization) lives is always changing. At times, it is turbulent. Prolonged equilibrium dulls an organism's senses and saps its ability to arouse itself appropriately in the face of danger.

Equilibrium by Default

Consider the dodo bird, now extinct. In its native South Pacific habitats, the dodo enjoyed a stable and congenial environment safe from predators. Lulled into a state of equilibrium during a prolonged evolutionary cycle, this docile and defenseless fifty-pound bird became incapable of flight. Abruptly, it became fatally vulnerable to sailors and settlers with firearms.

The dodo was not alone. Isolated for 40 million years, the island continent of Australia fostered a stunning array of marsupials, rodents, and lizards. Many became extinct when Europeans introduced foxes, cats, goats, other mammals, and their parasites. In just 200 years, 80 percent of the biodiversity unique to Australia vanished.[4] In Hawaii, prolonged isolation gave rise to species of plants and bird life that lacked the defenses found in more diverse environments. There was no threat from indigenous browsing animals, so plants bore no toxins or thorns. Many species of birds found it more convenient to nest on the ground. After the introduction of rats, pigs, goats, and mongooses, 88 percent of Hawaii's native bird life and 10 percent of its plants disappeared.[5]

Among commercial parallels, shuttered factories in the rust belt, the victims of minimills and of agile Asian competitors, are the industrial equivalents of extinct species. They are relics of prolonged equilibrium and insufficient variety.

Life scientists call this tendency of isolated populations *genetic drift,* and it is universal among living things.[6] Unless, or until, an environmental upheaval is both real and recognized, the drift of any species is to specialize or refine its winning formula. Finches in the Galápagos Islands evolved specially curved bills to harvest the seeds of an indigenous plant. Genetic drift in organizations becomes evident when more and more energy is dedicated to tweaking a strategy that maintains the status quo.

Equilibrium by Intent

For anyone immersed in equilibrium, it is not easy to recognize it as a threat because it often wears the disguise of an advantage. It is concealed inside strong values, or a coherent and close-knit social system, or a well-synchronized operating model.

In their best-selling book, *In Search of Excellence,* Tom Peters and Bob Waterman listed the qualities that, in their view, contributed to the success of forty-three excellent companies.[7] Since the book's publication, managers have sought to emulate those desirable traits. Chief among them were: clear corporate vision; strong values; and a great deal of internal consistency among other elements—otherwise known as *organizational fit.* Given the authors' emphasis on the latter trait, the book may have been better named *In Search of Equilibrium.*

Within five years after the book's publication, half of the forty-three companies were in trouble. At present, all but five have fallen from grace.[8] One of this text's authors, Richard Pascale, collaborated in developing the Seven-S Framework—a management tool highlighted in the Peters and Waterman book. The Seven-S Framework identified the key levers that make organizations tick. The levers can be characterized as hard factors—strategy, structure, and systems— and softer aspects—style, staff (i.e., people), and shared values. The seventh "S" is skills. The Framework was conceived as a descriptive tool and was intended to help executives assess how each organizational component was operating with the rest.

The message was implicitly prescriptive in its support of organizational fit. As we eventually came to understand, excessive imposition of "fit" meant that it was impossible to change any single element of the system without changing every other element. Unwittingly, we had actually encouraged managers to pursue the very equilibrium that would prove their undoing.

Consider IBM, which was one of the companies featured in *In Search of Excellence.* In 1993, Louis V. Gerstner, Jr., the company's new chief executive officer, asked James Cannavino, a senior executive, to take a hard look at the strategic planning process. Why had IBM so badly missed the mark? Cannavino dutifully made his way through shelves of blue binders that contained 20 years' forecasts, trends, and strategic analyses.

"It all could be distilled down to one sentence," he told Gerstner. "We saw it coming. . . . Our strategic planners foresaw the impact of

PCs, open architecture, intelligence in the network, computers on microprocessors, even the higher margins of software and declining margins in hardware." Pursuing the issue further, Cannavino turned to IBM's Operating Plans. Did they reflect the shifts the strategists had projected? "These blue volumes [three times as voluminous as the strategic plans] could also be summarized in one sentence: '*Nothing changed.*'"

Cannavino added:

But the most important piece to the puzzle was a secret only insiders would know, a dose of arsenic to our diet of cyanide, and it was administered during the year-end financial reconciliation process. When we rolled up the sector submissions into totals for the corporation, the growth of new products never quite covered the gradual erosion of margins on our mainframes that was taking place. This shortfall, of course, was the tip of an iceberg that would one day upend our reliance on the IBM 360 as the centerpiece of our business platform. But facing this possibility would have precipitated a great deal of turmoil and instability. Instead, year after year, two of our most senior executives simply went behind closed doors, quantified the gap, and raised prices to cover it.[9]

■ ■

Chris Langton, one of the pioneers of complexity science, has deepened our insight into the way equilibrium comes about. He programmed a series of simulations analogous to a beehive in which individual virtual "bees" were given simple rules to follow. When the rules became too rigid or too numerous, the beehive froze into inactivity. A little elasticity in the rules generated a repeating pattern in the hive; a few changes would ripple through the system, but the hive then reverted to its original state and the same pattern emerged again and again. In both instances, the rules evoked order and equilibrium.

With no rules, the opposite phenomenon occurred. The hive dispersed. But there was yet another set of rules described by arcane, hard-to-pigeonhole algorithms that proved most interesting. Along with some regularity, there was a flow of nonrepeating patterns. The algorithm was defined in such a way that it generated disturbances in its own regularity. Patterns would propagate in the honeycomb, disaggregate, and then recombine in perpetually novel ways. The "hive" always had enough internal variety to keep it from being locked into itself.[10]

Let's look at Japan in the beehive context. In 1998, the nation of Japan experienced banking losses equivalent to 60 percent of its gross domestic product (GDP).[11] But, as with Langton's rigid rules for most of the 1990s, Japan's culture and institutions steadfastly resisted altering the parameters that might have fostered the disequilibrium necessary to reset the economy on a more vibrant footing. As a heavily networked society, Japan's version of Langton's rules was:

1. Redundant workers must not be laid off.
2. Government should shore up failing companies with public works spending.
3. Banks should carry an inflated value of loans on their books rather than taking write-downs.
4. Banks should never allow a business to fail by forcing nonperforming borrowers into insolvency and passing the losses on to investors.

The rules limited the network's flexibility. When a national or corporate culture such as Japan's (or IBM's) is "so thick you can cut it with a knife," all those dense connections fuse like chemical bonds rather than flexing like a permeable network.

Neither IBM nor Japan failed to respond effectively to an equilibrium threat because of indifference, laziness, or inefficiency. Rather, these systems did not recognize an equilibrium threat. It is difficult to do so when one is immersed in equilibrium, and harder still to arouse oneself to the proper level of response. A fish takes for granted the water in which it swims; when it learns about land, it is usually too late. When a long period of stability lulls a company into equilibrium, that condition is tantamount to a death sentence.

So why don't all living systems spiral into the thrall of equilibrium and die? Because two countervailing forces are at work to promote instability and thwart equilibrium. One is the threat of death through the eternal Darwinian struggle for survival; the other is the promise of sex, by which we mean recombinations that introduce genetic diversity. Let's take a look at each.

The Threat of Death

In 1839, when Charles Darwin set forth from England aboard the H.M.S. Beagle to study the ecological system of the Galápagos Islands off the coast of Ecuador, he expected to find a stable, natural community living at peace with itself in an isolated habitat. Instead, he encountered turmoil and relentless imbalance as species encroached on one another.[12] Darwin summarized these surprising discoveries in the last chapter of The Origin of Species:

> In looking at nature, it is most necessary never . . . to forget that every single organic being around us may be said to be striving to the utmost to increase in numbers; that each lives by a struggle at some period of its life; that heavy destruction inevitably falls on many. The face of nature may be compared to a yielding surface, with 10,000 sharp wedges packed close together and driven inwards by incessant blows, sometimes one wedge being struck, and then another with greater force.[13]

One of Darwin's most important contributions was his observation that species (by which we mean living systems) do not evolve of their own accord. Rather, they change because of the forces—indeed, the threats—imposed on them from the environment. Having said that, it should also be pointed out that many species seek avenues of survival that do not escalate into full-blown life-or-death struggles with others. Most species seek means to cooperate, coevolve, and coexist. Even within species, one finds many examples of altruistic behavior. Among mammals and insects, individuals regularly sacrifice themselves for the good of the whole.[14]

Life scientists call these dynamics of survival "selection pressures." Selection pressures intensify during periods of radical upheaval. Most species, when challenged to adapt too far from their origins, are unable to do so and disappear. But nature is a fertile and indifferent mother, more dedicated to proliferating life in general than to the perpetuation of any particular species. From the vantage point of the larger complex adaptive system, selection pressures constantly enforce an ecological upgrade. The mutations that survive fit better in the new environment.

Reflecting on the competitive corporate landscape of the past decade or two, we can readily identify with Darwin's wedge imagery. New rivals are constantly converging on the same market opportunity, and they clamber relentlessly over one another, seeking a better position in the economic food chain.

Whole sectors decline or disappear entirely. Office-supply stores are swept away by Staples, and the largest and most established bookseller, Barnes & Noble, is badly shaken by Amazon.com. The examples speak to the ubiquity of selection pressures as they play out on the corporate landscape. There are no safe havens. From cell phones to cotton seeds, pharmaceuticals to payroll systems, herbicides to hot sauce, soap to software, it is a Darwinian jungle out there, and it isn't getting easier.

Like all complex adaptive systems, corporations must be ready for a sudden confrontation with the inexorable hazards of natural selection. Widely admired leaders such as General Electric's Jack Welch have devised ingenious techniques for sounding the Darwinian call to arms. It is interesting to analyze GE's well-publicized methods from the disequilibrium perspective. In 1980, when he succeeded Reginald Jones, a popular and highly respected CEO, Welch found GE's many businesses too comfortable in their oligopolistic markets. "I wish I did not have to play the hand I was dealt," he confided to Richard Pascale, who worked with him extensively in the early 1980s. "Yes, these businesses are generating reliable earnings," he worried, "but they lack a competitive edge."[15] To shake this complacency, Welch announced that every business must be number one or two in its industry or it would be divested, and he proved true to his word. Flagship brands such as GE's Small Appliances, Mobile Communications, and Factory Automation were put on the block. Throughout this huge corporation, one could feel a rush of adrenaline.

Next in Welch's arsenal of disequilibrium-generating devices was "Workout." Characterizing GE as "an overweight slugger up against nimble street fighters,"[16] Welch unleashed a process through which lower-level employees could shine the spotlight of public scrutiny on the most aggravating bureaucratic policies and redundant work practices. Workout (which might be thought of as "Theater for Disequilibrium") fostered a series of public events at which senior corporate officers were subjected to straight feedback from the troops. Then, under continuing employee oversight, they were expected to take decisive action in eliminating hindrances. Following Workout, Welch turned his attention to the pace of change. In 1992, he launched the Change Acceleration Process in which the top 100 executives in every business were trained to be change agents and were then given an essential business project designed to both internalize and demonstrate their skills. "When change within a business is slower than that without," Welch observed, "you're in real trouble. We can't predict the future but we can learn to react a lot faster than our adversaries."[17] Sound familiar? Welch provided us with a down-to-earth restatement of the Law of Requisite Variety.

Most recently, Welch's emphasis has been on Quality—not a new idea, to be sure, but implemented in half the time normally required for a company-wide program and aspiring toward exacting outcomes. Each of GE's initiatives shares a pattern: Amplify survival threats and foster disequilibrium to evoke fresh ideas and innovative responses.

The Promise of Sex

Complex adaptive systems become more vulnerable as they become more homogeneous. To thwart homogeneity, nature relies on the rich structural recombinations triggered by sexual reproduction. Sex is decisively superior to evolution's other major alternative for species replication: parthenogenesis.

Parthenogenesis (the process by which some plants and worms conceive offspring through self-induced combinations of identical genetic material) yields offspring identical to their single parent. That process is of little help when a species desperately needs a novel mutation to stave off disaster.[18]

Sexual reproduction maximizes diversity. Chromosome combinations are randomly matched in variant pairings, thereby generating more permutations and variety in offspring. Oxford's evolutionary theorist, William Hamilton, offers a simple explanation of why this benefits a living system.[19] Enemies (such as harmful diseases and parasites) find it harder to breach the diverse defenses of a population generated by sexual reproduction than the relatively uniform defenses effected by parthenogenesis. By mingling genes, males and females arm their offspring with novel DNA combinations. Microbes equipped to pick the locks of one generation of a particular species discover that the cellular tumblers have been changed in the next. When the bubonic plague swept through Europe in the fourteenth century, it decimated 30 percent of the population. Subsequent waves of the deadly contagion claimed only a fraction of that number.[20] Sexual reproduction had distributed protective antibodies to most of the progeny of the first wave's survivors. The majority of the next generation's population was protected when the bacteria returned for an encore.

At the London School of Economics, Alex Trisoglio has studied the connection between disease and genetic diversity. He observes:

Recent study of evolution, both in the natural world and in computer-based complex systems, has demonstrated the surprising result that the presence of parasites in a system accelerates evolution dramatically. A parasite will find a way to take advantage of a host; the host will evolve a way to protect itself; the parasite, in turn, will find a new line of attack. In such "evolutionary arms races" the ability to change more rapidly than the other organism is truly the only sustainable competitive advantage. Recent work suggests that this Red Queen effect, which is named after the character in *Alice in Wonderland* who runs as fast as she can just to stay in the same place, may even be responsible for the evolution of sex itself![21]

When Jack Welch challenges each GE business head to (1) hire 30 to 60 people with e-commerce or other nontraditional backgrounds, (2) protect them from the organization's immune defense response, and (3) come up with viable "Destroy-Your-Business.com" options within six to nine months, he is fostering precisely the kind of arms race between a parasite and host that Trisoglio describes.[22]

Along with the unique advantages it bestows, sexual reproduction introduces a significant drawback: It dilutes a winning formula. Because the genetic cards are always being shuffled, successful parents cannot ensure that their winning talents will be inherited by their progeny. As the breeders of racehorses know all too well, mating the filly that won the Preakness with the stallion that swept the Kentucky Derby does not guarantee an offspring that will win the Triple Crown.

Human Intention and Change

In the natural world, the dichotomy between genetic uniformity, which perpetuates a winning formula, and genetic diversity, which dilutes the formula, is resolved by evolution and chance. In the business world, it's an important matter of choice.

This trade-off also represents an excruciating paradox. Companies must weigh the benefits of introducing new genetic material—say, in the form of new hires—against the possibly disruptive effects on a smoothly running operation.

It is critical to protect the reliable core of an organization's business platform while one simultaneously plants and nurtures the seeds of revolutionary change. One way to do this is to carefully cultivate the fringes. Here we adopt another process from nature. The "verge"—

the boundary between forest and savanna, or the intertidal zone along the ocean's edge where no single species dominates—is known to foster the most prolific rate of mutation. Alex Trisoglio states:

> The fringes are the source of most truly innovative ideas in cultures, economies and organizations. By promoting an active fringe, which may appear uneconomic or positively anti-systemic, an organization can ensure that it is continually testing for new ideas and possibilities. The management challenge is that much fringe activity will create no value at all, whereas the occasional idea can revolutionize the company. As a result, assessing cost-effectiveness for fringe activity in general can prove difficult. A second problem is recognizing when the fringe has created something so important that it no longer deserves to be on the fringe.[23]

Xerox PARC (Palo Alto Research Center) is a case in point. The Xerox R&D lab invented ALTO (which many regard as the first personal computer), the first commercial mouse, Ethernet (predecessor of the Internet), many of the basic protocols of the Internet, client-server architecture, laser printing, and flat-panel displays, to name a few of its numerous contributions.[24] Yet because the rest of the mainstream organizations did not recognize (and would not embrace) the revolution at the fringe, Xerox was left in the backwater of the major new wealth-creating opportunities of the past thirty years. This legacy will surely one day warrant a place in the corporate hall of shame.

Every molecule in the human body replaces itself every seven years.[25] What endures are the genetic instructions that direct new cells to sustain the physical presence. Just as the body's molecules replenish themselves by moving in and out of the system, so must an organization revitalize itself by utilizing new members and diverse ideas. Both human and corporate bodies are rejuvenated by fresh and varied genetic material.

Exchanges of DNA within social systems are unfortunately not nearly as reliable as those driven by the mechanics of reproductive biology. True, organizations can hire from the outside, bring senior officers into frequent contact with iconoclasts from the ranks, or require engineers and designers to meet with disgruntled customers so the former can learn from the latter. But the enemy of these mechanisms for exchanging metaphoric DNA is, of course, the existing social order. Like the body's immune defense system, the social order identifies foreign influences and seeks to neutralize them.

Equilibrium enforcers—persistent social norms, corporate values, and orthodox beliefs about the business—often nullify the sought-after advantages of diversity. An executive team may recruit an outsider to gain diversity, then regress into behavior that nullifies the advantage by listening stereotypically ("There goes the techie again," "Ah—the feminist point of view"). The new token "genetic material" often finds itself frozen out of important informal discussions in which the real business gets done.

Of the six companies forming the cornerstone studies of this book, Sears most powerfully exemplifies these dangers. Almost all employees of Sears began their careers as teenagers working as stock clerks or sales personnel. They left for college or stints in the armed services, then rejoined the company to climb the management ladder. The average length of service of the 5,000 top managers is twenty years—the outgrowth of a conscious policy to hire at entry level and promote exclusively from within. When Arthur Martinez took over in 1992, he was the first chairman in 110 years to come from outside Sears, and only one of his top 100 executives was an external hire.[26]

Sears provides a stark contrast to the design for diversity one finds in Silicon Valley. Job swapping is the norm, not the exception. (It is perhaps the only region on earth where one can change companies without changing car pools.) The valley behaves like a "company," and the companies located in the valley are like "divisions." In its entirety, it is a superorganism; ideas, employees, capital, and technology flow rapidly within the system. This activity is not without its costs, but the turmoil contributes to the region's intellectual and economic vibrancy.

When management thinker Gary Hamel was asked whether he thought IBM had a chance of leading the next stage of the information revolution, he answered: "I'd need to know how many of IBM's top 100 executives had grown up on the West Coast of America where the future of the computer industry is being created, and how many were under forty years of age. If a quarter or a third of the senior group were both under forty and possessed a West Coast perspective, IBM has a chance."[27]

Chance or Choice?

Conscious learning and intention define a watershed in our exploration of what the science of complexity means for business—a line of divergence between humans and the rest of nature. Nature disturbs equilibrium through the threat of death and the promise of sex; it nudges species into an arena where chance mutations can thrive. Clear parallels exist between human systems in general and businesses in particular. But humans have an important advantage. As self-knowing and intelligent entities, companies, at least in theory, are capable of recognizing danger (or opportunity) in advance and mobilizing to take appropriate action. They can wield the power of human intention.

The role of human learning and intention in evolution reignites a debate that had, for the most part, been laid to rest by Charles Darwin. In the early nineteenth century, French zoologist Jean Baptiste Lamarck studied biological adaptation. His work, a precursor to Darwin's, argued that species proactively caused their own *genetic* evolutionary change. Lamarck concluded that species exhibit an inherent tendency to evolve more complex strategies for survival over time. (This much was subsequently shown to be correct.) Lamarck's more controversial assertion was that species do so through the *genetic* transfer of *both* physical traits and *learning* to their offspring[28]—an assertion that was discredited by Darwin's discoveries. Evolved mammals exhibit intentionality and transfer experience to their young, but this is not captured genetically nor is it bestowed automatically on the next generation. "Evolution through learning" anthropomorphizes what is better explained by random mutation and natural selection.

Human beings are extremely well equipped with consciousness and the capacity of foresight. To a greater extent than other species, they *can* lift themselves by their anticipatory bootstraps. But the biggest difference, of great significance to business, is that human learning is codified and can be passed down, via the social system, to future generations. In this sense, learning becomes part of the "genetic" structure. Lamarck may have been wrong about species, including humans, at the individual level, but he was right insofar as human social systems not only learn behaviors but incorporate them into their cultural DNA.

All this can become a blessing or a curse. Human systems are capable of discontinuous leaps in learning that would have been regarded as unimaginable, given the previous institutional trajectory. This was certainly the case at Monsanto and in the transformation of the U.S. Army. Within these institutions, learning was incorporated into the skill base of future generations. Sears exemplifies how resistant the old DNA can be to the infusion of new genetic material.

The above discussion might lead us, in balance, to an optimistic prognosis for humanity in general and organizations in particular. In theory, humans are endowed with conscious awareness. They are capable of intellectually grasping a threat before it materializes and, through the exercise of intention, responding it before it is too late. Finally, as we have discussed, human systems can incorporate these valuable lessons into the DNA of the organizational memory—at least in theory. In reality, the actual track records of many business organizations give cause to ponder. History seems to better support Winston Churchill's apt observation that "mankind will occasionally stumble over the truth, but usually we pick ourselves up and carry on."[29]

Our collective failure to translate conscious awareness into effective organizational response is captured in the declining survival rate of the Fortune 500 over the past twenty-five years. During the relatively tranquil period from 1976 to 1985, only 10 percent of those listed fell by the wayside (they failed to grow as rapidly as their peer group, merged or were acquired, or, in a small fraction of cases, went bankrupt). Skip to the more turbulent period from 1986 to 1990, when the attrition rate jumped to 30 percent. In the next five years, 1991 to 1996, the attrition rate rose again, this time to 36 percent.[30] It is reasonable to assume that most companies on the Fortune 500 list (1) would have preferred to remain there (e.g., organizations that were acquired would have preferred to have been the acquirers) and (2) were aware of the competitive threats in time to take corrective action. The question becomes: Why didn't they do so? Truer to Darwin's theories than we would wish, learning and proactive response did not take place. A significant percentage of organizations failed to mobilize the level of response needed to sustain themselves.

Now consider this stark contrast. Over the past 100 years, the health sciences have almost doubled human longevity in the industrialized world whereas corporate longevity has actually decreased. Even if we exclude the large subset of companies that perish before completing their first five years in business, the average corporation lives only half as long as the average human being![31]

The lessons of nature and the specific principles of living systems do not constitute a miracle drug that cures all these ills. But when an organization needs to fundamentally reinvent itself and sustain high levels of responsiveness and agility, the insights of living systems allow us to see more deeply into the challenge and provide more promising avenues for success.

As we will witness at Hewlett-Packard, Monsanto, Shell, and the U.S. Army, the principles of complexity can be translated into practical designs for the purpose of revitalizing organizations. That statement isn't a metaphor. It isn't speculative. It isn't astrophysics. Readers may even be familiar with many of the techniques employed, but the above applications had distinctly encouraging results. In another realm, many of the herbal remedies used centuries ago are finding their way into modern pharmaceuticals. The active compounds remain constant, but the forms and potency are vastly improved. A systemic understanding of bacteria, viruses, body chemistry, and genetic structure (which enables scientists to identify trace ingredients, replicate them, and intensify their potency) was needed to achieve the inroads against disease that have taken place. The principles of complexity provide a similar means of tapping the active ingredients of familiar management techniques and making them much more powerful.

The practical means of applying the principles of complexity are at hand. Resistance to implementation is found less in the workforce than among executives and managers. Opposition is anchored in the assumptions of social engineering and the machine metaphor, which, as discussed in Chapter 1, deny that organizations are living systems and withhold some of their most potent means of mobilizing their resources and sustaining their vitality.

When a roadway exists and one wishes to transport a load, harnessing a horse to a cart makes a great deal of sense. In a condition of greater uncertainty, such as a horse race, jockeys typically relinquish more initiative to their horses in the final stretch. And when they become lost on an unfamiliar mountain trail after dark, wise riders simply give their horse its head. In each case, the horse is a living entity. Conditions determine the optimal degree of freedom given to this living entity and, in particular, the extent to which tapping into the full potential of the horse's native intelligence is desirable.

Organizations are very much alive, however we choose to manage them. Whether we approach them with a script defined by social engineering (that is, consistent with the traditional machine model) or regard them as living systems will depend on the circumstances we encounter. Specific criteria will help us to evaluate the situation and determine the type of leadership required.

Human Intention and Adaptive Leadership

The six organizations that form the cornerstones of this work—British Petroleum, Hewlett-Packard, Monsanto, Sears, Shell, and the U.S. Army—differed radically in the immediacy of the threats they were facing, yet all were mobilized by a defining act of human intention. Conventionally, we refer to this as "leadership." Yet, curiously, the six corporate leaders shared almost no personal traits in common:

John Browne, Managing Director (at the time of the case), British Petroleum's Oil Exploration Unit (cerebral and instrumental);

Joel Birnbaum, Senior Vice President and Director of Hewlett-Packard Laboratories (visionary warrior);

Robert Shapiro, CEO of Monsanto (professorial and conflict-averse);

Arthur Martinez, CEO of Sears (analytical and abrupt);

Steve Miller, Managing Director of Oil Products at Shell (approachable and consensus-oriented);

General Gordon Sullivan of the U.S. Army (charismatic and deeply inquisitive).

None of these men led in a conventional fashion. Each unleashed his organization's *distributed* intelligence. All but Martinez and Browne came fully to terms with their organizations as living systems.

Ronald Heifetz, Director of the Leadership Education Project at Harvard's John F. Kennedy School of Government, observes that leadership is frequently equated with authority.[32] This is misleading. A great many people in authority do not provide leadership; conversely, some people who had very little formal authority have changed the world through extraordinary acts of informal leadership. Jesus Christ, Buddha, Mohammed, Mohandas Gandhi, Martin Luther King, Jr., Mohammad Yunas, Nelson Mandela, and Susan B. Anthony come to mind.

Heifetz makes a distinction between "technical (i.e., operational) leadership" and "adaptive leadership."[33] The former entails the exercise of authority and is an entirely appropriate response in conditions of relative equilibrium. Operational leadership works best when the problems faced can be dealt with by drawing upon a preexisting repertoire and exploiting it with more speed, quality, or scale. Operational leadership goes hand in hand with the tenets of social engineering. A solution is devised from above and rolled out through the ranks. If a company is in crisis; if downsizing, restructuring, or reducing costs is called for; if sharpened execution is the key to success, then operational leadership is the best bet.

Most business situations, of course, are rarely either/or propositions. Often, businesses face operational and adaptive challenges simultaneously. Even when the organization at large is in the midst of a full-blown transformation, there are usually pockets of activity where conventional management practices work best. At Sears, transformation was necessary in frontline service delivery in the mall stores. But the highly profitable Sears credit card division was not facing such radical change in its segment and was appropriately managed in a traditional manner. The U.S. Army sought transformation in combat methods (using information technology to improvise on the battlefield). For the most part, its other mainstream activities—procurement, logistics (The U.S. Army Matériel Command), and the conduct of basic training (i.e., boot camp)—proceeded along conventional lines, unscathed by the turmoil elsewhere.

The point is: Over time (and even concurrently), organizations need evolution *and* revolution. When they have been limited exclusively to the restrictive precepts of social engineering, they have been handicapped and largely unsuccessful in unleashing authentic revolutionary change. The principles of living systems offer a powerful new recourse. The trick is to clearly identify the nature of the challenge and then use the right tool for the right task.

Making Happen What Wouldn't Happen Otherwise

As we have noted, living systems usually respond to disequilibrium threats by attempting to restore stability. In a leadership context, employees rely on those in authority to orchestrate a response (usually drawn from a routine that has previously been proven successful). If the traditional repertoire is appropriate for the present challenge, the organization copes successfully. The system resides secure in the knowledge that it is doing more of what it already knows how to do.

Problems arise, however, when a species (or organization) misapplies a traditional solution to an *adaptive* problem. In this situation, the current repertoire of solutions is inadequate or just plain wrong. In nature, the alpha male silverback mountain gorilla draws its troop together in a tight circle and behaves aggressively toward rival males or other natural threats. This traditional solution works effectively— unless the troop is facing poachers armed with guns, tranquilizer darts, and capture nets.

Adaptive leadership "makes happen what isn't going to happen otherwise." It is a surefire recipe to disturb equilibrium. Consider a problem for which traditional solutions are unsuitable and a novel solution must be found. An example might be Barnes & Noble's threat from Amazon.com or Native American tribes' loss of hunting grounds to the encroachment of Caucasian settlers. What is predictable in these situations? The individuals affected will look to figures of authority. More often than not, those in charge take the bait, try to provide the answers (drawn from traditional success routines), divert attention to easier problems, or tread water—all the while allowing the initial threat to intensify. In the 1930s, a weary British public, still exhausted after World War I, looked to Prime Minister Neville Chamberlain to find a way to stop Hitler without involving England in another war. Britain had no appetite for rearmament.

Chamberlain played his part, seeking to maintain equilibrium in the British social system through a policy of appeasement. He signed the Munich Treaty, acceding to the German occupation of Czechoslovakia. The long period of appeasement did not end until Hitler's invasion of Poland. By then, the German war machine was ready to take on the world. Initially, Chamberlain gained authority by taking the problem off the shoulders of the British people and carrying it for them. His prompt loss of authority when this solution failed is the other side of the quid pro quo.[34]

Leaders are to a social system what a properly shaped lens is to light. They focus intention and do so for better or worse. If adaptive *intention* is required, the social system must be disturbed in a profound and prolonged fashion. Magnifying a threat or utilizing organizational devices to propagate "genetic diversity" then becomes important. Adaptive leaders don't move on an issue too quickly or reach for a quick fix. Rather (taking actions quite the opposite of social engineering), they emphasize mobilizing followers deep within the ranks to help find the way forward. This is achieved, as Heifetz describes it, by (1) communicating the urgency of the adaptive challenge (i.e., the threat of death), (2) establishing a broad understanding of the circumstances creating the problem, to clarify why traditional solutions won't work (i.e., sustaining disequilibrium), and (3) holding the stress in play until guerrilla leaders come forward with solutions (i.e., making room for genetic diversity). This sequence generates anxiety and tension.[35]

Adaptive leaders can be frozen out when followers don't want to face the bad news (e.g., Churchill's warnings to the British public about Hitler prior to World War II). Churchill was written off as a hawk and an eccentric for five long years as Hitler rearmed Germany, pursued technological advances in airplanes and submarines, and otherwise mobilized an increasingly militant German nation.[36]

Followers often turn to authority as a bulwark against the associated uncertainty and risk. "The essential work of adaptive leadership is to resist these appeals," states Ronald Heifetz. "Instead, they must (1) hold the collective feet to the fire, (2) regulate distress such that the system is drawn out of its comfort zone (yet contain stress so it does not become dysfunctional), and (3) manage avoidance mechanisms that inevitably surface (such as scapegoating, looking to authority for the answer and so forth)."[37]

The concept of adaptive leadership, necessary when an organization is challenged to do what it has never done before, sheds considerable light on the organizations discussed in this book. As we proceed, the distinction between *adaptive* and *operational* leadership will be a recurrent theme.

Disturbing equilibrium through the mobilization of adaptive intention is an unnatural act, especially for executives who have risen through the ranks and have been rewarded for their competence in exercising authority. The big payoff of the living systems point of view is that what is remote and unnatural within the traditional frame of reference becomes sensible and accessible within the complexity mindset. In the next chapter, a review of the unfolding events at Sears contrasts how two chief executives sought to mobilize intention and the consequences of their actions.

DISTURBING EQUILIBRIUM AT SEARS

In 1995, 110-year-old Sears, Roebuck & Company generated the greatest appreciation in shareholder value among all the companies listed on the *Fortune* 500. That same year, its chairman, Arthur Martinez, was selected by *Business Week* as one of the top twenty-five managers of the year. In 1997, *Fortune* listed Sears among its Most Admired Companies and declared it "the most innovative general merchandise retailer." In 1998, the National Retail Federation awarded Martinez a Gold Medal for his remarkable turnaround of the venerable retailer.[1]

All this notoriety reflected authentic cause for celebration. After four decades of continuous retreat during which its market position was cut in half by aggressive rivals such as Wal-Mart, Circuit City, and The Limited, Sears' retail business was restored to profitability. In the process, it had clawed back two points of market share, worth about $2 billion in incremental revenues.[2]

But peel the onion a layer deeper and you will find a curious paradox: Martinez actually added very little to the mix of strategic initiatives and merchandising tactics implemented by his predecessor, Ed Brennan.

The paradox is easily explained: Brennan inadvertently preserved his company's moribund equilibrium. Martinez understood that the disruption of that equilibrium was essential to revitalize the company. Unfortunately, through inattention and inaction near the end of Martinez's tenure in the late 1990s, equilibrium reestablished itself and Sears once again began to sink.

From its founding in 1880, and through the next seven decades, Sears was run successively by three very strong and accessible chief executives. Its operating model was fueled by a vibrant tension between the home office and the sales territories that was encouraged and harnessed by its CEOs. In addition, a system of checks and balances kept the buying staffs and the equally strong territorial managers on their toes. Like a standing wave one encounters when white-water rafting, Sears thrived as a dynamic, ascendant enterprise. Its "molecules" within were continuously shifting and changing.[3] Then, during a succession of caretaker chief executives, this precise tension was lost. Territory managers ran the stores as barons and effectively stonewalled strategic direction from headquarters. This myopic focus thwarted Sears' ability to respond to the early threats posed by Wal-Mart and Toys "R" Us. Many Sears managers dismissed these competitors as "too small to worry about" or "not a problem in my region."[4]

The rise and demise of Sears captures in detail how an organization gets in its own way. As in many unsuccessful attempts to reshape companies, Brennan exemplified the mistake a well-meaning figure in authority can make, despite the fact that he is *doing* everything right. Brennan failed to disturb equilibrium and tap into the energy and ideas in the ranks. As a result, he was unsuccessful in changing what Sears was *being*: a stodgy, conventional retailer.

Ed Brennan's tenure could not be faulted for want of initiative. He sold the Sears Tower in Chicago, he slimmed down headquarters, and he moved the central organization to an open campus in the Chicago suburbs. He launched Brand Central, allowing non-Sears appliances, with labels such as GE, Maytag, and Panasonic, to be offered alongside the Sears brands. He diversified into financial services through the acquisition of Dean Witter (for $609 million) and Coldwell Banker (for $202 million), and he invested $1 billion to launch the Discover Card. In 1993, when he sold these assets, they were valued in excess of $15 billion; their cumulative profits had accounted for 70 percent of Sears' consolidated earnings for the preceding five years.[5] Brennan streamlined the buying organization, gradually reduced employment by 48,000 people during his tenure, simplified logistics, reemphasized women's apparel, and piloted new formats such as stand-alone automotive outlets and home furnishing and home improvement stores.[6]

Missing, however, was the deep-seated revitalization of Sears' tradition-bound culture. Brennan was the consummate social engineer. He failed to awaken a living system that could breathe life into his many initiatives.

As a complex adaptive system, Sears had drifted a long way from the vibrancy that prevailed from its founding in 1880 through its stature in 1956 (when General Robert Wood retired as chief executive officer). Sears was losing its appeal among its own workforce as well as its customers. As noted above, a constructive tension between the buying staffs and the strong field organization gave way to feudal parochialism.

Beginning in the early 1970s, Sears was not noticing (or responding to) changes in shopping habits. These trends included fewer mall visits by two-career families and, importantly, encroachment by aggressive competitors such as the category killers—discount stores and Home Depot. Sears did not truly acknowledge Wal-Mart as a competitor until 1992.[7]

Brennan tried to correct the excesses of decentralization. But, as is common with most machine-model remedies, the pendulum had swung too far. He eliminated the position of territorial manager altogether and reduced almost all other echelons in the regional hierarchy. Once powerful store managers were relegated to "keeping the lights on and the doors open." "As a result," states one store manager, "our knowledge at the fingertips was lost. Brennan's recentralization ushered in an era of 'drive-by merchandising.' 'Experts' from headquarters would visit a store three times a month and believe they understood your local market better than you did."[8] Under enormous pressure to meet their margin targets (and threatened by the prospect of further layoffs), each individual on the store management teams hunkered down and attended to their own patch. Resignation permeated the organization at every level. One regional manager characterizes the atmosphere as one of "salute-and-obey. Directives came down from above and we did our best to follow them."[9]

As a consequence, the stores became a merchandising hodgepodge. Poor service and out-of-stock conditions alienated customers. Many of Brennan's efforts to achieve sweeping changes at Sears became snagged in the concertina wire of the stores' defensive perimeters. A regional manager reports: "There was no maneuvering room to make sensible market decisions. As bad press began in the 1970s, there was widespread depression and eventually an unwillingness to admit at cocktail parties that we worked at Sears. It all seemed so big and complex and out of control. We felt defeated and powerless."[10]

Sears' initial operating model had been fueled by tension between the home office and the field sales outlets. This kept the system honest (i.e., equilibrium was continually disturbed) and it was mediated by a succession of three very strong and accessible chief executives whose careers spanned the first sixty-eight years of Sears' history. They were not threatened by contention; they encouraged it and harnessed it.

Long before Ed Brennan succeeded to the chairmanship, the former blend of initiatives and controls had given way to norms of compliance and acquiescence. It was widely understood that to push back or resist one's boss's directives was "not being a team player." In addition, Sears' extremely lucrative pension programs (heavily weighted toward the final two decades of service) and career moves every eighteen months (subject, of course, to pleasing the boss) fostered compliance and effectively suppressed all meaningful conflict and disruptive ideas. "It was a corrupt system," says a longtime executive.[11] Martinez had to alter these patterns dramatically to restore Sears' vital signs.

The defining feature of a complex adaptive system is its ability to learn. Sears had become so immersed in denial and complacency that its ability to learn was marginalized. Beginning in 1974, negative reports of business analysts were brushed off as "mean-spirited journalism and biased reporting." When Sears was accused of widespread fraud in 1990, following a California sting operation that documented fraud in 85 percent of its visits to Sears auto centers, forty-four states subsequently filed suit. The public relations nightmare was exacerbated by avoidance and stonewalling.[12]

Arthur Martinez recognized dangerous stagnation (i.e., equilibrium) and employed virtually every disruptive device that has been discussed thus far. Launching a campaign for genetic diversity, he issued guidelines that 20 percent of all managerial vacancies in mall stores were to be filled from outside, as were vacancies elsewhere in the Sears system. He "zero-based" the top 150 jobs and induced many incumbents to take early retirement. At the apex of the pyramid, five of the top eight executives were displaced. These moves, combined with other actions, slimmed down the bloated bureaucracy at headquarters.[13]

We have previously mentioned that Brennan's tenure was characterized by operational leadership. Within the mall stores, he focused on merchandising and better execution. He sought to restore confidence by assuring employees and investors that all was under control. Taking the opposite tack, Martinez unbalanced the status quo by confronting the organization with its chronic failure to keep its commitments. He shook the organization to its core by shifting the locus of responsibility for initiatives and innovation to the ranks below.

In a textbook application of adaptive leadership, Martinez took several decisive steps. Addressing his top fifty executives, he pointedly observed: "Yesterday's peacock is tomorrow's feather duster." He reviewed the past five years' declining performance, juxtaposing actual quarter-to-quarter results with highly optimistic (and unrealized) projections. "We're going to start telling ourselves the truth," he continued. "I hold no one responsible for the past. But beginning today, when we make commitments, we're going to track them, keep them, or know the reason why."[14]

Although we are emphasizing adaptive leadership, let us not lose sight of the fact that a successful leader will develop and maintain a crucial tension between adaptive and operational leadership. To re-state an earlier point, operational leadership—the exercise of authority and the appropriate use of existing business skills—is always an important component of leadership. Doing this exclusively is problematic. Martinez exhibited both types of leadership. In closing down Sears' catalog business (debated for years but caught in a thrall of indecision), downsizing another 50,000 employees (deep pruning was done at the top), *insisting* (not just suggesting) that Sears mall stores accept Visa and MasterCard, and trebling the merchandising budget for women's apparel, he was exercising operational leadership. He urged other major business activities, such as logistics and credit card operations, to improve through conventional approaches.[15]

In the mall stores, Martinez faced a larger problem: an army of 300,000 demotivated sales personnel and stocking clerks. Many of these primarily part-time workers lacked a high school diploma.[16] Ignored, frustrated, and undermanaged for years, these employees were resigned and demoralized. Yet, in their daily contact with customers, this population could do the most, in the shortest amount of time, to arrest Sears' decline. Reenergizing this cadre was an *adaptive* challenge. Management couldn't gain the new desired behavior by edict. It needed to enroll these frontline employees so that those on the sales floor would be motivated to seize, each day, opportunities to improve customer loyalty.

Martinez elevated the urgency of this quest. He called for a quadrupling of Sears' margin (which would bring it to industry parity) within two years, and for a 15 percent improvement in customer satisfaction. None of these discontinuous goals was attainable through a business-as-usual approach.

Then came the hard part. As exemplified during Brennan's tenure, most organizations are submerged in a numbing but familiar drift toward homeostasis. It is like resisting being awakened from a sound sleep when you hear a strange noise in the house. In the fog of semi-consciousness, you try to get your mind to focus: Is it an intruder or the cat? Organizations are resistant to undertakings that pull them out of their familiar equilibrium. When the leader focuses on an issue and strives to generate urgency surrounding it, the guaranteed first line of defense is for the organization to turn back to the leader for an answer. "We need a plan," ". . . clear direction," ". . . more resources" are verses in this predictable refrain.

Many erstwhile leaders would have taken the bait. Martinez did not. He assembled what became known as the *Phoenix team* (as in "rising up from the ashes"). His top 100 managers convened one or two days a month for more than a year. Dedicated teams and task forces were spawned at these meetings. They became the innovators who pushed the envelope and provided an infusion of energy and ideas. From the very beginning, Martinez made it clear that he did not have the answers but he believed they could find them together.[17]

He challenged one team to explore Sears' long-ignored franchise with female customers. The outgrowth of this effort was the fantastically successful "Softer Side of Sears" campaign. Another team sought imaginative new ways to tap into the latent ideas and potential of the sales staff. This work stream led to literally thousands of "Town Hall meetings" attended by all permanent full-time and part-time employees. One or more Town Hall meetings were convened by each of the 800 stores in the system.

At these daylong events, an innovative new visual device (called a "learning map") was used to convey the competitive context and to evoke dialogue about Sears' problems with its customers. Almost two-thirds of Sears' 300,000 employees participated in these events.[18]

A learning map is a visual device which pictorially represents the business situation. (A visual depiction, it turns out, is far more effective than words alone in helping a community of people establish a common ground.) Discussion of what the picture means evokes dialogue, which in turn lays a foundation of business literacy. By generating a shared perspective and fostering work toward common goals, the visual aligns a dispersed or heterogeneous group of stakeholders.

Typically, a learning visual is six feet wide and four feet high. Sketched images of the real world—customers, competitors, factories, and stores—portray a strategic scenario. Seeded here and there are charts and statistics—essential details that capture the current circumstances.[19]

Small groups cluster around the multiple copies of the learning visual that are posted around the periphery of a room. "New Day on Retail Street" (Figure 3.1), the title of the map used in the initial round of Town Hall meetings at Sears, pictured a typical Main Street, USA. Readers of the map picked up, in the lower left-hand corner, a circa 1950 Main Street bordered by a traditional nuclear American family. The easily identified route then passed a billboard indicating the sharp decrease in shopping-mall visits per year, curved upward around a 1970s graveyard of former competitors, and entered a 1980s Main Street lined with category killers such as The Gap, The Limited, and Wal-Mart. Taking each significant icon in turn, the participants discussed the images and related them to their own experience. Over several hours, they learned about and internalized the competitive situation in a way that would have been impossible from a consultant's report or a manager's presentation.

A learning visual creates "line of sight" understanding and provides an overview of the strategic context. It enables employees on the shop floor to see the direct connection between what they do and the overall corporate results. This connection is pivotal when adaptive work is required. At Sears, the learning visual led to the joint discovery of new solutions and innovations that were not likely to be identified and driven down from above.

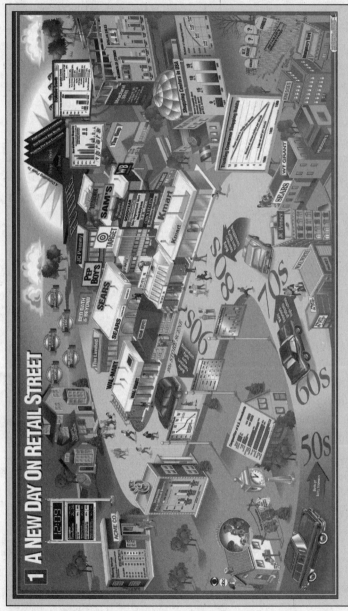

Figure 3.1   Root Learning Map

51

Martinez and the Sears task teams did not adopt the Town Hall meeting and the use of learning visuals out of any particular affinity toward workplace democracy or a fondness for employee participation. Rather, they were influenced by a parallel workstream which had uncovered important corrolations driving in customer behavior. One of the Phoenix task teams had commissioned a study through a consumer statistical research spin-off of the University of Michigan. The evaluation demonstrated that a 5 percent improvement in employee satisfaction caused a 1.3 percent improvement in customer satisfaction. This, in turn, correlated strongly with customer retention and volume and resulted in a 0.5 percent increase in store revenue. Further, the study showed that the payoff was fairly immediate. Only three business quarters were needed to cycle between an initial jump in employee morale and improved revenues and margins.[20]

Statistically defensible findings (later replicated by faculty at the Harvard Business School) neutralized, if not overcame, skepticism within Sears' managerial ranks. But, interestingly, the compelling evidence had a downside. Its very persuasiveness eliminated the company's need to undergo a corresponding shift in faith, with respect to the nature of adaptive work. Management did not come to terms with the necessity of regarding the 300,000 mall workers as a living system. There was never deep-seated buy-in to the ongoing importance of distributed intelligence and the need to cultivate it appropriately. This lapse turned out to be critical over the long haul. Neglect of it led Sears back into another downward spiral of performance.

Notwithstanding the problems lurking on the road ahead, the learning visual was used with great effect. The aim had been to engage and mobilize the 300,000 people who were mostly in the part-time sales staff. Sears recognized that its sales personnel were crucial to providing customers with a better shopping experience. But how, after years of neglect and managerial indifference, could this huge army be mobilized? An edict such as "Be Nice to Customers" would be greeted with derision. Furthermore, it was widely acknowledged that sales floor service performance was adversely affected by numerous systemic problems in distribution, warehousing, stocking, and store operations. How could these shortcomings be identified and corrected?

Imagine a 50-year-old sales clerk who has worked in the children's clothing department at Sears for ten years. She arises at 7:00 A.M. each morning, commutes an hour by bus, and, once at work, performs a variety of sales-related tasks in her department. She is unaware of how much money Sears makes on each transaction, the nature of competition, or what affects her customers in the larger context of shopping trends and demographic shifts. Yet, after she attends one Saturday Town Hall meeting held for her department and her entire store, the sales clerk and her team learn:

- The competitive environment has changed radically.
- Customers shop less, want far better service, and have many options.
- Sears makes 2 cents on each dollar—not 45 cents, as many workers had believed.
- Each clerk can make a difference.

As employees work their way through the learning visual, they acquire literacy—a fundamental knowledge base—in the business situation. Later, in the Town Hall meeting, each team is asked to focus on what it can do, within its own department in the store, to improve customer retention.

Over a twelve-month period, similar sessions were conducted in all 800 Sears mall stores. More than a half-million suggestions were generated. Cumulatively, these ideas and remedies contributed to a dramatic improvement in Sears' image among customers. They are assigned considerable credit in adding 9 percent to Sears' sales in one year and doubling store profitability.[21]

Sears rebounded; it reached and then exceeded its initial goals. Martinez's early moves dramatically disrupted the complacency and equilibrium that were inhibiting Sears' performance. When the organization began to view its past repertoire as suspect rather than sacrosanct, it was motivated to address the profound challenge of authentic transformation and renewal.

One senior executive's reflections on the repercussions of this employee awakening make the disruption to Sears' conservative management structure tangible:

> Traditionally, as in most companies, senior Sears executives would travel to the field for store visits. As part of the routine, executives, accompanied by escorts, would meet with store employees. These were obligatory in nature. The meetings were focused around the visiting executive. Ritual requests for employee input were made, followed by one or two tame responses. It was all choreographed "inside" of the prevailing hierarchically-based culture. The informal covenant was: "You (senior executive) ask questions, we (the employees) answer, and little happens."
>
> After four months of Town Hall meetings centered around conversations of what drives profitability and customer satisfaction, I visited the stores again. Before the meeting was even kicked off, an employee rose and confronted me. The issue was not around traditional employee concerns (e.g., working conditions), but rather about the business: "I [employee] have an out-of-stock situation with a hot-selling dress in my department. I have asked three people in the buying organization for help, and, to date, I have gotten nowhere. I'm frustrated and so are my customers! What will you do to help?" The employees proceeded to take over the meeting and our dialogue continued in this fashion until it was time to leave.[22]

Martinez's efforts, particularly with the Phoenix teams' task force initiatives and the Town Hall meetings, successfully broke through Sears' equilibrium. And this breakthrough ignited employees' commitment to the company's adaptive challenge.

The Sears story continues to unfold. During his first four years, Martinez made enormous strides. Employees were assuming more responsibility for sales floor success, experiencing an increased sense of power, and identifying more authentically with the corporation's aspirations and challenges. Employees at all levels were feeling they could make a difference and their contributions would be valued. Martinez encouraged constructive contention that had previously been silenced at Sears. He aggressively encouraged his organization to learn from customers, suppliers, and competitors.

When Martinez began at Sears, he had the advantage of a honeymoon. It is one thing to engage in radical acts of adaptive leadership when you are new to a job; any early improvements are greeted with delighted surprise by stakeholders accustomed to disappointment. But this status has a half-life. Once Martinez took the helm, missteps, when they occurred, could no longer be assigned to the old regime. A series of embarrassments and setbacks in 1997 and 1998 took the wind out of Sears' sails just as the mall stores were making headway with adaptive change.

It was revealed that Sears Automotive was (inadvertently) selling barely used, once recharged batteries and representing them as new. Its credit card division was violating bankruptcy statutes. The company was accused of reneging on insurance commitments (Sears was subsequently upheld in the courts), and former employees demonstrated in front of its mall stores. In each of these instances, Martinez confronted the problems squarely, admitted to wrongdoings, and settled with those who had been injured.[23]

As discussed earlier in this chapter, Martinez was persuaded that "improving employee satisfaction," as a way of improving customer satisfaction (and, in turn, revenues and margins in the mall stores) would lead to Sears' redemption in the marketplace. But, as noted, both he and his senior management team fell victim to doing the right things without internalizing the accompanying living systems insight. Martinez took a series of actions consistent with living systems theory but, at the end of the day, he did not exhibit any deep-seated conviction that tapping into the collective intelligence of frontline sales personnel was essential to sustained success. Failing to comprehend the entire enterprise as a living system that would always drift toward equilibrium, he managed to power through a one-time episodic shift but did not create ongoing adaptive capability.

There were some mitigating circumstances. Martinez was distracted by several embarrassing situations and lawsuits. He was deeply involved in repositioning Sears' new market entrants—Parts America, Orchard Supply, and Sears HomeLife Furniture (which remain in stiff competition with Auto Zone, Home Depot, and Crate & Barrel). The mall stores officially reported to a business unit head to whom Martinez had delegated full accountability for the turnaround. Still, the unrelenting challenge of adaptive leadership is to manage the level of distress in a way that keeps the entire organization constantly aware that discontinuous results can only be achieved by discontinuous means. Martinez did not sustain this awareness. His compromises, particularly with the command and control executive who headed mall store merchandising and the president of the mall stores (who allowed old Sears ways to persist), sent mixed messages to management and implied that it was acceptable to retreat into a comfort zone.

An example of a mixed signal that adumbrated trouble ahead was the limited preparation offered to mall store managers who were responsible for introducing the first round of Town Hall meetings to 800 stores. At the senior levels of Sears, a carefully constructed program for these sessions was put in place. Based on the principal of "see one, do one, teach one," all seven regional vice presidents received two days of intensive training as did the teams of 7 district managers that reported to each vice president. The two-day district manager sessions were conducted by Sears headquarters staff in each of the regions around the country. But that's where it ended. The store managers themselves (twenty per district) were trained unevenly by district managers. At times, as little as two and one-half hours were allotted to covering both the Town Hall meetings design and the learning visuals. Notwithstanding this lack of preparation, the learning visuals were effective. Yet, the larger issue of management's lack of involvement in the critical activity of mobilizing employees was reflected in the stores' diminishing attendance. Most stores participated in the first round of Town Hall meetings (using the "New Day on Retail Street" learning visual), but only half the stores hosted the second round of Town Hall meetings six months later, when the second learning visual ("Sears Money Map," a Monopoly-like game that communicated Sears' sources and uses of funds) was introduced. By the third round, store participation had dwindled to 30 percent. Steven Kirn, director of this effort, states "The learning maps were a powerful tool that we did not leverage to the fullest. We dropped the ball on this one."[24]

Behind the scenes, Martinez faced a problem of alignment. His two key lieutenants, the executive vice president of Retail Stores and the senior vice president of Merchandising, had never authentically bought into the mobilization of employees that Martinez had unleashed. Over the ensuing months, the two senior executives issued edicts to squeeze costs and hold margins—all reasonable measures, but imposed in a fashion that eroded employees' hard-won faith. Did customer service really matter and was employee input truly valued? Once again, the answers became shrouded in doubt. When Martinez discovered these reversals, he did not confront those involved. Instead, he tried to persuade and cajole, waiting for a consensus that never came. Belatedly, he reorganized the top three posts and terminated the services of the two wayward executives. By then, most of the employee commitment—as well as the stores' vibrancy, so evident two years earlier—was gone.

The Martinez era came to a close with more of a whimper than a bang. But this much is clear: Sears, whatever its future, is very much a complex adaptive system. It reflects (1) the ever shifting struggle between equilibrium and innovation and (2) the unending tension between the preserving forces of tradition and the transforming forces of change.

There is no permanent victory in this eternal cycle of life and death. Rather, species and organizations cope—some better and some worse—with the challenges as best they can. Understanding living systems does not decisively win the game but, most assuredly, it improves the odds.

PART TWO

CHAPTER 4

SURFING THE EDGE
OF CHAOS

The edge of chaos is a condition, not a location. It is a permeable, intermediate state through which order and disorder flow, not a finite line of demarcation. Moving to the edge of chaos creates upheaval but not dissolution. That's why the *edge* of chaos is so important. The edge is not the abyss. It's the sweet spot for productive change.[1]

The first fire ant arrived from South America before World War II. Naturalist Richard Conniff has extensively documented the fifty-plus years of war against this species—how pushing it to the edge of chaos evoked its astonishing array of survival strategies. To date, the fire ant is winning, having proliferated and expanded from its initial beachhead in Miami to occupy 260 million acres in eleven states. Cameo appearances in Phoenix, Arizona, and Santa Barbara, California, were thwarted (at least temporarily) by exterminators.[2]

The galvanizing force behind these extermination efforts is the ants' sting, which afflicts about five million Americans a year. The venom from a single ant is milder than a bee sting. The problem is that, like eggs at the supermarket, the stings tend to come in dozens. The ants self-organize to do it in concert. (They actually send a signal and sting all at once!) Toddlers falling into fire ant mounds have died of their stings. The ants kill newborn calves. "They swarm over bedded-down fawns," states Conniff. "When they try to lick them, they are stung inside the stomach, where autopsies have found ants by the hundreds." From island bird sanctuaries off Corpus Christi, Texas, where fire ants threatened pelican colonies by eating their hatchlings alive, to road accidents where, according to Conniff, they often get to human victims faster than an ambulance, or to the drastic reduction of biodiversity, where fire ants have diminished the population of nesting birds, reptiles, mammals, and other ants by as much as 90 percent, this species has adapted brilliantly to circumvent hazards, exploit opportunities, and thwart all efforts to control its territorial encroachment.[3]

At the individual level, fire ants behave as classic "agents" in a complex adaptive system. Entomologist Douglas Hofstadler writes: "Individual ants are remarkably reflex-driven. Most of their behavior can be described in terms of the invocation of one or more of about a dozen rules in the form 'grasp about with mandibles,' 'follow a pheromone trail' (scents that encode 'this way to food,' 'this way to combat,' and so on) in the direction of an increasing (or decreasing) gradient, test any moving object for 'colony member scent' and 'sting it if it is not,' and so on."[4]

This repertoire, though small, is continuously evoked as an ant moves through its changing environment. An individual ant is at high risk whenever it encounters situations not covered by the rules. Most ants—worker ants, in particular—survive at most a few weeks before succumbing to some situation not covered by the rules.[5]

How have colonies of fire ants managed to multiply and thrive in the face of a $172 million campaign to eliminate them? Chalk it up to the ants' survival instinct, seemingly amplified in direct proportion to humankind's efforts to eradicate it. The fire ant appears to thrive at the edge of chaos.[6]

Frontal assault commenced in 1950, when the U.S. Department of Agriculture (USDA) sprayed 27 million acres with the pesticide heptachlor. "The spray killed fire ants—along with reptiles, mammals, birds, and fish, plus livestock and pets," states Conniff. Heptachlor became one of Rachel Carson's chief targets in *The Silent Spring*. Humbled by negative publicity and convincing evidence that fire ants rebounded much faster than the other species drenched in the insecticide fog, the experts sought an environmentally benign pesticide—mirex. Commencing in 1970, this "perfect pesticide" was sprayed by bombers over 130 million acres. The spraying, Conniff notes, "was discontinued 16 years later when shown to be a potent killer of crustaceans and a possible carcinogen with a particular knack for concentrating in human fat tissue."[7]

All the while, and notwithstanding setbacks from this massive Vietnam-scale assault, the fire ant, like the wily Viet Cong, dug in and improvised. How? The answer lies generally in advantages that inhere in all social species, and specifically in the fire ants' remarkable capacity to generate ingenious defenses.

When the ants' environment is benign, there is one queen per colony. Conniff points out that "queen" is really a misnomer for a reproduction machine that lays sixty to one hundred eggs per hour (a level of output that replicates the queen's own body weight every twenty-four hours) and continues this for perhaps six years! This is the equivalent of a 120-pound woman giving birth to a half million eight-pound babies a year. As environmental adversity intensifies, rival queens will live together in a communal nest until the colony reaches a critical mass, at which time the worker ants will execute all but one of the queens.[8]

When the environment becomes outright hostile (that is, nearer to chaos), surviving colonies strive to rebuild their army of workers, which occasionally triggers warfare between colonies. Conniff notes that some fire ant free-for-alls escalate. Workers steal rival colonies' eggs and larvae, often hauling the disputed booty across a 100-foot-wide battlefield. The human equivalent would be an adult who carries his or her own weight twenty-five miles at a full run in broiling sun.[9] Gradually, the weaker colonies merge into larger ones. Walter Tschinter, an ant researcher at Florida State University, has observed: "[The] losing queen joins the surrender party in parade as her former workers carry her eggs to the conqueror's nest. . . . Since her defecting army represents the spoils of war and gains her entry to the new community, she may, with luck, survive the regicides and regain her supremacy because the community of ants seems to determine which queen survives not by genetic loyalty but fertility."[10]

Perpetual life on the edge has fostered even more remarkable innovations. As the pesticide wars escalated, researchers discovered *permanent* multiple-queen colonies that often had sustained twenty to thirty queens. When one queen died, these colonies never skipped a beat. Some had 300 queens, all laying eggs. In these instances, colonies were packed together in extraordinary densities. Instead of the normal distribution of forty mounds per acre, the super-colonies clustered 400 mounds (22.6 million ants per acre or 519 individuals per square foot). This density has a huge impact on foraging efficiency. In single-queen colonies with the usual spacing, workers usually show up at a food source in two minutes. In multiple-queen colonies, they arrive in just twenty seconds.[11]

Human beings aren't ants, and organizations aren't ant colonies. But when productive agitation runs high, innovation often thrives and startling breakthroughs can come about. This elusive much-sought-after sweet spot is sometimes called "a burning platform." The living sciences call it the edge of chaos.

Andy Grove, the Chairman of Intel, has had a long-standing acquaintance with this realm. He embraces it as part of his executive tool kit. His skills at the edge have been honed by several incidents in Intel's history: the forced march from semiconductors into memory chips (DRAMS) as Intel shifted from a me-too clone of Texas Instruments and Fairchild to define a distinct competitive advantage; the retreat from DRAMS to microprocessors (when Asian price reductions and Japanese quality destroyed Intel's market niche); and, more recently, the branding of the Pentium chip, which alienated Intel's largest customers (the PC manufacturers) by establishing a retail franchise with end users.

Microprocessors, the mother lode of information technology, are not only the expensive brains of personal computers and workstations. They are becoming increasingly important to intelligent automotive controls, cell phones, and consumer electronics of all kinds. The wealth-creating potential of microprocessors has been a magnet to Intel's competitors. Every new Intel offering sparks an arms race with clone suppliers seeking to introduce a cheaper alternative. Grove recalls:

By the mid-nineties, a PC price war, abetted by the Asian economic crisis, had shaved $100 off the average price of a computer. We had to face the disturbing possibility that the pace at which we could introduce a new microprocessor (premium prices for a year, then priced for the middle market a year later, and finally value-priced for the low end) was collapsing. We had to speed up this cascade. A new product that used to migrate to the bottom of the market over three years needed to get there in twelve to eighteen months to retain our competitive edge.

As you try to make sense of the new landscape [i.e., formulate the adaptive challenge], I've learned it is important to move the organization quickly from denial to acceptance of change [i.e., disturb equilibrium]. Doing so usually involves two phases. First, you must experiment and let chaos reign. That's important because you're not likely to successfully stumble on the answer at the first sign of trouble. Rather, you have to let the business units struggle and watch the dissonance grow in the company [i.e., manage the level of distress]. As this unfolds, you enter the second phase of change, which I describe as the Valley of Death [i.e., the edge of chaos]. Doing away with established practice and established people—tearing apart before you can put together something new—is not fun. It is wise to refrain from talking too much about where this is all going in the early stage. Talking prematurely about changes that disrupt people's lives and are not truly believed can undermine efforts before you really know what you're doing. But once they are in place [i.e., the adaptive challenge has been met], it is essential for leadership to speak clearly about what the changes mean and what the organization is going to do. At this point, you are at the other side of the Valley of Death and you can describe the future that lies ahead.[12]

As we have discussed in preceding chapters, innovations rarely emerge from systems with high degrees of order and stability. Systems in equilibrium lose diversity and give rise to the sorts of problems one encounters in incestuous communities and centrally planned economies. On the other hand, completely chaotic systems—riots, the stock market crash of 1929, or the Chinese Cultural Revolution of 1965–1976—are "too hot to handle." Productive inroads must wait until things settle down a bit.

When a complex adaptive system is moved toward the edge of chaos—when hurricanes and typhoons roil the deep seas, or fires rage through forests or prairies—the potential for generativity is maximized. Hurricanes recharge the oceans with oxygen and nutrients, and replenish carbon dioxide in the atmosphere.[13] Fires, we learned in our discussion of Yellowstone, cleanse a forest and make room for new life. In fact, fires have been found to be absolutely essential to the regeneration of the tall grass prairies of the Great Plains. The biodiversity inherent in prairies is stifled when fires are suppressed.

Norman Packard, of the Santa Fe Institute, coined the term "edge of chaos" to define a fertile domain for revitalization. "The ghost in nature's machine," he wrote, "almost seems to be purposefully piloting the system to the edge of chaos."[14] The components of a system at the edge of chaos are far from a condition where they lock into place, yet their level of excitation is not so extreme that the system dissolves entirely. Nobel laureate Herbert Simon views transformation as a shift in identity.[15] The edge of chaos is the precondition for transformation to take place.

Many scientific disciplines—microbiology, neuroscience, ecology, paleontology, economics—have found evidence in support of Packard's speculations. The edge of chaos is the locus of all sorts of innovative activity. Paleontologist Stephen Jay Gould, whose discoveries have popularized the term "punctuated evolution," accumulated fossil evidence that challenged Darwin's gradualism. Gould has documented that major environmental disturbances, such as asteroid impacts or radical shifts in weather, can trigger the proliferation of new species and accelerate adaptation within species.[16]

Microbiologists have shown that both the frequency and the density of mutations increase as the evolutionary challenge becomes more complex. Geneticists have observed a sharp increase in mutations of genetic structure when disturbances to the parent gene approach a point of criticality (i.e., near the edge of chaos).[17] Beyond this point, the gene rapidly disintegrates. Summarizing the accumulating evidence, geneticist Stuart Kauffman writes: "Darwin believed that mutations and natural selection would improve the flexibility in biological systems over time through the accumulation of a succession of minor variations just as tinkering can improve technology. But networks near the edge of chaos have the flexibility to adjust at an accelerated rate and trigger cascades of change."[18]

But why "the edge"? Wouldn't it suffice to disturb equilibrium but give the edge of chaos a wide berth?

Edges are important to life; in fact, we are drawn to them. They define a frontier that tells us we are about to venture farther than we have ever gone before. "As long as one operates in the middle of things," states science writer William Thompson, "one can never really know the nature in which one moves."[19]

The visual cortex of our brain directs our eyes to look for edges, helping us to distinguish figure from background and consequently to get our bearings. Living systems generally push up against the edge as a way of determining how much turbulence is enough. The yellow light of a traffic signal triggers motorists' response. They either apply the brakes or accelerate through the intersection. The yellow light is analogous to the "edge." It stimulates heightened awareness and generates a burst of adrenaline and mental activity. Drivers can then avoid ending up in cross traffic in the intersection, which would be analogous to outright chaos.

Consider your own way of coping with deadlines. Fortunately, many if not most of us marshal our cognitive and psychological energies to meet them. Typically, when they are still far in the future, we experience no urgency; we may even feel complacent. But if the deadline is imminent and we know we cannot meet it, we experience unproductive stress and mental gridlock. Too much stress causes us to oversimplify, jump to conclusions, become paralyzed, or default to old habits and prior success routines.[20] We learn from experience how to make constructive use of an upcoming time limit; we know that an unmet deadline will evoke an optimal level of adrenaline, tension, and creativity. Many people experience their most productive moments near this temporal edge of chaos.

On Purpose: Images of Life at the Edge of Chaos

On Purpose, a nonprofit consulting partnership, provides these images of life at the edge of chaos:[a]

- Swarms. Lots of individuals buzzing around, taking collective and independent action. (At Intel, Andy Grove turned to his R&D community of 650 best-in-class engineers and challenged them to invent breakthrough chips *and* halve cycle time. Teams formed and dispersed. The solution came by designing a means to decrease the functionality and cost of the chip architecture rather than banking on the learning curve for manufacturing and distribution within a compressed twelve-to-eighteen-month time frame.)
- Jungles. Connections are messy, overlapping, webbed, and redundant. (Intel's R&D community reached across technology, manufacturing, and sales in helter-skelter ways to drive the discovery process. At its climax, this crisscrossing seemed chaotic, was uncoordinated, and contained a lot of duplication.)
- A mad scientist's lab. Lots of half-finished prospects exhibit serendipitous connections, evidence of false starts, and occasional breakthroughs. (Intel's discovery process generated ten dead ends for every breakthrough. There was no orderly funnel through which ideas were screened and the "bad" ones could be quickly vetoed. Proposals that looked weak at the beginning finished strong, and vice versa.)

---

[a] Cleveland, et al., op. Cit., p. 26.

Navigating the Edge of Chaos

Many managers are uneasy with the idea of drawing an organization away from its comfort zone and skirting the abyss called chaos. Understanding the practical do's and don'ts of these excursions reduces apprehension. The journey is, in fact, far less reckless than it may first appear.

The distinctions and terminology that have evolved within the disciplines of complexity science serve as aids in navigating the shoals of chaos. Analogously, these devices function like the navigational charts, compass, sextant, and propulsion system needed to pilot a vessel. Adopting three distinctions of science helps us navigate near the edge of chaos in the business world:

1. *Attractors,* analogous to a compass, orient a living system in one particular direction and provide organisms with the impetus to migrate out of their comfort zone. (Chapter 5 describes how experiences at Monsanto have demonstrated the practical application of attractors.)

2. *Amplifying and damping feedback* serves like the throttle of a propulsion system; it causes a process of change either to accelerate or to slow down. The revitalization of British Petroleum's Oil Exploration unit, described in Chapter 6, demonstrates how amplification can be used to push a system out of equilibrium and toward the edge of chaos. BP's Oil Exploration unit also used damping controls to prevent the system from spiraling into confusion and nonperformance.

3. *Fitness landscapes,* used by ecologists and other life scientists to map the relative competitive advantage of species, are more useful as visualization devices than the traditional two-dimensional diagrams of inputs/outputs and feedback loops that one encounters in systems dynamics. Monsanto illustrates how an organization moves over its fitness landscape, modifying the topography as it goes.

Attractors: They Move You in New Directions[21]

Attractors appear in three forms: point attractors, cycle attractors, and strange attractors. Think of them as magnets that draw a complex adaptive system in a particular direction.

1. *Point attractors*, most commonly found in the inanimate world, lure systems to a stable position of rest. A pendulum swings but eventually settles at the lowest point and stops. Entropy is an example in nature. All living things are drawn eventually to this point of total stillness.

A point attractor in commerce is a monopoly or an extremely stable market niche. For instance, Vulcan Materials sells crushed stone, gravel, and rock asphalt in Alabama. Conveniently, Vulcan controls most of the gravel quarries in the state and has a lock on the base material used for roads as well as the aggregate used in making concrete. As long as Vulcan's prices are below what it costs to haul gravel in from a neighboring state, Vulcan owns the market.[22]

2. *Cycle attractors* move systems into loops of predictable but dynamic patterns. An expanding population of rabbits in a particular area attracts a corresponding increase in the fox population until most of the rabbits have been eaten or have retreated. This precipitates a decrease in fox numbers, and, in turn, creates conditions for the resurgence of rabbits.

In commerce, we see cycle attractors in the varying numbers of fans whose attendance at professional sporting events is governed by winning or losing seasons, or in the beverage consumption patterns driven by the perpetual cycle of prizes, promotions, and price wars between oligopolistic rivals such as Coca-Cola and Pepsi.

The above descriptions of point and cycle attractors are provided in the spirit of completeness. Strange attractors, the third type, are of greatest interest to complexity theorists and are most relevant to applications in business.

3. *Strange attractors* lure systems to the edge of chaos.[23] The strange attractor in the earlier discussion of fire ants arises from the interplay between the survival instinct and a hostile environment. This instinct exists within all species but is catalyzed by the fire ants' ecosystem as extermination efforts intensify. Strange attractors do not occur in a species in isolation; instead, they arise from the interaction between an organism and its environment. For reasons not well understood, this evokes a quest of unusual scope and scale. If this sounds more like science fiction than science, readers' misgivings are not entirely unfounded. That's what makes these attractors "strange"!

"Strange" is an unsettling term. As noted above, however, it is an apt adjective because such attractors have an unfathomable property. Black holes, with their infinite power to attract and compress, are an example in nature—as is gravity, which exists, simultaneously, nowhere and everywhere, and eventually curves in space.

A particular mystery is how strange attractors come into existence and then shape events. They operate like a magnet among iron filings: Multiple nodes within a system align with one another and coalesce into a pattern.

A cursory look at the chain of events that led to the global treaty to eradicate land mines might reach the superficial conclusion that Princess Diana's highly publicized visits to maimed victims in Afghanistan, which highlighted the chronic danger to children crippled many years after the end of hostilities, acted as the strange attractor. Wrong. Nor did the global consortium of public and private agencies, which publicly declared their intention to outlaw these devices, precipitate the treaty. The key to understanding the emerging consensus to outlaw land mines is also the key to understanding all strange attractors: There is no single, unitary cause, no "it." The strange attractor for the land mine treaty was catalyzed by all of the above factors, reinforced by:

1. The power of global communications to bring the suffering of Angolan and Afghan children into the living rooms of the industrialized world.
2. Human empathy for the suffering of innocent land mine victims.

3. New technology that makes it possible to locate and defuse land mines.
4. A new communal spirit among nations, which facilitated stakeholders' taking constructive action on a compelling humanitarian problem.

Fritz Roethlisberger, the late professor at Harvard Business School and a pioneer in the field of organizational behavior, once observed: "Most people think of the future as the ends and the present as the means, whereas, in fact, the present is the ends and the future the means." Translated, Roethlisberger tells us that a strange attractor—for example, the campaign to outlaw land mines—informs and alters what people do now. In that respect, the future is the *means* to alter behavior. The new behavior shapes the ends, which in turn alter the future, and the spiral continues.

One doesn't creep up on a big future. Rather, the future is boldly declared and serves as the catalyst for all that follows. When President Kennedy announced his moonwalk vision, there were no solutions to the problems that lay ahead: Congressional approval, appropriation of funds, technological breakthroughs, and the rejuvenation of the National Aeronautics and Space Administration (NASA), which had languished for years in the internecine rivalry of Army versus Navy versus Air Force rocketry programs.

Despite these many problems, the strange attractor—the impetus in this unique case—was a collection of emotions and aspirations: desire, excitement, curiosity, power, a quest for knowledge, a competitive wish to be the first country to accomplish a moonwalk, and imperialistic lust. Leaders and ordinary citizens alike were inspired to work toward accomplishing miracles in Congress, in laboratories, and across the nation. Putting a man on the moon by the end of the 1960s acted as a powerful force that drew opposing factions into a single mission. Those involved undoubtedly lived at the edge of chaos. Some of their experiences on the edge have been represented in movies about the space program and in autobiographies of astronauts.

Frequently, when we look back on crucial experiences that have changed our individual lives, our nation, or even the world, we tend to regard those particular events as destined to transpire, as though nothing could have prevented their occurrence. Perhaps we think of Christopher Columbus's journey to America with that kind of hindsight; maybe we view the space program as being inevitable. We can, almost always, justify the "inevitability" of any event or outcome, but not because the situation was, in fact, predestined. Instead, we are analyzing and reviewing these breakthrough conundrums retrospectively. *What we did, how we acted, and what methods we employed* appear to be the only logical course. But that perspective ignores the crucial issue of how enactment on behalf of a powerful goal alters the structure of reality.

Drawn by the strange attractor, we evolve, perhaps temporarily, into individuals who are different and better, which suddenly and unexpectedly increases the odds of our making a future aspiration a reality. *Being* the right way makes *doing* the right thing a lot more likely.[24] And for that outcome we can thank strange attractors, which sometimes galvanize organizations—which is to say, all of us—to achieve greatly.

The question now becomes: How does one create a strange attractor in a business context? The technical term for the vision and values dreamed up by the CEO and headlined in annual reports and on office bulletin boards is "bullshit" or "future schlock." Too often, such pronouncements have been authored by a CEO or an elite group operating in relative isolation and unduly influenced by management fads, altruism, or navel gazing. When the future schlock is disseminated to the workforce, the bewildered and amused employees don't understand why their chief executive officer would circulate awkward statements on television tapes about a future that their collective experience says will never be. The taped recitations offer little that resonates with the employees' souls and sensibilities. Further, such trite incantations are often honored in the breach. The business-as-usual music does not jibe with the new lyrics.

The vision-and-values proclamation issued by David Whitwam, CEO of the Whirlpool Corporation, is a concrete example of this type of disconnect. His glossy package evoked precisely the employee incredulity we are describing.

> Vision: Whirlpool, in its chosen lines of business, will grow with new opportunities and be the leader in an ever changing global market. We will be driven by our commitment to continuous quality improvement and to exceeding all of our customers' expectations. We will gain competitive advantage through this, and by building on our existing strengths and developing new competencies. We will be market-driven, efficient, and profitable. Our success will make Whirlpool a company that worldwide customers, employees, and other stakeholders can depend on.
>
> Objectives: Whirlpool is dedicated to achieving global leadership and to delivering exceptional shareholder value. Our goal for "total return to shareholders" is to be in the top 25 percent of large, publicly held corporations. This will be done by achieving "very satisfied" customers throughout the world. To assure this, our global business operating goals are: customer satisfaction, total quality, and growth.

When Whirlpool asked employees to evaluate the vision, only 20 percent thought it was valuable and believable. "A substantial majority," states communications researcher Sander Larkin, "said, 'We didn't trust you before and we don't trust you now.'"[25] Why? Because the Whirlpool statement did not resonate with the experiences and street smarts of the workforce; it lacked the imagination and inspirational quality that motivates people to reach beyond themselves. Imposed from above, the vision and values were seen almost as satire.

In contrast to Whirlpool's proclamation, Ford Motor Company's declaration to employees and customers—"Quality is Job 1"—was powerfully energizing and motivating. It represented a radical break from Ford's shoddy quality, and the mantra was reinforced continuously, in words and in actions, from the highest echelons to the factory floor.[26]

It accomplished wonders.

An assessment of Ford's success alongside Whirlpool's failure sheds light on strange attractors. Their emergence takes a lot more than charismatic leadership and a sexy aspirational slogan.

Philip Caldwell and Donald Peterson, the top leaders at Ford, were decidedly not charismatic, but the emergence of a strange attractor seems to have little to do with leadership style. It has everything to do with an organization's latent appetites, which are already present but await articulation. The leader, who may sense the dormant energy, catalyzes it—in effect, seeding the clouds with iodine crystals. When the raindrops materialize, was it the crystals or the cloud that ended the drought?

A strange attractor is never milled from new material. It is already in the woodwork. That is what makes it both strange and powerful. It isn't something a leader "gives" or "does" to followers. It is emergent. The attractor comes into existence because it resonates from sympathetic chords in the environment, the times, the organization's members, and a leader who can express the challenge in a way that invites others into a dance that is being choreographed as it is performed.

To summarize: (1) strange attractors are cogenerated—they arise through the convergence of many factors within the organization and its environment; (2) they materialize when what is already present is expressed in a way that provides shape and substance; (3) they flourish in an environment of adaptive challenge and tend to atrophy when subjugated under the heavy hand of social engineering; and (4) they foster breakthroughs and outcomes that are unforeseen and unimaginable.

A close look at Monsanto reveals these dynamics at work.

CHAPTER 5

MONSANTO: WALKING ON A TRAMPOLINE

We have chosen Monsanto as an illustrative case study. Why, given the growing controversy surrounding genetically altered crops and foods? Simply, Monsanto's transformation between 1993 and 1999 is instructive on several levels. It exemplifies much of our discussion of adaptive leadership and the power of a strange attractor to disturb equilibrium. Monsanto moved to the edge of chaos in order to alter its identity and transform its culture.

By 1999, opposition, globally and within the scientific community, to genetically modified crops and foods had slowed Monsanto's momentum considerably. We will address this outcome in detail in this and later chapters.

To begin at the beginning, we need to trace the firm's initial, highly successful reinvention of itself. In three years, Monsanto radically altered its portfolio, took on and surpassed competitors many times its size, and quadrupled its stock price. Today, having merged with Upjohn to form Pharmacia, it continues to rank well among its peers in most comparisons.

Monsanto's CEO, Robert Shapiro, engaged in both operational and adaptive types of leadership. He employed operational leadership to downsize staff, divest some business units, and pursue strategic acquisitions to reorient the company. He exercised adaptive leadership to generate new products and capabilities within the company.

When Robert Shapiro became CEO of Monsanto in March 1993, he inherited a low-growth, highly cyclical company with primary assets in petrochemicals and agricultural commodity products. Reminiscent of Hernando Cortés, burning his ships to focus his soldiers' attention on the conquest of Mexico, Shapiro divested Monsanto of its $3.8 billion mainstay chemical business to rededicate the company's energies as a pioneer in life sciences. Exploiting Monsanto's liquidity and borrowing capacity, he invested $8 billion to secure life sciences patents, know-how, and technology and so acquired some of the world's largest seed companies.[1] There was no turning back.

An avid follower of the emerging science of complexity, Shapiro was one of the first senior executives to visit the Santa Fe Institute. The exposure kindled ideas that gave shape and substance to Monsanto's reinvention journey. CEOs' offices often have a credenza displaying the latest business books. (Indeed, the comprehensive selection is usually so current that one wonders if it is perpetually updated by the same nightly service that waters the plants.) Shapiro's credenza displayed only multiple copies of the same volume: Kevin Kelly's *Out of Control,* one of the first books to discuss the self-organizing properties of nature. Rarely could a subordinate exit Shapiro's office without being given a copy. *Out of Control* provided a template that inspired Shapiro to lead in a fashion that unleashed the distributed intelligence of Monsanto.[2]

Significantly, when Monsanto underwent its reincarnation as a "Life Sciences Company," it leaped a chasm as wide as the one Sears would have spanned had Martinez sought to shift from a mall retailer to an e-retailer. That a mediocre Midwestern chemicals manufacturer even considered taking on the likes of Zeneca, Novartis, and Dupont is remarkable.[3]

None of Monsanto's subsequent success was preordained. External threats in the down cycle of the chemical business were compounded by internal cultural barriers. Monsanto was conservative, tradition-bound, politicized, and notorious for its parochial silos. Consistent with industry practice, its separate fertilizer, herbicide, and insulation divisions ran independent bulk processing operations. As is generally true in commodity businesses, the focus was more on cost than on customers.[4] Although technological innovation was a component in the bulk processing value chain, it remained a low priority. Along with research, it was more visible in the annual report than in the mainstream operations of the company.

Shapiro came to Monsanto through the acquisition of Searle Pharmaceuticals. In a reverse acquisition, Monsanto obtained Searle as a high-tech, high-growth asset, and former Searle CEO Shapiro became Monsanto's new CEO.

Shapiro had reckoned with the strategic challenges of melding the two companies but not with the cultural differences. "My 'welcoming' E-mail from Monsanto employees about the way this place worked made 'Dilbert' look good," he reported soon after his arrival. "They were repeatedly telling us, 'We're prepared to sacrifice your ideas and commitment for your obedience.'"[5]

Shapiro recognized an immediate need to radically shift this organizational mindset, to cultivate talent, ingenuity, nimbleness, and technological skills, and to become more "Silicon Valley" than "St. Louis" (where Monsanto is located). Divesting the chemical business and resetting the portfolio toward life sciences was the easy part. Because most acquisitions fail, the success of yoking Searle to Monsanto would depend on a thoroughgoing transformation. To do this, Shapiro needed to upend Monsanto's traditional hierarchy and unleash the potential in the ranks.

Shapiro was drawn to the notion of "strange attractors." The concept evoked the unfathomable possibilities of the big future that

Monsanto so desperately needed. Strange attractors are cogenerated; they cannot be conjured forth by top-down pronouncements. All this jibed with Shapiro's sensibilities and leadership inclinations.

Shapiro passionately believed Monsanto's "strange attractor" would emerge through the intersection of new developments in bioengineering for food and agriculture, more powerful computers that could apply these breakthroughs in plants, and Monsanto's unique market knowledge. He chose the forum of Town Hall meetings to introduce these ideas and begin a dialogue. Over a six-month period, Monsanto's entire scientific and professional cadre attended these meetings. The sessions exemplified how the ingredients of a strange attractor are introduced, kneaded, and shaped by conversation. The process can galvanize an organization to move toward the edge of chaos.[6]

Picture one of the first of these sessions—a large workshop in Chicago, in 1995, attended by 300 of the company's informal leaders. Standing on a raised dais, pacing back and forth, and speaking into a wireless microphone in his lapel, Shapiro seems at ease—like someone trying to talk through a problem in your living room. He tells his audience:[7]

Here's what bothers me. There are almost six billion people in the world but the global economy works for only one billion of them. Even for the favored group (and the two billion that are about to join it), there are rising expectations as to the amounts, choice, quality, and health of food. At the other end of the continuum, at least one and a half billion of the world's population are in real trouble. Eight hundred million of these are so malnourished that they cannot participate in work or family life and are on the edge of starvation. Finally, over the next thirty years, most of the additional people joining the planet will be born in poorer places.

The system we have is unsustainable. We burn a lot of hydrocarbons, waste a lot of stuff. There is not enough acreage on earth to provide for humanity's food needs using traditional technology. In developed countries there is the interesting challenge of aging. The elderly consume a lot of health care as technology offers more costly interventions. Fewer people in the workforce end up supporting the higher bill for those who are old. This, too, is politically unsustainable.

Food is shifting from an issue of fuel and calories to an issue of choice. With growing nutritional and environmental consciousness, food must inevitably command a larger share of mind.

These problems for humanity can also be seen as a trillion-dollar opportunity. These are all unresolved problems. It isn't just a question of modular extensions of what we have (via technology and innovations in distribution). We need to reinvent our approach fundamentally.

Biotechnology is a profoundly different avenue for agriculture and human health. And information technology provides enough of a difference in degree that it represents a nanotechnology. Biotechnology is really a subset of information technology. It does not deal with the information that's encoded electronically in silicon but with the information that is encoded chemically in cells, not used for E-mail or spreadsheets but information that tells what proteins to make, when to make them, and how to make them. The rate of increase of knowledge in this field puts Moore's Law to shame, doubling every twelve to eighteen months. We will map the entire human genome by 2005, and will understand most of the functionality of the genome in this same period.

I believe our agriculture and health care systems will be revolutionized by the intersection of biotechnology and information technology. There is something of great consequence in the convergence of these technologies with our market knowledge, and I want you to help me discover what it is.

Shapiro's words resonate with the audience and provide a glimpse of a strange attractor in the making. It's a little like galactic dust coalescing into a star. The interplay goes something like this: Shapiro points to pieces in the puzzle (life sciences breakthroughs, agriculture, information technology, market knowledge); listeners relate his words to their own experience and fill in the blanks with their detailed knowledge of the business; Shapiro focuses on the *unsustainable* problems facing humanity—immense challenges that cry out for nontraditional solutions.

Many in the room are moved at the prospect of contributing to the elimination of world hunger and chronic suffering. Those from Searle understand the relevance of their expertise in life sciences and bioengineering; those from traditional Monsanto see the usefulness of their knowledge of the food and agriculture industries—the mindset and methods of farmers, and the value of their suppliers and channels of distribution. Others in the audience bring threshold proficiency in the information technology needed to simulate genetic permutations and identify plant applications.

Shapiro's words are a sketch, an architect's rendering, not a blueprint. Old-timers and newcomers begin to locate themselves in the ambition. Shapiro continues:

> The key to the future will be pulling networks of these disciplines together. Ciba Geigy is attempting this in their merger with Sandoz to form Novartis. Novartis is larger than we are in agriculture, nutrition, and pharmaceuticals. Hoechst and Zeneca will get there. Even Dupont recognizes it is no longer sufficient to be big.
>
> Whether they or we or others will pull this off will depend on four key attributes: Foresight (see ahead), Insight (see deeply), Speed, and Courage. The degree of commitment needed will be of heroic proportions—much more than the normal doggedness and persistence that have been our ethic for years. We need a design at Monsanto where heroism can happen, and that's what we're embarking on today.
>
> In pharmaceuticals and biotechnology, there are short life cycles. If you are two years late, it's a commodity. Searle's Cox II [an inhibitor that arrests inflammation in arthritic joints] is an example. If we're six months ahead of Merck, there are big dollars in it for us. If we're behind, we're in trouble. The cost of R&D is so high that we have to capture large market share and premium prices to survive. It is no longer enough to be a player at the table. If we play the same game as the big guys play, the chances are high we will lose. Therefore, the question is: Can we play a different game or play the old game differently?
>
> What is the design that lets us play a different game? Better foresight? Deeper insight? Greater speed? How can we operate with dramatically more efficient internal process than they do, have richer collaborations than they do, come to decisions faster than they do, execute faster than they do? And what about more courage? Is it possible to design a Monsanto where people are somewhat braver, somewhat more honest, and somewhat less territorial so that we have a genuine competitive advantage?
>
> When we compare the ordinary days in our life with those when times were great, most of us feel we operate at 50 percent of our potential most of the time. But the efficiency we lose together is 50 percent × 50 percent

× 50 percent until it's nothing. In fact, I think that organizations like Novartis and Dupont—and Monsanto—operate at 10 percent of their potential. If we can learn to operate at 20 percent of our potential, we are twice as good as the competition. If they get to 20 percent and we get to 30 percent, we are 50 percent better.

I hope these musings will become more than a monologue and become a conversation. *Conversation* is a strategic element, a source of competitive advantage. Our success is likely to turn on the quality of conversations we have, more than any other single factor. So let's get into a conversation together and see if we can put flesh on the bones of what I've discussed this morning. What are the arenas of potential? What are the linkages between technology and market knowledge? How can we self-organize to pull this off?

"Hold on," you may be thinking. "How does this differ from a vision? What's 'strange' about this 'attractor'?"

The answer doesn't lie in Shapiro's words but in the meeting hall. Imagine a participant who was present that day—a veteran of many years logged in Monsanto's business-as-usual. Life in the core business was not very exciting. Searle had some potentially exciting pharmaceuticals in the pipeline, but the remainder of the company's portfolio—NutraSweet and Roundup herbicide (the big revenue contributors)—didn't provide a lot of reason to run to work in the morning.

As Shapiro begins to talk about the future, the future begins to alter the present. He isn't pontificating. He isn't lecturing about cost reduction or shareholder value. He's thinking out loud about the world, the human condition, and how biotechnology could profoundly alleviate the challenges facing humanity. This resonates with many listeners, perhaps evoking forgotten passions and tarnished ideals set aside or compromised long ago in the wear and tear of corporate life. His message strikes a meaningful chord. It poses professional challenges. He rekindles employees' purpose and pride. And he's probably right. *Someone* will exploit this intersection of biotechnology, information technology, agribusiness, and market knowledge. Why not Monsanto?

The company has strength in all these areas. Further depth in information technology will need to be acquired, and the challenge is still a long shot. But over the course of the day, participants begin to identify practical possibilities. The level of buy-in and excitement is palpable.

These public statements, silent conversations (inside people's heads), and subsequent small-group discussions gave birth to Monsanto's strange attractor. As the process unfolded, employees repeatedly asked Shapiro to give a more definitive shape to his "vision." He refused to do so. "It will only get in the way," he countered. "People will take it too seriously. It needs to come from us."

Shapiro's Town Hall meetings launched what became known as Monsanto's Growth Initiative.[8] Following his opening address, participants assembled from a cross section of businesses and disciplines, and from diverse geographical locations and technological backgrounds. Teams self-organized around opportunities that had enough potential to attract volunteers. In the months ahead, specific arenas of opportunity took shape. Later, volunteer effort narrowed these to specific options with business plans to exploit them.

Pierre Hochuli, Monsanto's former Director of Research and Shapiro's Growth Initiative czar, reflected on those heady times:

> Shapiro was the master of the Town Hall process. People were energized. We had 3,000 proposals out of the first Chicago meeting alone.[9]
>
> Shapiro also sought to align and energize the executives who ran Monsanto's major business units and their key staff counterparts—what Shapiro called our "beehive model": a core group of thirty-two executives organized into a flexible SWAT team rather than their traditional functional structure. Each cell was codirected by two senior managers—one from technical and the other from the commercial side. We trained them in straight talk, courage, trust, and truth-telling. [Historically, Monsanto had been a very political place.] The beehive design was Shapiro's direct translation of Kevin Kelly. As it took shape, it altered our resource allocation process. Acquisitions were made as the inquiry began to inform us where our future lay.

People gave it 150 percent. They were still doing their day jobs, then working a second shift on the Growth Initiatives, reaching across our formidable functional boundaries and subverting organizational barriers. We were worried about stress and burnout. But Shapiro believed that people would be willing to carve into their personal life and work more productively on the job if we tapped into their passion and made work meaningful. It was total havoc, total chaos. Real tensions arose because all this buzzing about was crisscrossing traditional lines of authority. Bosses no longer felt they had their finger on the pulse of what was going on. There was duplication and confusion. Mostly, we just endured it. But we did name a group of ten executive sponsors, called "Turbo Chargers," to support and shepherd the teams, help them consolidate overlapping topics, break logjams, and provide air cover and resources. Each of the arenas (e.g., Food and Health) generated specific business ideas. Three hundred such ideas were funneled down into business proposals for Phase I funding. Six months later, fifty of these ideas warranted more serious Phase II pilots. Five matured into significant revenue streams today.

The energy we unleashed was awe-inspiring and the innovations were extraordinary. We witnessed the unlikely cross-business combination of our carpet manufacturing (which weaves nylon fiber) and our cardiovascular leadership in Pharmaceuticals. We patented an inert vascular skin graft that leads the market today.

Shapiro's articulation of a strange attractor served to catalyze the collective intelligence already present in Monsanto. Likely and unlikely combinations and recombinations of people within Monsanto generated innovative, novel products and services. For example, a low-level IT person on the team developing Roundup-resistant seeds contributed the idea of *licensing*. A familiar concept in the world of software, it was way outside the box in agriculture. Yet, it turned out to be pivotal. Roundup-resistant crops would halve our sales of herbicide. This had a negative impact of $500 million on our business—a deal breaker. We'd been searching for a way to recover our R&D investment in genetically altered seeds, but we kept running into a dead end. You couldn't price the first batch high enough (and after that, farmers would grow their own seeds from our stocks!). But with licensing we could sell the seeds over and over again and not lose control of our patented technology. We explored this idea with the big industrial cotton growers and they bought it. We were off and running.

Over the course of eighteen months, probably 10,000 of Monsanto's 30,000 employees were drawn into these initiatives in one way or another. The company felt alive again—the first time in anyone's memory![10]

The impact of Monsanto's initial success was significant. The share price rocketed from $16 to $63 as analysts came to regard Monsanto as the stalking horse for the new Life Sciences industry. McKinsey, the consulting firm, pronounced Monsanto's reinvention as one of the most rapid and thoroughgoing in business history. Because the company accomplished its metamorphosis by taking the imperatives of living systems literally rather than metaphorically in its approach to change, its achievements are particularly noteworthy.

Within three years following Monsanto's introduction of genetically modified seeds, farmers had shifted 50 percent of all cotton and 40 percent of all soybeans grown in the United States to disease- and herbicide-resistant crops. American cotton growers alone reduced herbicide consumption by $1 billion.[11]

But mounting objections to genetic modification in Europe significantly slowed and, in some cases, reversed Monsanto's future. On one hand, advocates argued that genetic modification provided crops with higher nutritional value, antibodies against human disease, and enhanced plant resistance to disease. More targeted herbicides and insecticides means less use of them. Further, combining targeted herbicides with herbicide-resistant crops reduces tilling, which, in turn, lowers soil erosion and the contamination of water supplies. On the other hand, critics contended that bioengineered crops could induce biopollution. Use of the technology could lead to and perpetuate an agrarian monoculture (i.e., an industrially uniform agriculture) rather than one predicated on diversity. Insect resistance and other unforeseen effects warn that nature inevitably responds to intervention with counter developments.

Monsanto tended to dismiss these concerns initially—writing it off to a political backlash. But eventually Shapiro demonstrated his understanding of critics' concerns:

When you start talking about large-scale introduction of dramatic traits in combination with each other, you are dealing with systems that are so complicated that no one can effectively model them. You can start with running field tests—just as when you introduce a new drug, you run clinical trials to see if people really keel over. But, just as the human body is a subtle and complicated thing, it may be that only one time in a million some side effects happen. And your testing won't reveal that. It has to be out there first. So what you have to keep asking yourself is: "Suppose the worst happens. What are the consequences?"[12]

By October of 1999 the consequences of the environmental concerns were apparent. Shapiro, speaking at the Greenpeace's annual conference, stated:

Our confidence in this technology and our enthusiasm for it has, I think, widely been seen, and understandably so, as condescension or indeed arrogance. Because we thought it was our job to persuade, too often we forgot to listen.

Whatever the final outcome in the global debate, Monsanto's reinvention of its portfolio owes a good deal to the application of a living systems change model and to the power of its strange attractor.

Given the benefit of hindsight, the risks of pursuing Monsanto's strange attractor with single-minded determination become far more evident. Shapiro bet the company on the life sciences strategy, borrowed heavily, and counted on a strong price/earnings multiple to find his acquisitions. But the impact of the global controversy was significant. Revenues were suppressed, stock value plummeted ultimately forcing Shapiro into a merger with Upjohn. In the new entity, renamed Pharmacia, Shapiro is the nonexecutive chairman with no direct operating responsibilities. He stated:

There are two things that most of us feel. We feel hurt and we feel angry. We were really proud to get out front the way we did. In retrospect, it seems incredibly naïve, but it's the truth. We had real leadership. We had worked hard to do it. We had shown faith in this science when others were dubious, and it all seemed to be working. So we painted a big bull's eye on our chest and went over the top of the hill.[13]

Many share Shapiro's sense of loss. A significant transformation was achieved, but it appeared short lived. There was a sense in the ranks of shooting for the moon and ending up in geosynchronous orbit. As Pierre Hochuli observes,

> Our convictions about the future have had a huge impact on our company, the industry, and agriculture in general. But it has also made us thoughtful about the price to an organization and its people of starting with a big bang, gaining momentum, and not having the staying power to see it through.[14]

A Partial Grasp of Complexity

The story of Monsanto's rise and fall dramatically demonstrates the enormous benefits that accrue when a company embraces complexity. It also shows the perils of ignoring some of its implications. The story for the biotechnology industry is in some ways just beginning, but Monsanto's chapter is highly significant for this as well as other industries. A deeper look from the perspective of complex adaptive systems reveals lessons for businesses of all kinds.

Like so many technological changes, genetically engineered crops were created as solutions to certain problems—and these solutions came to be seen by some as problems in themselves. Monsanto's exuberant confidence in the technology's promise came to be seen by increasing numbers of people as arrogance in the face of mounting concerns. The impression of arrogance was strengthened by what were viewed as inadequate, if not dismissive, responses to these concerns.

From a scientific point of view, concerns about biotechnology's impact on ecological integrity increased alongside concerns about its safety for human health. The concerns that ultimately proved fatal for Monsanto's "Bt" products are an example.

Genetically modified (Bt) potatoes and corn require dramatically reduced levels of pesticides. But serious questions arose about rapid evolution of insect resistance to the pesticide once it is part of the plant, which would end the usefulness of a pesticide considered to be so safe when sprayed as it is used by organic farmers. The issues of unforeseen effects on other species intensified when tests demonstrated the negative effects of Bt pollen on monarch butterflies. Concerns about "escape" of genetically altered species into the wild and the resulting creation of "super-weeds" drew increased public attention when the creation of one such plant was verified only one year after the introduction of another Monsanto herbicide.

Most of the concerns had surfaced early; Monsanto was not blindsided late in its development process. What was Monsanto's response to these concerns? As the concerns took the form of a rapidly deteriorating "public opinion," they were regarded as public relations problems. Or, the issues were delegated off as regulatory issues.

Europe's confidence in their regulatory agencies hit a low in the wake of mad cow disease, but even in the United States, there was an emerging view that the regulatory system's rules and definitions were no longer adequate to the complexities of biotechnology. In a *New York Times* article on the subject in late 1998, a reporter detailed this regulatory puzzle: "The FDA does not have jurisdiction, [for example] over the Bt potato because it is considered to be not a food, but a pesticide and hence its regulation is the province of the EPA. The potato's safety was thus judged by standards less exacting than those for foods. Pesticides carry very strict labeling regulations. But for the purpose of *labeling,* the potato was transformed back into a food, regulations which require detailed nutritional information but *prohibit* mention of any presence of pesticides."[15]

Monsanto's director of corporate communications, Phil Angell, spent much time in Europe and the United States telling people about the FDA's assurances of safety. When asked about the problems of regulating for safety and the related issue of labeling, he said, "Monsanto should not have to vouchsafe the safety of biotech food. Our interest is in selling as much of it as possible. Assuring its safety is the FDA's job."[16]

The question here for the purposes of our examination is not the safety or lack of safety of genetically engineered foods. The question is that of Monsanto's accountability both for the long-term impact of its products as well as for taking criticism seriously. By October 1999, Shapiro's statement at the annual Greenpeace conference (quoted above) demonstrated a shift in Monsanto's attitudes toward its critics.

Gordon Conway, president of the Rockefeller Foundation, has spent his career spearheading the development of sustainable agriculture in the Third World. In his view, biotechnology has a necessary role to play in ending hunger and reducing suffering. For example, there are 100 million children who suffer from Vitamin A deficiency: millions are blinded and at least two million die each year. Genetically modified rice could end this problem.

Thus, Conway stunned observers and participants in his June 1998 board meeting by sharply criticizing Monsanto's efforts and making public his recommendations the following day. He criticized Monsanto for its disregard of the consumer and public opinion and thus jeopardizing the very possibilities he (and Shapiro) see for the role of biotechnology in the end of hunger.[17]

Conway talked about the need to convene forums, credible scientifically and politically, in which all varieties of stakeholders can be in dialogue about the difficult dilemmas and trade-offs inherent in these issues. Beyond controversy about the ownership of the genetic code is the question of to whom these decisions ultimately belong. Monsanto's treatment of public concerns as *public relations* problems served to drive the biotechnology issues into an adversarial stalemate that amplified the extreme views on both sides.

Lessons Learned

We have seen the power of a strange attractor at Monsanto. What are other lessons to be learned? The science of complex adaptive systems is a framework for inquiry. What then can it tell us about what happened? What are the lessons—not just for Monsanto, or even for the biotechnology industry, but for companies in general? The lessons in our view have to do with extending the principles of CAS beyond the boundaries of the company itself.

We have previously explored the ways complex adaptive systems become more vulnerable as they become more homogeneous. Homogeneity causes insularity. As we have seen, cultivating heterogeneity within a system is essential. But how a system connects with its "external" world is also a key source of that system's health. Connectivity is not just about good relations with those outside the company. It impacts the quality of strategy and design and has direct bearing on a company's success.

Biotechnology presents just one example of issues that are too complex to address without a design for broadening the participation of people with diverse concerns and stakes in the questions. Seeking out the views of scientists and government regulators, people affected in different ways by the product help everyone imagine and design for unintended consequences. To talk only to oneself as a company will lead to strategic vulnerability.

Ford provides an example of a company that recognizes the advantage of getting out ahead of regulations. In May 2000, after eighteen months of meeting with advocates of social responsibility and environmentalists, William Ford, Jr. took the unprecedented step of admitting that sports utility vehicles emit more pollution than cars, contribute to global warming, and can be dangerous to smaller vehicles. He then expressed Ford's commitment to designing SUVs that are safe and clean.[18] Unlikely collaborations have sprung up between such adversaries as the Natural Resource Defense Council and Dupont. New collective intelligence about sustainable products and processes is being developed through these uneasy but productive relationships.

The lessons of complexity take us beyond the questions of connectivity to the fundamental question of a company's identity. Does this company identify itself entirely as a system unto itself battling for survival? Or does it view itself as a part of larger complex adaptive systems? The answer to that question changes substantially how executives think about the development of strategy. The insight that a company is part of a larger interdependent system does *not* diminish the competitive aspects of its task. However, it does reduce certain risks (such as the unintended consequences illustrated by Monsanto's experience). We can no longer afford to look at our businesses as atomistic agents alone in a world to which we connect only through competition.

These lessons apply for activists as well. Activist organizations can be equally dismissive and arrogant, contributing in their own way to the creation of stalemates. There is a role for adversarial strategies, whether they be those of regulators, activists, or companies. But there is an increasingly critical role for an entirely different approach that starts from the point of view that sustainable solutions must work for all parts of what is actually a complex adaptive system—a system that includes business, activists, and consumers.

As we heard from Shapiro and countless others, the emerging global view is that "sustainability" is the challenge of this century. The theory of sustainability is that it is constituted by a trinity of environmental soundness, social justice, and economic viability. If any of these three are weak or missing, the theory of sustainability says that that practice will not prove to be sustainable over time. To achieve any measure of sustainability, activists as well as executives will have to think in longer and broader terms. But it will also require that they suspend the certainty of their narrower positions. Acting consistently with this view of sustainability offers the potential for surprising integrations of seemingly irreconcilable interests.

AMPLIFIERS, DAMPERS, AND THE SWEET SPOT[1]

Feedback is the means by which a system talks to itself. Damping feedback monitors threshold functions. Amplifying feedback evokes, or draws attention to, new possibilities. Studies have shown that the olfactory cells, which provide mammals with their sense of smell, delicately tune receptors to dampen out familiar smells and rapidly amplify receptors with new smells. In this way, the brain is alerted to new dangers or opportunities. The analogy is apt and relevant to business.

As we have seen at Monsanto, strange attractors move organizations toward the edge of chaos. Amplifiers and dampers allow navigating close to the edge without going over it. Damping mechanisms work like the thermostat in a house. Temperatures stay within boundaries through the use of an electromechanical device that continually guards against their being "too hot" or "too cold." Mechanisms that amplify feedback do the reverse. The shriek you hear when a microphone gets too close to a loudspeaker is an example. The signal is amplified until it oscillates to a piercing level.

Amplifiers, Dampers, and British Petroleum

In 1989, John Browne was named managing director of British Petroleum's exploration unit, but his new job title was more impressive than the outfit he inherited. BP Exploration (BPX), an also-ran among the major petroleum companies, had discovered no major new oil fields in over two decades. Its bloated staff of 14,000 (primarily geologists, geophysicists, and reservoir engineers) was compartmentalized into warring tribes in Glasgow, London, and Houston.[2]

Intense, intelligent, and reserved, John Browne takes quiet pride in staying two moves ahead of anyone he is likely to encounter. New to his job as head of BPX, he faced a daunting challenge. Unlike his prior assignments in BP's commercial activities, the overhaul of Exploration did not play to his strengths. To begin, BPX was much more like a research lab than a refinery or a distribution network. Billions in investment capital turned on the arcane art of interpreting seismic readings that gave tantalizing hints of the earth's hidden wealth. The problem was that there were only a few oil treasures left.

Researchers have reckoned that the planet has no more than 300 unidentified geological domes and, based on historical averages, only one in twenty of these contains oil reserves the size of the North Slope of Alaska or the North Sea. Arithmetic leads to the sobering conclusion that perhaps only fifteen megafields are still to be found. These will most certainly be elusive—hidden away in inaccessible ocean depths or in geopolitical hot spots such as the former USSR or offshore Vietnam.[3]

Two developments in the late 1980s reduced some barriers to discovery: (1) *glasnost* and (2) groundbreaking technology in satellite-based seismic surveys. Suddenly the deep oceans, as well as formerly restricted geographic areas, were fair game. The oil industry was gripped by its own gold rush—the "endgame" of oil exploration. Success would accrue to those who had (1) the diplomatic skills to gain access to politically inaccessible parts of the world, (2) the business acumen to negotiate for the most promising acreage for seismic tests, and (3) the technical expertise to beam seismic data from remote locations on earth to satellites and thence to centers of excellence in the developed world where shrewd minds could interpret them and make multimillion-dollar bets on where to develop test wells.

After three months on his new job, Browne had grasped the endgame scenario and its implications. Based on industry benchmarks, he readily concluded that his organization could shed 10 percent of its workforce and not miss a beat. (Among other things, BPX's operations in Glasgow, an accident of history, could be consolidated, eliminating one of the regional silos.) This was the stuff of operational leadership; initiatives could be decreed and executed through the exercise of authority.

But Browne was also aware of the adaptive challenge. He recognized that the most important task, by far, was to inject new energy into the lackluster BPX team and motivate rival geographic regions to cooperate. This task could not be accomplished by edict. Although a social engineer at heart, Browne knew he needed a different approach.

The kickoff event began with BPX's top one hundred assembled in a hotel ballroom near Heathrow Airport. Consultants from McKinsey presented the strategic logic of the endgame scenario. Browne announced a downsizing of 10 percent (1,400 professionals) and a consolidation of operations in Scotland and London. All of this was received, not surprisingly, with a clammy and resigned silence. Those present were the survivors of many new bosses and a long legacy of strategic iterations, downsizings, and restructurings. The unspoken sentiments were: "B.O.H.I.C.A.!" (Bend over, here it comes again.) "Keep your head down and this too shall pass."[4]

But what was to follow that morning was something unique to the participants' experience. It demonstrated how amplifying devices can evoke disequilibrium and move an organization toward the edge of chaos. After the noon break, Browne returned to the podium and made a startling admission:

You have all been through many strategy presentations, downsizings and restructurings. I think these moves I've outlined make business sense and can be driven from the top. But that's the easy part. Absolutely nothing is going to change unless the organization changes. We are going to have to be much more astute and nimble to have any chance of getting our part of those last fifteen major oil fields. If we do, our share price will reflect it and we can maintain our independence. If we fail, we will be swallowed up by the bigger fish.

I am not an "explorer" [a technical term for petroleum geologists and geophysicists]. But even if I were, I need your help. We've got to figure out how to do this together.[5]

Browne's words and demeanor conveyed an adaptive challenge. Inviting the participants into the conversation was the first installment in a sequence of amplifying activities. Participants divided into teams and were asked to conduct an organizational audit. Using the Seven-S Framework described in Chapter 2, each of seven teams was given one of the "S's" (e.g., systems or structure) and asked to discuss in detail how it was manifested in BPX, both formally and informally. The second step was to assess how this picture jibed with the attributes of an organization that would succeed in the endgame.

Most teams began cautiously. But as the anecdotes and war stories multiplied, intensity grew. The picture wasn't pretty. So involved and heated were the conversations that more time was consumed than was allotted.

A moment of truth: If the work was to be taken seriously, more time was necessary. But the meeting was to end at 5:00 P.M. Participants had plane reservations, appointments, and families. In a stark departure from precedent, Browne asked those assembled to stay into the evening and give the audit as much time as it deserved.

Significantly, this request was an amplifier. It's a small thing to add a few hours to a meeting. Yet it sent a big signal: "Browne is in earnest." "However buttoned down he might appear, John Browne is prepared to improvise." "Perhaps it isn't all choreographed," participants speculated. Browne's simple act conveyed that the issues were more important than the logistical nightmare of rescheduling flights and finding hotel accommodations on no notice. Sometimes, small events can become defining moments in the amplification of organizational energy.

Later that evening, each team reported its sobering and ugly conclusions. Nearly every facet of BPX's way of working was at variance with what was required if the unit aspired to winning the endgame.

"There was certainly no euphoria in the room," one participant recalls. "We had to endure a pretty grim portrayal of ourselves. But while tough to hear, it cleared the air. In the morning session, we were saying to ourselves, 'Nice, but it is never going to happen.' The audit made clear why this was true. We could see how organizational habits and protocol held us back. 'So I'm not crazy after all,' people were thinking. 'The way this place works makes it impossible to succeed. Short of a thoroughgoing reinvention of ourselves, we're stuck.'"

Organizational audits amplify sentiments for change. Straight uncensored talk about "the way things *really* work around here" allows a lot of hidden conflict and frustration to surface in a constructive way. Having teams present their findings to one another sparks debate and dialogue. The room gets smaller. The atmosphere changes from a "theater with performers" to a "conversation among colleagues." Attendees shift into the mode of uncovering the truth for themselves rather than relying on the boss to tell them. The locus of initiative shifts from the podium to the convention floor.

"The audit had, in effect, generated a real-time case study of the business," says Browne, "and it showed us the size of the mountain we had to climb. But I worried that this refreshing sense of clarity would have a half-life of about twenty-four hours."[6]

Browne's next move turned up the amplification dial considerably. He immediately assembled his top eight officers and distilled the previous day's audit down to "Nine Big Problems." Then he announced that, within six weeks, a slightly larger group of 120 would reassemble to develop a journey map for addressing these problems.

BPX, in the business of deciphering plate tectonics, had adopted near-geological time cycles for the pace of its daily operations. Nothing of consequence happened without six months' notice. The announcement of an obligatory three-day offsite during the busy fourth quarter of the year—in the midst of a restructuring and downsizing, and with only six weeks' warning—was greeted with incredulity and outrage.

One of the most effective of all amplifiers is to overload an organization so that it cannot continue to conduct business as usual. This strategy served Browne well in his journey toward the edge. There was immediate pushback to the proposed meeting. "Bad timing," "Postpone it," "Overkill," "Let a small task force do it," groaned the strident chorus. But, consistent with the essential tenets of adaptive leadership, Browne did not waver. He sustained the level of distress. "This [adaptive] work *is* the essential work of the business," he responded.[7]

An edgy group of 120 reconvened six weeks later. They had previously divided into teams, and one of the "Nine Big Problems" was assigned to each group. The choice of individuals comprising teams aimed to reflect the political and substantive hurdles that needed to be addressed. If a proposed solution could survive the debate within the team, it had a chance of surviving in the organization.

For example, one team was assigned the problem of recovering (or divesting) BPX's $16 billion of unrecoverable oil reserves. These assets existed on the books, dragged down financial metrics like return on investment (ROI), and could not be recovered economically by conventional methods. The task could have been delegated to a team of maverick geologists who might have converged on an unproven technology as a new silver bullet. Instead, Browne insisted that the team also include more sober-minded reservoir engineers and reserved members of the finance staff, all of whom marched to the conservative tune of brisk asset disposition. Some of these constituents had no romantic attachment to recovering oil as a technological challenge.

On the first day, the teams rolled up their collective sleeves and actively grappled with the underlying nature of the problems. By the second day, deep-seated philosophical differences and mistrust among coworkers could no longer be politely sidestepped. But, amazingly, by the third day, teams started to converge on a game plan. Their assignment was not to *solve* the problems but to scope out an approach for their ultimate resolution. The objective was to identify milestones, a course of analysis, and any pilot tests that might be necessary to eliminate the problems in the months ahead.

In the closing session, representatives from each team were allotted fifteen minutes at the podium to describe the impasses they encountered, the progress made in their deliberations, and their proposal going forward. One participant described the experience:

> I went to the workshop with a chip on my shoulder. It seemed like overkill. The meeting couldn't have been scheduled at a worse time. But work did get done over the three days. The biggest surprise was the way it came together at the end. One of the first groups had a poorly handwritten overhead on the screen. Its contents impacted us personally and we couldn't read it without getting up close. So people just got up and crowded to the front of the room and stayed there, standing, as each of the subsequent teams presented. We listened to guys we knew and trusted describe these big problems and how they might be attacked. The cumulative effect was eerie—almost galvanizing. You began to say, "Wow, we actually might be able to do something here. If each of these teams delivered the goods, this could be a different place."[8]

Although the workshop ended on a high note, John Browne noted again that the half-life of optimism is short. To sustain the intensity and focus (i.e., introduce another amplifier), he announced that each team needed to proceed at full speed on the plans that had been outlined. He asked the teams to get to work on their analyses, field trips, and pilots, and be able to summarize tentative findings and recommendations in a "green paper" (i.e., a malleable variant of a white paper) due in ninety days.

For the balance of November and December, little occurred, but directly after the New Year, soundings were quickly taken. "Is Browne serious?" "Do we really have to write a green paper?" "How big a deal is this?" "Is the ninety-day deadline firm?" When answers reconfirmed Browne's commitment, all hell broke loose. Executives obliterated huge chunks of their January calendars, departed on benchmarking field trips, visited competitors and suppliers, and hosted conversations with experts.

Beleaguered executives complained that they didn't ". . . have time to do our jobs." Browne's answer: "Perhaps solving these kinds of [adaptive] problems *is* the job of senior managers. Maybe we should be delegating more of the routine stuff to develop the ranks below."[9]

At this juncture, disequilibrium was manifest and it began to trickle down to lower levels. "What's going on up there?" became the question in the trenches. "These guys are acting differently, delegating more, seeking our input."

BPX's excursion near the edge of chaos became palpable in January. It culminated in a defining event in Phoenix, Arizona, six weeks later. At the Phoenix meeting, each team had a four-hour slot, only fifteen minutes of which could be used to reiterate findings and present the proposals summarized in the green papers (which everyone was expected to have read beforehand). The balance of the time was for discussion. The design of these sessions engaged participants in the "soft underbelly" of each team's recommendations—the most radical, difficult, or controversial aspects. Instead of a sales pitch with pro forma approval, the aim was to understand what had made the "Big Problem" both big and unsolvable. Shifting the most controversial aspects of each problem to the forefront served as an additional amplifier.

Not surprisingly, the sessions sparked tension and debate. Each closed with a plenary discussion in which Browne and his top team questioned, challenged, and distilled each proposal down to next steps, deliverables, and resources required. Decisions were not made on the spot, but the ramifications were identified. Examples of damping feedback surfaced: reaching closure, defining boundary conditions, sizing up necessary commitments and the means of tracking results.

One participant recalls:

> Those days were intense. The third session often went until 10:00 P.M. Then Browne and his top team would stay up to 1:00 or 2:00 A.M., deliberating on what had been proposed, reaching resolution, and committing resources. Each morning began with Browne reporting on the decisions reached on the proposals of the day before. [Again, manifestations of damping feedback.] But what became apparent at Phoenix was that somewhere along the way we were different. There was energy, possibility, debate, openness. You could sense a renewed appetite for excellence.[10]

Utilizing the simple devices of (1) overloading the organization beyond its business-as-usual carrying capacity, (2) using deadlines, public scrutiny, and other action-forcing events to sustain disequilibrium, and (3) identifying the adaptive challenge (but not stepping in to save the organization from it), Browne amplified disequilibrium and moved his organization out of its frozen state. Damping mechanisms such as milestones, resourcing, and deliverables brought closure at the end of the process.

Browne's exercise of adaptive leadership made many attendees uncomfortable. At times, the intensity and pace of collateral activity felt chaotic. But the approach generated fresh solutions and the commitment to execute them. The momentum was sufficient to reverse BPX's fortunes in oil exploration. Browne's turnaround of BPX became a defining event in his career. After one brief collateral assignment, he was positioned to move into his current role as Chairman of British Petroleum.

The Map: Fitness Landscapes[11]

Biologists use the term "fitness" to describe the success of an organism. We will use it to describe the competitiveness of an enterprise.

Fitness depends on numerous interrelated factors that can combine in a vast number of ways.

There are three types of fitness landscapes, and each can be used to characterize familiar competitive scenarios:

1. *Gradual,* such as the undulating terrain of northern France (or, in a competitive business context, the set piece of the 1960s).
2. *Rugged,* such as the topography of Nepal (present-day competition in cellular phones and e-commerce).
3. *Random,* such as the topography of the moon, where the random impact of meteors rather than the logic of plate tectonics shaped the surface (economic panics such as the stock market crash in 1929).

Higher degrees of fitness are depicted by linear height on the landscape; a loss of fitness is visualized as going downhill in this three-dimensional territory. Thus, when a threatened species, such as the North American coyote, is driven from its traditional habitat by human extermination programs, it descends the fitness landscape toward the edge of chaos. It must learn to cope with different terrain, climate, and rivals, and to find new sources of food. Coyotes have become urbanized in many sections of the country. Once established in a new territory, a coyote begins to master its new environment. This adaptation may, in fact, lead to overall prospects for survival that are better than those in the original habitat. In this context, the coyote's fitness has increased. It has carved out a niche on a superior fitness peak in the foothills above Malibu and Beverly Hills.

Biologists describe a species' or population's struggle to secure a niche as a long climb uphill, where "uphill" means better adaptation. When a species reaches a *subsidiary peak* (called a *local optimum*) on the fitness landscape, it may choose to remain there. Biologists call this perch on the fitness landscape a *basin of attraction*—a rest stop during the eternal competitive journey in which equilibrium is only temporarily restored.

Species become stranded on intermediate peaks or basins of attraction. Because there are no suspension bridges to get to the higher peaks on the horizon, the organism must "go down to go up." (This image is useful because most organisms don't do this voluntarily.) To do so, there must be sufficient internal unrest and instability; otherwise, an organism would not opt to leave its intermediate peak and suffer the indignities of the valley—low margins, undifferentiated products, customer defections, loss of competitive advantage—on the gamble of reaching a higher perch on the fitness landscape.

We have established that living systems are driven out of a basin of attraction by discomfort (either external or internal). Companies may encounter employee unrest and attrition, customer defections, or loss of margins or market share. These factors often generate so much stress that an intermediate basin of attraction is abandoned. Moving from peak to peak and choosing the right peak are major challenges. A few companies pull it off, but not many.

Honda, which built its reputation making racing motorcycles, subsequently used what it learned about high horsepower and low weight ratios (a necessary combination in racing) to create the breakthrough Supercub. It applied the knowledge and respect gained from the Supercub to launch a global motorcycle brand. Then it branched into automobiles. Today, it dominates the world in the manufacture of small, efficient internal-combustion engines for motorcycles, automobiles, garden tractors, lawn mowers, and power generators. These achievements, and Honda's standing in each category, can be visualized as a succession of ever-higher fitness peaks.[12]

In Chapter 4, we described Intel, a spin-off from Fairchild, which achieved its first competitive advantage (i.e., fitness peak) as a manufacturer of semiconductors. It migrated to DRAMS (memory chips) and then to microprocessors, and is in motion again in an effort to establish its brand in retail channels.

Given some hindsight, these journeys from peak to peak seem straightforward. But knowing when and where to move and how to choose the right peak often constitutes one of the most stressful gambles in an executive's career and a company's life. At the edge of chaos, bets are placed on the whole company. Significantly, this is also when you most need to draw on the collective intelligence of the entire organization. Most frightening of all (as is the nature of adaptive work), the pilgrimage is figured out as it unfolds.

Kevin Kelly, Executive Editor of *Wired Magazine,* states:

> Organizations, like living beings, are hardwired to optimize what they know and not to throw success away. A company expends great effort to move its butt uphill, or to evolve its product so that it is sitting on top, where it is maximally adapted to the consumer environment. Companies find devolving (a) unthinkable and (b) impossible. There is simply no room in most enterprises for the concept of letting go—let alone the skill to let go—of something that is working, and trudge downhill toward chaos.
>
> And it will be chaotic and dangerous down below. The definition of lower adaptivity is that you are closer to extinction. Finding the next peak is suddenly the next life-or-death assignment. But there is no alternative (that we know of) to leaving behind perfectly good products, expensively developed technology, and wonderful brands, and heading down to trouble in order to ascend again in hope. In the future, this forced march will become routine. The biological nature of this era means that the sudden disintegration of established domains will be as certain as the sudden appearance of the new. Therefore, there can be no expertise in innovation unless there is also expertise in demolishing the ensconced. In the [network economy], the ability to relinquish a product or occupation or industry at its peak will be priceless. Let go at the top.[13]

Value Added?

Appraising the value of fitness landscapes as tools for business requires stepping back to reflect on the alternatives. Historically, we appraise a firm and its strategic options through a SWOT analysis (strengths, weaknesses, opportunities, and threats) or some variation on this theme. This approach has its roots in an organizational theory called *systems dynamics.* Systems theory spans forty years, from Forrester's path-breaking work in the 1960s to Peter Senge's treatment of "learning organizations" in the early 1990s.[14] The insights from systems analysis are often represented by vectors, diagrams, inputs and outputs, and feedback loops. The underlying aims are: to be as comprehensive as possible in anticipating all inputs and outputs, and to think through unforeseen consequences. The particular contribution of systems analysis is in spotting counterintuitive second- and third-order effects and in forcing a systemic perspective.

This deterministic approach lends itself to social engineering. It emphasizes the need for consistency, congruence, fit, and alignment among (1) different parts of the system, (2) different systems, or (3) the systems and their environment. The underlying premise is: "If we can get a complete picture, we can figure it out."

Complexity science represents three major steps beyond systems thinking:

1. Theoretically, systems thinking can address nonlinear events (such as increasing returns or the links among increased employee satisfaction, customer satisfaction, and profit). In practice, it is rarely used to do so. It tends to be applied in situations where linear dynamics obtain (that is, where effects are proportional to the cause). In contrast, complexity science concerns itself with nonlinear effects where very small perturbations at the start may lead to avalanches.

2. Complexity science is not built on the assumption (or even the temptation) that one can proactively control what will happen. Rather, it emphasizes nimble reactions: Expect the unexpected. The focus is on broadly understanding and coping with the world as it unfolds in real time.

3. The living systems view does not focus only on the path of an organism as it maneuvers across the competitive landscape. Complexity also concerns itself with the way the landscape itself changes as the organism moves across it. Systems dynamics conceptualizes the challenge as mapping causal factors that move a system from point A to point B. Complexity regards the journey as walking on a trampoline. Each step alters the

whole topography. What was "up" at the start may be somewhat "down" farther along the route, and the ascent may become far steeper as the destination draws near.

Consider an example in nature. Four billion years ago, bacteria
emerged as the first form of life on Earth, and they flourished in a
biosphere without oxygen. The primary constituents of the atmosphere were hydrogen sulfide gas, carbon dioxide, water, and small
amounts of methane and ammonia. Widespread volcanic activity and
lightning storms combined these ingredients with the carbon in the
earth's crust to form organic compounds—amino acids and sugar.
These compounds became the first settlers' food source—as long as
they lasted.[15]

Bacteria are a Malthusian nightmare. Any single-parent bacterium
can produce a billion offspring a day. Exponential rates of increase in
the numbers precipitated life's first food crisis: Bacteria consumed
food faster than the atmosphere could renew it. But mutations
among some descendants circumvented the food shortage; they
learned to manufacture their own food from more abundant ingredients. They combined light and chemicals to generate enough energy
to break down hydrogen sulfide gas and gain access to hydrogen—a
new dietary staple. This development marked one of the earth's most
important metabolic innovations: photosynthesis.[16]

Over the next 200 million years, the earth's volcanic activity re-
ceded and the supply of hydrogen sulfide was diminished. Once again,
the blue-green microbes, the wiliest of bacterial organisms, sought another substance for sustenance. This time it was water—abundant and
packed with hydrogen. Amazingly, they devised a way to crack the
safe of this very stable molecule to get at the goodies.[17]

Break apart H_2O and the residual oxygen is, of course, the "waste
product." Initially, oxygen was an insignificant fraction of Earth's
atmosphere, but over the next 100 million years it accumulated,
reaching present-day levels of 20 percent. Oxygen, it turns out, was
highly toxic to many of the initial colonizing bacteria. Thus, on the

journey to improve their fitness (i.e., as rival microbes sought advantage by securing new food supplies), some bacteria inadvertently altered the landscape so radically that they precipitated the extinction of the pioneering species. Talk about walking on a trampoline![18]

This oft-told story of the planet should resonate with many businesses. Traditional retailers such as Barnes & Noble sit on a "local peak" of the bookselling landscape and set their sights on what appears to be the more desirable peak of e-commerce—in this example, the peak occupied by Amazon.com. Barnes & Noble plots a course to get to that peak. Along the way, e-commerce attracts an enormous amount of media attention and wanna-be contenders. The excitement solidifies Amazon.com as the business platform of the future, a label that publicly increases the value of its franchise. And Barnes & Noble, as it strives to build an e-commerce channel of its own, is still rooted in its lower peak because of its embedded base as a traditional bookseller. Amazon.com's peak seems to grow higher, until, perhaps, the hype about e-commerce begins to slacken. Investor interest diminishes, stock prices fall, and e-retailers like Amazon.com (which have yet to show a profit) face a day of reckoning. Retrenchment takes place as they endeavor to do so. For Barnes & Noble, still at midcourse in the journey, the new peak loses altitude and becomes less desirable.

No illustration of how the landscape can change is more compelling than the recent experience of Monsanto. The initial success with genetically improved crops (and the speed at which these innovations were adopted in the United States) catapulted the enterprise to a new peak—and inadvertently put it into the crosshairs of a public relations nightmare. Monsanto was the darling of Wall Street one day, the instigator of "Frankenstein Foods" the next. How this turnaround emerged is illustrative of the cascades and avalanches that can occur in living systems.

An unrelated crisis in Britain, triggered when tainted beef from France was found to be carrying an infectious agent that caused mad cow disease, led to several deaths. No links to biotechnology, genetically modified foods, or Monsanto were ever suggested or considered viable, but this threat to public health was not well managed by the British counterpart to the FDA. Adding fuel to the fire, European Union authorities, almost simultaneously, suffered a similar embarrassment when it was disclosed that health officials knew about, but did not alert the public to, toxins in Belgian poultry products. The alarm that spread throughout Europe was intensified by a loss of public trust in the institutions ostensibly responsible for protecting consumers. Opposition within the scientific community mounted. All prior assurances by these agencies were now suspect; notable among them were earlier pronouncements that genetically modified crops and foods were safe. There was a generalized distrust of biotechnology, global corporations, and government watchdog agencies. In the midst of these developments, "walking on a trampoline" became a very apt image for Monsanto.

■ ■

Fitness landscapes are useful tools in navigating the edge of chaos. Their principal advantage over more traditional journey maps are twofold:

1. The landscape imagery makes clear that one must "go down to go up" if the goal is to reach a higher fitness peak. The human disruptions and distress associated with this truth are often the most undermanaged aspect of corporate change efforts.
2. As Monsanto illustrates, the landscape changes as soon as there is movement on it. For many highly volatile industries, "walking on a trampoline" has a ring of truth about it.

Beyond the Edge?

The edge of chaos, a realm of uncertainty and discomfort, maximizes the generativity of living things. We have explored how several distinctions used by the life sciences can be applied as human systems endeavor to safely navigate across this domain: attractors as a magnet, amplifiers, and dampers to speed up or slow down, and fitness landscapes as maps. Using these devices, leaders can awaken an organization and unleash its potential. In this unfrozen condition, new ambitions and possibilities take form. Complexity science calls this "self-organization and emergence." It is to that subject that we now turn.

PART THREE

CHAPTER 7

SELF-ORGANIZATION
AND EMERGENCE

Self-Organization and Emergence

Self-organization and emergence are two sides of the same coin of life. *Self-organization* is the tendency of certain (but not all) systems operating far from equilibrium to shift to a new state when their constituent elements generate unlikely combinations. When systems become sufficiently populated and properly interconnected, the interactions assemble themselves into a new order: proteins into cells, cells into organs, organs into organisms, organisms into societies. Simple parts networked together can undergo a metamorphosis. "A single ant can't fight off a wasp. A single brain cell is a simpleton—but a few tens of millions (or billions) of them can perform miracles," observes science writer Neil Gross.[1]

Emergence★ is the outcome of all this: a new state or condition. As we have seen, a colony of fire ants has emergent capabilities and

---

★ On first acquaintance, "strange attractors" (discussed in a preceding chapter) and "emergence" seem confusingly similar. Think of strange attractors as a magnetic field and emergence as the aligned pattern of iron filings when placed in that field.

constitutes an organism weighing 20 kilograms, with 20 million mouths and stings. A jazz ensemble creates an emergent sound that no one could imagine from listening to the individual instruments. Kevin Kelly reminds us: "Ants have shown us that there is almost nothing so small in the world that it can't be made larger by embedding a bit of interaction in many copies of it, and then connecting them all together."[2] Two hundred years earlier, Adam Smith had the same thought in mind. As one of the pioneers of a new discipline of economics, he called our attention to the "invisible hand" and its aggregate effects as a mercantile force. But Smith recognized that individual choice did not explain everything. In addition, individuals, as members of communities, generate fiduciary relationships and dependencies. All of this, he noted, sums to a more complex emergent phenomenon: an economy.[3]

Lowly bacteria have much to teach us about self-organization and emergence. Reproducing every twenty minutes (a single parent spawns a billion offspring in a day) endows bacteria with an awesome cycle-time advantage in nature's marathon of mutation and selection.[4] A significant deviant might occur only once in a million, and a million of these might perish. But with the breeding multiples stacked in their favor, it's a good bet that the microbes will get there first. They were the first, for example, to evolve and perfect self-organization as a strategy of survival. And, as we will see, the emergent structures they've devised are so versatile and efficient that we might wonder whether, in time, bacteria might indeed inherit the earth.

Take a familiar manifestation: dental plaque. This amazing substance is a bacterial community called a "biofilm." Researchers have found biofilms almost everywhere—they foul machinery, clog pipes, and contribute to many medical conditions such as kidney stones, chronic ear and urinary-tract infections, and gum disease. Experts at the National Institutes of Health now believe that biofilms are implicated in two-thirds of all human bacterial infections.

Dental plaque is a powerful (and scary) example of self-organization and emergence. Researcher Ellen Licking writes:

> At its earliest stages, this strange thing called a biofilm is little more than a layer of cells attached to a surface. But as the bacteria grow and divide, something wondrously conspiratorial happens. When enough of them—a quorum—have gathered, they send signals around, telling each other to reorganize. They begin to arrange themselves into an array of pillars and mushroom-shaped structures, all connected by convoluted channels that deliver food and remove waste. They become, in other words, not a simple collection of bacteria, but a spooky kind of communal organism with its own defense capabilities and communication system.[5]

The result? As this self-organizing structure matures, the emergent community is one thousand times more resistant to antibiotics and toxic chemicals (e.g., fluoride, chlorine, ammonia) than were the individual bacteria on their own! Why? Bacteria in a biofilm protect themselves by communally sharing life-giving proteins (equivalent to four people sharing the same liver) and then redirecting the now-surplus proteins to form a protective layer on exterior cell walls. Proteins that once served as receptors for antibiotics disappear or become inert. Toxic chemicals can't get through the gel-like shield secreted by the bacteria, which (as we are reminded during semiannual visits to the dental hygienist) form a stone-hard layer of armor that must be chipped off with steel or shaken loose with a needle-thin pulse of ultrasonic energy.

The Japanese have developed an environmentally friendly detergent in which the cleansing action is powered by dirt-eating communities of bacteria. It is the top selling laundry powder in Japan. Self-organizing armies of bacteria are used daily for: (1) bioremediation (to clean up oil spills or remove toxic chemicals like lead and cyanide from rivers and lakes); (2) bioleaching (to extract ore; the process now accounts for about 25 percent of U.S. annual copper production); (3) biosensors (to monitor the toxicity of rivers and signal danger with phosphorescent colors); (4) desulfurization (of

Examples in Nature: Bees and Beehives

Self-organization and emergence play such profound roles in nature that some believe they are to life what relativity is to physics: the organizing logic that explains a great many other things. We see self-organization and emergence in colonies of bees. Let's take a quick look at both.

Swarming is a marvel of self-organization. Entomologists use videotapes to capture the patterns of messenger bees as they return to the hive and report on the sites they have visited. More messengers join the dance, each advocating a particular option. The hive becomes agitated. Self-organization takes the form of a buzzing consensus, the emergent outcome of which is a swarm. The bees leave their old hive en masse and head for the new location, having mysteriously preselected their future home based on the information conveyed in the rival dances.[a]

Swarming is actually a modest example of a hive's self-organizing capabilities. More remarkable is the communal behavior that holds the internal hive temperature at a near-constant 98 degrees Fahrenheit, which is accomplished through a fascinating repertoire of specialization and coordination.

In the summer, worker bees diversify their roles. Some continue to collect pollen to maintain the colony's food supply. Others bring water droplets into the hive and deposit them on the brood combs. Still others beat their wings near the comb to stimulate evaporative cooling. Another cadre of workers locates itself on a buzzing vector between the brood comb and the hive's entrance. Coordinating like a fire brigade, its job is to fan the hot exhaust air out the opening.[b]

In the winter, workers seal off crevices and openings with comb material. As cold weather intensifies, the bees assemble their body mass around the brood comb to form an insulating layer. The colder it gets, the more tightly the blanket of bees knits together. Each bee generates 0.1 calorie of heat per minute. Thus, a typical hive of 20,000 bees can infuse the brood comb with 2,000 calories a minute, which is comparable to the energy expended by a toaster oven. As a result, in winter or summer, the brood combs are kept within a one-degree variance of the optimal temperature.[c]

[a] E. Capaidi, et al., "Orientation Flight of Honeybee Revealed by Radar," *Nature*, No. 403. 2000, pp. 537–540; Edward O. Wilson, op. cit., pp. 92–98; Karl von Frisch, *The Dance Language and Orientation of Bees* (Boston, MA: Harvard University Press, 1993), pp. 269–277.
[b] Wilson, *ibid.*, pp. 306–309.
[c] *Id.* p. 308.

coal, to reduce acid rain); (5) fixing nitrogen (in plants); and (6) creating substitutions for chemicals (in making snow and in arresting frost at temperature-sensitive vineyards and citrus groves).[6] The diversity of these applications suggests the practical importance of our newly acquired ability to harness the self-organizing and emergent potential of one of the "simplest" forms of life.

What self-organization and emergence can do for bacteria, they can also do for business. These properties enable a system or organization to tap its own latent potential to defend, innovate, and transform itself.

The Self-Organization and Emergence of Tupperware

Direct sales organizations (Tupperware, Mary Kay, Avon) and many volunteer, activist, and self-help organizations [Greenpeace, The Sierra Club, the National Organization of Women, MADD (Mothers Against Drunk Drivers)] harness self-organization in very practical ways and are perpetually maintained by their members.

Tupperware, a remarkable example of self-organization and emergence, was the pioneer of an archetype.[7] The story began after World War II, when the United States witnessed a proliferation of products sold door-to-door (much like today's assault by catalogs and e-commerce). Among these enterprises was a New England-based tool retailer—Stanley Home Products. One of its sales representatives was notorious for heavy drinking and absenteeism, yet he consistently performed above quota.

His regional sales manager, Brownie Wise, sought an explanation for this paradox of low input and large output. She found that the salesman did, indeed, spend most of his daytime hours in taverns, but when his peers went home at night, he went to work. He cajoled friends, neighbors, and barroom acquaintances to host informal get-togethers in their own homes. In that friendly setting, relaxed "guests" had fewer defenses against a sales pitch. Humorous, lighthearted selling, aided by peer pressure, generated more revenue in two hours than a whole day spent knocking on doors.

The puritan values of Stanley Home Products were severely taxed by this unseemly and unprofessional approach, and the hard-drinking sales representative was dismissed. But Brownie Wise recognized the kernel of genius in this selling approach and began to look for a product that would lend itself to the "home party" concept.

Enter Earl Tupper—engineer, former DuPont chemist, and inventor of a line of plastic containers with a special patented seal. The problem was that the advantages of Tupperware (superior materials and a unique seal) made the product more expensive than the seemingly comparable plastic containers sold in supermarkets. Tupperware's attributes were not easily discernible to homemakers.

Tupper's fledgling enterprise was near insolvency when Brownie Wise approached him with the idea of home parties. Shortly thereafter, as president of Tupperware, she reintroduced the product through the home-party setting. The fledgling Tupperware organization, already "unfrozen" by a threat of insolvency, was receptive to reinvention. The system was open to the idea of recruiting, training, and encouraging the right people to sell Tupperware through home parties across the United States.

The new concept dovetailed with an emergent development in American society, and Tupperware found a way to catalyze it. During World War II, many women had worked in defense industries and elsewhere, replacing the men in uniform. When the war ended, society (and husbands) expected them to return to their homemaking chores. Most did, but others were restless. Selling Tupperware on a self-employed, part-time basis appealed to homemakers who sought a way to earn extra money and an independent outlet for self-esteem.

To women who were being praised for little more than a hand-knit sweater or a good meatloaf, Tupperware offered a whole new avenue of self-expression. One Tupperware dealer wrote a poem that concluded: "Yes, dear God, I believe in thee./But now, at last, I believe in me."

"If we build the people, they'll build the business," was Brownie Wise's mantra.

Tupperware is fueled entirely by self-organization. Each dealer is self-employed and must find others to host home parties. Those who excel as hosts are recruited to become dealers. Highly successful dealers (those who recruit a network of successful hosts who also become dealers) become team leaders of protégé dealers. The team leader receives a commission on her dealers' sales. The arrangement is essentially a pyramid scheme in which social capital and economic incentives are the binding agents.

The success of these self-organizing networks is a force to be reckoned with. Over the span of five decades, Tupperware has encircled the globe and reached into virtually every facet of American society. More than 80 percent of all American homes have at least one Tupperware product.

Self-organization requires discipline. Accordingly, Tupperware has made a science of "having fun." Its 200-page guide book details games, ice breakers, upbeat formats for monthly rallies, and myriad schemes for identifying prospective hosts for home parties.

Tupperware dealers train and motivate hosts at monthly rallies that are carefully orchestrated to generate inclusiveness, build self-esteem, award every success, and lure potential recruits into the Tupperware ranks. Among the recent genre are "rush-hour parties"—events held in offices. Workers are invited to stay for a get-together an hour after closing. (They miss the drive home in heavy traffic and make up half of the lost hour by virtue of a faster commute.) In exchange for their time, they play games and examine some products they might need.

Tupperware has also discovered that self-organization and emergence can be exploited to enlarge the product category and guide research-and-development expenditures. Clever games at parties offer prizes for the most imaginative new uses of a product. Ideas elicited from customers and dealers have contributed to Tupperware's technological leadership in the field (it introduced the first ovenproof and microwave-proof plastic bowls) and have significantly boosted market share. Today, Tupperware is the largest plastic container supplier in the world. Sales exceed $2 billion globally, and the company earns 40 percent before taxes on its assets.

Undreamed-of Paths, Unimagined Places

Self-organization in business relies on the intelligence that exists in every part of a complex adaptive system (in the mind of every employee) and makes it possible to tap this resource and release its formidable potential. That capacity, in turn, allows companies to seize opportunities and solve problems as they arise. Self-organization and emergence are the twin engines of adaptive work. Through these capacities, a company can explore new, previously undiscovered paths to reach a desired destination or new and previously unimaginable destinations.

New Routes

Remember when antibiotics were expected to sound the death knell for pneumonia, strep infections, and a host of other bronchial ailments? Forget it. Bacterias' amazing abilities to (1) mutate and multiply, (2) self-organize into potent and drug-resistant communities, and (3) generate emergent collective defenses allow this worldwide community to regularly outmaneuver every new antibiotic within a predictable three-year cycle.

Viruses are on a par with bacteria in their ability to circumvent the human immune system. It is not just figuratively but *literally* true that it is easier to put a man on the moon than to cure the common cold. The flu virus regularly evolves new routes to foil the escalating sophistication of the immune defense response. The most recent "new route" of the influenza virus utilizes a stealth technology: it hides before it begins to infect the host, which gives it a greater chance to breed a critical mass for the invasion.[8] Bacteria require three years to circumvent the latest antibiotic; viruses typically out-maneuver vaccines within a year. A previous year's immunization shots are largely ineffective because the microbe has mutated to a form not recognized by the human immune system.

New Destinations

Nature has demonstrated repeatedly that the most radical possibilities open up when intraspecies cooperation takes place. Within a species, innovation typically fosters new routes. Across species, new destinations often arise from improbable combinations. Some of the most radical innovations in biotechnology are taking place in unlikely crossovers such as between fish and mammals, fungus and insects, animals and plants.

Tacit cooperation occurs more often in nature than many realize. The mistaken view that nature is brutish and fiercely competitive is vastly overstated (i.e., "survival of the fittest"). The phrase, erro-neously attributed to Darwin was, in fact, coined by sociologist Herbert Spencer to "explain" the social stratification and excesses of Capitalism in the late nineteenth century.[9]

Biologists have documented that nature favors cooperative traits over competitive ones. Cooperation is less wasteful from an overall systems standpoint. Competition destroys things. Cooperation allows multiple agendas to coexist and, at times, flourish. Ants coexist with sticky, insect-entrapping flowers in Latin America and with stinging caterpillars in Asia. They protect their hosts from other predators, are allowed grazing rights on the nectar of their flowering host, and drink the milk of the cooperating caterpillars.[10] In these instances, tacit cooperation allows one species access to an untapped food sup-ply and the other with a novel security apparatus. A fungus in the Amazon rain forests cannot breed or thrive without sunlight. In a decidedly one-sided variant of interspecies cooperation, it nestles on the back of an ant that scavenges the forest floor. The fungus infects the ant's brain and the earth-dwelling ant experiences an irresistible urge to climb to the top of the rain forest canopy. There the fungus consumes the ant and uses its proteins to jump-start its life as a flourishing tree-top dweller. For the fungus, this unlikely relationship provides escape from the inhospitable realm of the forest floor—a new destination.[11]

We grasp the distinction between new routes and new destinations by reflecting on the earlier Monsanto example. Monsanto's initial focus was on new routes: reinventing agriculture to meet humanity's needs through new routes in the life sciences. In fitness landscape terms, Monsanto was seeking a route toward a yet-to-be-defined life sciences "peak." Monsanto's competitors and market opportunities on this landscape were relatively familiar.

Then, as we discussed, the landscape itself changed as biotechnology, in general, and genetically modified foods, in particular, became the target of Greenpeace and environmental groups.[12] In the face of this disruptive shift, Monsanto endured a 20 percent decrease in its market value and was eventually forced to merge with Upjohn to form Pharmacia. But for the better part of a year, Monsanto continued to seek new routes toward its goal, blinded by persistence or denial from seeing the goal posts had been moved (or, arguably, torn down)! In fitness landscape terms, the game had changed. New destinations, not new routes, were called for.

We can only speculate as to what such a new destination might be. One possible scenario could entail Monsanto's shift in focus from "global-competitor-and-pioneer-in-the-life-sciences" to "convener-of-global-conversations-to-explore-proper-safeguards-for-bioengineered-crops-and-the-potential-use-of-bioengineered-staples-to-reduce-world-hunger." To be sure, this entails very different skills. But the shift *is* possible.

Twenty years earlier, another Midwest company, Motorola, made precisely such a shift from global electronic supplier of CB radios and other electronics to becoming a proficient orchestrator of antidumping legislation. Indeed, Motorola became so accomplished in the latter role (which involved building a competence in government relations) that it helped draft and steer legislation through Congress that created the office of U.S. Special Representative on Trade. In the process, Motorola provided the seed money and support to create the U.S. Semiconductor Association, an antidumping lobbying group in Washington. Through these efforts, the U.S. semiconductor and electronics industries have made huge strides in curtailing unfair trade practices.[13]

Arguably, Monsanto might undertake an enlargement in its strategic capabilities similar to that realized by Motorola. For example, it could orchestrate a global conference on "Bioengineering and World Hunger" comparable to the Kyoto Accords on global warming. At such an event, objective data could be presented on the risks and possible safeguards for bioengineered crops, the chain of social and economic consequences that flow from malnutrition, projected food shortfalls in vulnerable nations and scenarios of domestic and cross-border instability that arise in such circumstances.

In the context of such a conference, funding mechanisms might be explored through which developed nations pay a surcharge on bioengineered crops, which in turn underwrite the additional costs of distributing drought-resistant, disease-resistant, saline-tolerant and nutritionally enhanced seeds to needy populations. Alternatively, the financing for all this might be covered by the funds contributed by developing nations who, as a result of the Kyoto Accords, may pay a surcharge to offset the costs for burning more than their national quota of ozone-producing fossil fuels. Such innovations could provide avenues for bioengineered crops (with proper safeguards), to serve human kind in constructive ways.

In these scenarios, the *New Destination* includes many factors— transfer payments to populations in need and different stakeholders such as developing nations and environmentalists. The destination is no longer defined by Monsanto's superior height on a fitness peak as compared to Novartis and Dupont. Rather, Monsanto's fitness is determined by the extent to which it can convene global conversa-tions and generate policies that offer adequate safeguards against biopollution, and, at the same time, establish workable legal and eco-nomic covenants.

The Science of Self-Organization

How did we come to be as we are? What sequence of primordial events led to the creation of DNA, the complicated double helix that is the fundamental building block of life?

The closer one looks, the more improbable it becomes. For starters, unlike a computer, the human genetic system exercises most of its in-structions *simultaneously*. This means that the governing mecha-nism—the genetic system—parallel processes constituent elements with possibilities in the order of 10^{30}. How can all this simultaneous nonlinear activity settle down and replicate a species?[14]

In 1965, two French biochemists, Jacques Lucien Monod and François Jacob, won a Nobel Prize in Medicine for coming up with part of the answer.[15] They postulated that some of the cells of the body are regulators, including messenger ribonucleic acid (RNA). These regulators switch the DNA on and off, apparently at random, and play a determining role in shaping the destiny of any given cell to become part of a nerve, a muscle, or a nose. In effect, the regulators simplify *some* of the simultaneous or parallel processing and help nar-row down the options. Some, it turns out, but not nearly enough.

At the Santa Fe Institute, geneticist Stuart Kauffman had long been fascinated by this phenomenon. How, he asked, could so much seemingly random input give rise to reliable patterns? How, he wanted to know, could life as we know it have possibly evolved? He knew the odds were against it; even after the switching role of regu-lators was understood, far too many permutations were still possible. (Even after four billion years of experimentation, the earth has ex-plored only a tiny fraction of the possibilities that mutation and nat-ural selection might bring forth.)[16]

Kauffman believed that the explanation could be found in the science of complexity. Previously, we have shown how a complex adaptive system, when disturbed or threatened by some change in its environment, can be lured by attractors and feedback modifiers out of a state of equilibrium and toward the edge of chaos. Then the system becomes capable of redesigning itself into a new, more sophisticated form that is better able to cope with its problems and challenges.

This process of self-organization and emergence, Kauffman argued, must have provided a shortcut through the maze of possible genetic combinations to create life. To test his hypothesis, he built a simple simulation of a genetic system—an array of 100 light bulbs that looked something like a Las Vegas marquee. Messenger RNA causes the DNA to turn on or off, so Kauffman designed a computer program that would cause his bulbs to do the same Feedback and "learning" were simulated by controlling each "gene"—linking its behavior to, at most, two other "genes." Believing there was no need for further governing mechanisms, he speculated that random behavior would settle into patterns. This was not an obvious conclusion. The possible combination in Kauffman's simple arrangement of blinking lights was two (on or off), multiplied by itself 100 times— a total of almost one million trillion trillion possibilities!

When Kauffman switched on his device, the result was astonishing. Instead of generating patterns of infinite variety, as one would expect, the system always stabilized within a few minutes. Most of the lights were frozen on or off, and the rest of them migrated through a series of patterns. Kauffman recounts that "instead of wandering through trillions of permutations, this binary network quickly settled down and oscillated through a cycle of five or six or seven or, more typically as it turned out, ten states."[17]

A network of light bulbs isn't a complex *adaptive* system (only a complex one), but the same principle holds and the implications are far-reaching. "What if life was not just standing around and waiting until DNA happened?" Kauffman asks. "What if all those amino acids and sugars and gases and solar energy self-organized like the billboard of lights?"[18] In that case, DNA's appearance would not be a mathematical miracle, like a thousand decks of cards being dropped from an airplane and all landing face up. It would, instead, simply be the work of independent agents on the edge of chaos, under favorable conditions. The agents would be operating with neither too few nor too many rules, and would organize themselves so as to produce an emergent entity more evolved and complex than the component agents.

Networks = Nodes + Connections

Kauffman's experiments draw us to consider the relationship between self-organization and networks. Networks are comprised of two key ingredients: nodes and connections. Computer simulations have shown that the power of a network is proportional to the square of the number of nodes.[19] This mathematical relationship drives the geometric growth rates we have all witnessed in the usage of fax machines, personal computers, and the Internet.

Users of the Internet provide an illustration of a network in an emergent state. As icons of self-organization, they interact with no architect. No one is in charge; there are no formal rule makers or police. Users, as a community, evolve through self-organization. Emergence is evident in the growing number of roles the Net performs and the enterprises it fosters.

Curiously, the inner workings of the Internet are a microcosm of its larger existence. Think of each bit (or packet) of an E-mail message as bees in the hive of your PC. The hive swarms the instant you hit the SEND key. Routers on the Internet are the primary source of self-organizing intelligence. Like air traffic controllers, they direct each bee (or bit) and route it across global space, seeking the quickest route it can find.[20] At the other end, the swarm reassembles itself into a coherent message. As it turns out, the routers send some of the bees on what appears to be a roundabout route because the direct route is overcrowded. As Kevin Kelly observes: "A centralized switching system would never route a message in such a wasteful manner. But the

inefficiency of the individual parts is overcome by the incredible reliability of the network as a whole."[21]

The general principles of networks extend beyond the Internet
and beyond applications to information technology. The events at
Sears, British Petroleum, and Monsanto, which we described earlier,
harnessed self-organization and emergence by (1) increasing the
number of nodes (via Town Hall meetings and inclusion of larger-
than-usual populations of stakeholders), and (2) enriching the number and quality of connections (through designs that brought people
into relationship with each other that were based on a wider understanding of the business, and better cross-level and cross-functional
contacts). If data are volatile and untrustworthy and the interrela-
tionship of key factors is complex and poorly understood, tapping the
distributed intelligence of the entire system usually generates better
solutions than a central authority. In these situations, it is better to
enrich the connections among the nodes and let them play an instrumental role in evolving the way forward. Expanding upon a theme
from Hillary Rodham Clinton, it not only takes a village to raise a
child—it often takes a swarm to meet an adaptive challenge. The
chapter that follows provides a variety of illustrations of this concept
in action.

CHAPTER 8

SELF-ORGANIZATION AND THE CORPORATION

Visa, the largest credit card network in the world, took form in the late 1970s under the guidance of one of complexity's earliest corporate proponents, Dee Hock. As CEO, Hock applied the principles of self-organization to this struggling enterprise and, as they say, the rest is history.[1] Starting from behind, Visa seized a huge competitive advantage over its rivals and continues to extend its lead to this day. With almost 100 million cardholders and three-quarters of a trillion dollars of point-of-sale volume annually, Visa claims half of the credit card market. Its nearest rival, MasterCard, has 31 percent.[2]

Visa represents self-organization in almost a pure form. Its decentralized structure relies almost exclusively on self-interest as the primary incentive. The transactional nature of members' relationship to the clearing center and to one another suffices to cause the right things to happen and the simplest structures to prevail.[3]

To apply the concepts of self-organization and emergence broadly, we must demonstrate their relevance to social systems. Most organizations require that a balance be struck between self-interest and community interest. Transaction costs increase. Decision making can not be entirely delegated to the organizations' members.

We discussed earlier how the self-organizing potential of a living system is enhanced by (1) devolving power to the nodes, (2) establishing rich connections to form networks, and (3) enriching the value of those networks with information that sparks further evolution. The examples that follow will illustrate how these parameters play out in more complicated corporate contexts.

Imagine a continuum of complexity. We began with Tupperware and Visa, organizations in which self-organization and emergence are fueled largely by self-interest and manifest in the purest and most straightforward form. Mid-continuum are organizations that are highly dependent on the self-organization of members, but also rely on connections between participants that are based on both social as well as economic ties. Alcoholics Anonymous provides an example. Further along the continuum are larger societal systems. Silicon Valley will be used as an illustration. Finally, we look at a more traditional organization, the U.S. Army, which has explicitly harnessed self-organization and emergence as essential components of its day-to-day strategic capability.

Self-Organization and Self-Help

Self-organization and emergence play a pivotal role in the nonprofit sphere. Such entities usually pay very low salaries and rely extensively on volunteers. An analysis of the pioneer self-help group, Alcoholics Anonymous, reveals much about the formation and functioning of such organizations.

"AA," as it is known, was formed in 1935 through a chance encounter between a physician and a stockbroker, both of whom were recovering alcoholics.[4] Emergence needs a ripe issue. In this case, the issue was the problem of addictive drinking within a society that minimized, joked about, or denied its existence. Beneath this veneer festered a great deal of suffering. Societal awakening was necessary to redefine alcoholism as a disease. The condition also required innovative strategies for healing. As discussed earlier, such factors provide the grist for emergence.

Self-organization and emergence flourish with simple rules and structure. AA's founders invented such rules through the "12-step" process, an extraordinary contribution in its own right. Step one requires the alcoholic to openly admit to a problem with alcohol. Subsequent steps require each member to work methodically through a therapeutic program of self-acceptance and spiritual surrender. Alcoholics Anonymous also devised an elegantly simple structure and operating principles. The philosophy holds, among other things, that participants are a brotherhood and must share the burden of maintaining their AA chapter. AA intentionally operates from hand-to-mouth with no fund raising, grants, or publicity that might allow members to rest on their laurels. Each chapter is only as viable as its active membership. There is no hierarchy, no paid staff, and no endowment.

AA's 12-step program and its organizing principles have been codified by many similar organizations. In effect, it has become the DNA of a whole new organizational species.

In the 1980s, social scientist Gregory Bateson conducted an extensive study of AA. One of his most interesting observations focused on emergence. He found that AA's therapeutic intervention had no precedent; it was a quantum leap against the backdrop of the psychotherapeutic techniques of the time.[5] AA addressed an unmet societal need and ignited a contagion of interest. Within a few years of its inception, AA chapters could be found throughout the United States and in many other nations. This broad social movement just seemed to materialize out of thin air.

AA's institutional significance in the self-help sphere is comparable to the innovation of the Federal Reserve Board as a quasi-independent guardian of the U.S. economy. Over the past six decades, the AA model has fostered hundreds of self-help and activist organizations around the world. MADD (Mothers Against Drunk Driving) has almost single-handedly brought an end to lenient sentences for drunk drivers. MADD has catalyzed public awareness, altered the drinking norms of our society, and made the term "designated driver" a staple of our vocabulary.[6] Other self-organizing groups support victims of spouse and child abuse and patients facing the ravages of terminal disease. In the United States, two million people are involved with some aspect of Alcoholics Anonymous each day. Worldwide, at least thirty million individuals are directly involved with self-help organizations.[7]

The Emergence of Silicon Valley

Self-organization and emergence are not confined to any one company or industry. We find these factors at work in societies and economies. The thousands of highly specialized but tightly networked entrepreneurs who comprise the fashion industry of Northern Italy are an example.[8] A second is closer to home.

Self-organization in Silicon Valley occurs in two ways: (1) university scientists, entrepreneurs, and investors continuously self-organize to form start-ups; and (2) corporations, academic institutions, and venture capital firms self-organize to form strategic alliances, partnerships, and temporary project teams. *Emergence* likewise occurs in several characteristic ways. The Valley has been the spawning ground of emerging technology. Historically, it was the magnet that drew together the components and subsystems for personal computers. Today, it is a diverse coalescing site for the elements of biotechnology, microprocessors, and bioelectronics. The Valley has also fostered emergent business platforms such as e-commerce and, most recently, start-ups designed with an initial public offering (IPO) and imminent wealth creation in mind rather than near-term products, profit, or staying power. Finally, the Valley has been the source of emergent business practices—perpetual disequilibrium, fast pace, obsession with the big "after-next" idea—and a cauldron of talent and energy that seems continuously fueled by its own adrenaline.

Silicon Valley is home to one-third of the 100 largest technology companies created in the United States since 1965. The market value of these companies increased by $25 billion between 1986 and 1990 alone, dwarfing the $1 billion increase of their Boston-based Route 128 counterparts. Although the two regions employed workforces of roughly the same size in 1975, Silicon Valley businesses generated some 150,000 new technology jobs during the ensuing fifteen years— triple the number created along Route 128.[9] Venture-capital investments from January 1996 through the first quarter of 1997 were $2.8 billion in Silicon Valley as opposed to $700 million in Boston.[10] Over three decades, the Valley has grown to encompass 2,000 square miles. The region loosely includes Marin County, San Francisco, Oakland, Berkeley, Palo Alto, San Jose, and Santa Cruz.

Recently, McKinsey and Company conducted a survey to measure the growth of the high-technology sector in industrialized economies. In the United States, the revenues increased 14 percent between 1990 and 1998. The nearest rival was Germany, at 2 percent. Most of the U.S.'s astonishing growth was driven by Silicon Valley.[11]

"Historians will record 1971 and 1972 as the years the U.S. economy tilted west," writes Virginia Postrel, a columnist for *Forbes* magazine. "In those years, venture-capital firms began sprouting up in the region south of San Francisco to find young companies with information-technology products—often in the form of computers or their software—either on a desktop or on a silicon chip. Technology, silicon, talent, venture capital were the propellants of an engine that has generated more wealth in the past 20 years than the rest of the nation combined."[12]

As noted earlier, Silicon Valley combines the ingredients of emergence: sparks of innovation (including, but not limited to, the stream of discoveries pouring forth from Stanford University and the University of California at Berkeley); technology; capital; heterogeneity (intellectual and ethnic); and an upbeat and stimulating physical, intellectual, and spiritual climate. One interesting facet of self-organization in

Silicon Valley is the remarkable and ever changing set of partnerships. This pattern of cooperation and coevolution distinguishes the area from less successful counterparts along Boston's Route 128 and elsewhere. "On the East Coast," says one observer, "there's still the perception [a dying perception] that we can do it alone. 'We'll just keep adding people and keep the core competence in-house.'"[13] Important potential partners like the Massachusetts Institute of Technology (MIT) stand somewhat aloof from the entrepreneurial fray. Early on, Stanford and the University of California decided to join forces with companies. One of Stanford's first deans of engineering launched a program in which the school and nearby companies exchanged talent and co-managed projects in return for royalties—a program that continues to this day.

In Silicon Valley, both academic and business leaders actively cultivate strategic alliances. Among other things, this allows these institutions to cope with risk by sharing it. Species gain resilience by banding together, sharing resources, and working in tandem. If one leg of a network buckles, others can keep it intact.

This web of self-organizing relationships has become a conscious operating model for the Valley. It gives the region a meta-intelligence insofar as expertise and intellectual properties aren't just held within a company but are spread around through cross-pollination by firms and self-employed individuals. For example, Sun Microsystems, Inc., draws on independent programmers to develop applications for Java. Netscape Communications Corporation turns its new releases over at no charge to the Internet community (in return, the early users become the Beta test). A recent *Fortune* article diagrammed the labyrinth of financial holdings, joint board appointments, and common venture capital holdings among some of the more prominent Silicon Valley venture capital firms. On average, each of the twenty firms in the report had ten shared connections, and some, such as Netscape, had sixteen.[14]

Genetic mixing within the Valley is fueled by constant employee turnover. "When employees join a company, they are passionately committed to it," states a partner of one of the Valley's largest venture capital firms, Paul Koontz. But employees can magically lose that loyalty on very short notice. Then they "go and rev up an equally passionate commitment to somebody else."[15] With serial employment the norm, firms compete intensely; at the same time, they cooperate, learn from, and partner with one another.

■　■

The stories of AA and Silicon Valley contain the common features of colorful anecdote. Such illustrations have one shortcoming: They can relegate the application of living systems principles to the colorful fringe of the organizational world rather than to the mainstream of management experience.

The relevance and application of the principles of living systems are much more than a practice of last resort. In adaptive circumstances, these principles should be the first recourse. The U.S. Army adopted precisely this outlook.

There is method in our madness in featuring the U.S. Army to illustrate how enduring organizational capabilities can be built on the dual properties of self-organization and emergence. The Army is above suspicion insofar as it is highly unlikely that these ideas could be applied casually or permissively. Beginning in the late 1980s, several generations of the Army's senior leaders studied and consciously embraced the ideas of self-organization and emergence and began to apply them as an alternative model to the Army's command-and-control legacy. They have since distilled them down to protocols that have served the Army well in sustaining its vitality over time.

For many, the juxtaposition of *U.S. Army* with *self-organization* and *transformation* amounts to a contradiction in terms. Our stereotypes warrant reexamination. General Gordon R. Sullivan, recently retired Chief of Staff of the Army, explains:

> The paradox of war in the Information Age is one of managing massive amounts of information and resisting the temptation to over-control it.

The competitive advantage is nullified when you try to run decisions up and down the chain of command. All platoons and tank crews have real-time information on what is going on around them, the location of the enemy, and the nature and targeting of the enemy's weapons system. Once the commander's intent is understood, decisions must be devolved to the lowest possible level to allow these frontline soldiers to exploit the opportunities that develop.[16]

General Sullivan's words echo themes that we have discussed throughout this chapter.

Information-age warfare provoked the Army to harness self-organization and incorporate it as a central tenet of battlefield "doctrine" (the Army's term for *strategy*). The Army has pursued this by improving (1) the quality of the *nodes* (via higher-quality soldiers and superb training) and (2) the efficacy of *connections* that electronically tie together all the members of a fighting unit. Characteristically, the Army has codified these intentions so that these capabilities can be replicated.

The loosing of self-organizing impulses on the battlefield does not mean that tank crews fly helicopters or that soldiers spontaneously decide to support Kurdish rebels against Baghdad. To focus the lens of complexity, the Army invented an important managerial distinction called *Commander's Intent*. This is the foundation for action. Commander's Intent defines the scope of an engagement. The concept traces its origins to legendary General George S. Patton, a fatality of World War II. "Never tell people *how* to do things," he once said, "Tell them *what* to do and they will surprise you with their ingenuity."[17] (This philosophical difference, by the way, was at the crux of his clashes with British General Bernard L. Montgomery.) Under this construct, combat units are encouraged to improvise and initiate, but always within the larger structure of the Commander's Intent. When that intent is clearly communicated, fighting units can exploit opportunities that arise, or regroup when things don't go exactly as planned.

The Army brought urgency to its reinvention efforts by simulating a form of "competition" peculiar to a military monopoly. True, the Army has little direct "competition," insofar as armed conflicts are rare. Indeed, the Army's leaders are well aware of the fact that the military services languish during periods of peace and then misapply the last recent war's doctrine to the technology and unique tactical challenges of the next.

What is remarkable about the U.S. Army in the decades since the Vietnam War is that it has sidestepped this pitfall by making technological obsolescence "the enemy" in its quest for continuous renewal. The accuracy and lethality of smart weapons pose a diabolical challenge; the massing of troops and material (which is, after all, what armies traditionally do) accomplishes little more than providing one's enemy with a large and vulnerable target. In addition, the advent of distributed information allows the foot soldier or tank commander in the field to know roughly as much about what's going on as the generals in the command center. If this information is properly managed, soldiers on the front lines are able to make decisions in real time. Given the right tools, they can exploit opportunities and improvise in highly advantageous ways. This competitive advantage is squandered if one conforms to the traditional Army doctrine of first running all decisions past headquarters. Herein lies the case for self-organization.

"New routes" are important to the Army because, at the strategic level, new routes are needed to fight wars in the information age. At the tactical level, soldiers can devise new routes to victory on the battlefield.

One of the Army's most significant contributions to management practice occurs at three highly unusual U.S. Army training centers: (1) Fort Irwin, California (mechanized warfare); (2) Fort Polk, Louisiana (guerrilla insurgence); and (3) Hoenfelds, Germany (peace-keeping and humanitarian relief). These facilities are sufficiently remarkable to have been studied by senior executives from Shell, Sears, Motorola, and General Electric, as well as by senior delegations from every country in Western Europe, Russia, and most nations of Asia, Latin America, and the Middle East. Perfected over the past fifteen years, they are widely recognized to have almost single-handedly transformed one of the largest employers in the United States, in a manner that has great relevance for business.[18]

Let us zoom in on the training that is under way at the National Training Center (NTC) in California's Mojave Desert. Over a grueling two-week period, an Army brigade of 3,000 to 4,000 people (equivalent to a fully integrated business unit within a corporation), from bottom to top, go head-to-head with a competitor of like size in a simulation so realistic that no participant comes away unscathed. It alters forever the way executives lead and the way a front line performs.

Critical to the impact of the experience is a cadre of 600 instructors, one of whom is assigned to every person with leadership or supervisory responsibilities. These "observer/controllers," as they are called, shadow their counterparts through day after twenty-hour day of intense activity, provide personal coaching, and facilitate a team debriefing called an After Action Review (AAR). An AAR helps participants to understand what went wrong and how to correct the shortcomings. The AARs are in fact where the tank treads touch the terrain—exploiting the teachable moments of an exercise that ranges across 650,000 acres and costs $1 million a day.

A number of factors have contributed to the Army's extraordinary and sustained transformation. But observers inside and outside of the military agree that the NTC and its satellite facilities have been the crucible in which the transformation has come together. Since the NTC was established, more than half a million Army personnel have rotated through its programs several times. In fact, most upper and middle officers and NCOs have had as many as five NTC experiences. As one officer stated, "Before the NTC, we used to kid ourselves. The training was highly subjective. But the NTC experience leaves no room for debate. Day after day, you are confronted with the hard evidence of discrepancies between intentions and faulty execution, between what you wanted the enemy to do and what he actually did."[19]

One of the most remarkable aspects of the Army's transformation is that it has been sustained over a long period of time—it has weathered the vicissitudes of numerous executive transitions. Since the mid 1970s, the U.S. Army has had to respond to the sifting policies of six different Republican and Democratic administrations, eight Secretaries of Defense, ten Secretaries of the Army, and a succession of six different Army Chiefs of Staff (the top ranking general and de facto chief executive of the Army).

How could any organization successfully undergo a prolonged transition with its leadership deck continuously shuffled? Even under the most ideal circumstances (which those enumerated above surely were not), how can an institution with so many organizational constraints (public-sector disincentives; a booming economy that siphons off the best talent while the Army remains hobbled by frozen pay and benefits structures; a 60 percent annual turnover among the troops; severe downsizing; and a deeply entrenched command-and-control tradition) achieve the best-in-class status it now enjoys and fundamentally alter its leadership style and culture?

The short answer to these questions is that the Army has done a superb job of utilizing the guidelines enumerated in this and previous chapters. Through its orchestration of the six factors described below, it has cultivated a great deal of continuity in its reinvention efforts, despite shifts in funding levels and in policies at the top.

Specifically, these factors are:

1. *Disequilibrium* is guaranteed by the grueling twenty-hour-a-day schedule at the NTC. Humiliating defeats at the hands of a superior "enemy," physical exhaustion, and the relentless discipline of the AAR work to unfreeze the organization and move it far out of its comfort zone.

2. *The edge of chaos* is an apt image for the participants' experience. Disequilibrium is *amplified* by fatigue and by mounting evidence that success is dependent on how well fighting units can integrate their proficiency at routine maneuvers with a new requirement: their ability to improvise. *Damping* feedback is provided by the training that has preceded the NTC experience. Soldiers have been drilled to perform tasks under specific conditions to achieve certain standards. The AARs use specific battlefield events, supported by compelling and unambiguous data, to orchestrate "teachable moments."

3. *Strange attractors* are ingeniously exploited by the Army to avoid the historical trap of decline during peacetime:

- The Army perpetually reminds itself of the terrible humiliation of Vietnam and is determined not to repeat it. ("Never again" is a mantra taken deeply to heart.)
- By identifying "Information Age Warfare" and "The Digital Battlefield" as real and present dangers the Army stays focused on the threat of obsolescence.

These big-picture attractors, as important as they are, have not kept the Army from attending to aspirations that appeal to individual soldiers. Other attractors are "Service to Nation" (an important consideration to many who volunteer) and "Be All That You Can Be." The latter is more than an ad slogan. It resonates with the desire of many soldiers to discover their latent potential. The Army authentically sees itself as a developmental institution—one that helps recruits build strengths so that they can return to the civilian world with maturity, skills, and a sense of possibility that were not present when they enlisted.

4. The Army's journey over its *fitness landscape* has been discussed. Its leaders recognized the need to abandon the "basin of attraction": conventional weapons, doctrine, conscripted soldiers, and command from the top. They sought a new fitness peak where the topography is shaped by smart weapons, electronically networked fighting units, nontraditional missions (e.g., Serbia, Haiti, Rwanda), and models that exploit the distributed intelligence and initiative of the front lines.

5. *Nodes and connections* are strengthened by higher-quality recruits (a continuous struggle in a prolonged boom economy), and superb training. Superior equipment and electronic linkages increased the flow of information that matters: real time and big picture. All this was fused together at the NTC. There, under the glaring light of the AARs, each of the nodes must stand and deliver; in the blazing sun and numbing cold, true teamwork is born. Lasting mutual respect and deep human connections are forged under these conditions.

6. *Freedom and discipline* are enacted through the NTC process. Freedom is defined within the boundaries of the Commander's Intent: When soldiers understand the overall objectives of each engagement, they are free to improvise. As noted, discipline is enforced through vigorous training before attending the NTC. A second level of discipline occurs through the rigorous self-examination of the AARs.

Emergence Without 20/20 Hindsight

The capacity to spot what is *emerging* (before it unfolds) is the acid test of how well one grasps the concept of emergence. Without hindsight, it is much harder, of course, but the exercise sharpens the mind. The key is to focus on arenas where there is a lot of "noise" or "heat," and where conversations and structural inconsistencies resemble interstellar debris that hasn't quite coalesced into a planet or star.

Consider the consulting industry. For close to two decades, it has grown at a rate of 20 to 25 percent each year, and it currently rings up annual fees of $30 billion.[20] Accompanying this growth is a curious irony: Clients buy more and pay more—and *complain* more. They decry the expense, fear their dependence, and protest that consultants "borrow your watch to tell you what time it is." The incongruity between words and actions alerts us to the possibility of an emergent issue.

What's going on?

Corporate downsizings during the past two decades may provide a partial explanation. Companies have kept just enough staff to handle ongoing business operations. When a special project arises or an unexpectedly high demand occurs, outside resources are needed. Some tasks require special expertise: reducing cycle time; providing change architecture; implementing software for enterprise resource planning; researching possible acquisitions. Those internally responsible benefit from advice provided by those familiar with the widest range of up-to-date applications across companies and industries. Because such expertise is hard to find and expensive to retain internally, consultants are hired.

What is emergent here is the need for *knowledge services*. Anachronistic stereotypes of consultants obscure this bona fide need. "Knowledge services" provide an efficient solution to an emergent need.

Another arena in which we see emergence-in-the-making is in societal contradictions toward adoption. Five million qualified parents in the most affluent nations of the world stand eager to adopt children. And fifteen million homeless children, mostly in economically deprived nations, stand in desperate need of support. In Africa alone, in the past ten years, 10.4 million children have become orphans after their parents' death from AIDS. These children, having lost their mothers (and, in most cases, their fathers), are essentially abandoned.[21] Most live in the streets.

For such youngsters' physical and mental suffering is acute. Many die in spirit, many die in flesh. Yet adopting these children remains extraordinarily difficult and fraught with legal, emotional, financial, and diplomatic perils. Note again the preconditions for emergence: heat and noise, unmet needs, and structural incongruities.

The problems begin as soon as a poor nation allows wealthier outsiders access to its abandoned children. The demand for youngsters is so intense that, in a remarkably short amount of time, criminal networks emerge to steal newborn infants—who *have* indigenous natural parents—from hospitals and sell them. Destitute women are paid to have babies. As these cruel and inhumane second-order effects become apparent, nations typically close their doors to adoption. They often impose restrictions on prospective parents that are so onerous as to relegate the remaining children to an untouchable category—"a problem too difficult to deal with." Such has been the case in Vietnam, Romania, the Philippines, the states of Russia, and most of sub-Saharan Africa.

Juxtapose this emergent-issue-waiting-to-happen with the outlawing of antipersonnel land mines. It is useful to reflect on the common patterns.

The hazard of antipersonnel mines was intractable until a host of agencies self-organized. The visibility and voice of Princess Diana, who raised the issue to public consciousness, aided the cause. As a result of many factors, significant strides were made in restricting the use of land mines, and, in 1998, a Nobel Peace Prize was awarded to several leaders who helped bridge from this emergent need to a remedy. In the new decade, the disconnect between those who desire to adopt children and youngsters who desperately need a home is likely to achieve the status of "an issue whose time has come." When that occurs, global policies and humane remedies are likely to follow.

Caveats

Successful application of the principles of living systems theory to human social systems does not mean that people left entirely to their own devices will miraculously self-organize and generate emergent outcomes. Neither logic nor experience supports this conclusion. The excesses and destructiveness of the Chinese Cultural Revolution are a case in point. Mao Tse-tung failed to articulate an adaptive challenge. He launched the Cultural Revolution in 1966 to restore a vibrant communist society, resist rightist leanings, and rout out the "Four Olds": old thinking, old culture, old habits, and old customs. But there were no boundaries to this Commander's Intent. Mao's "Little

Red Book" provided ideological guidelines, but it lacked practical rules and behavioral limits for what became a prolonged uprising of the masses.[22] Many believe Mao intended that outcome. He prohibited education (middle school through university) for five years and ordered the military and the Party not to intervene in the rampages of the Red Guards. Insofar as unleashing the dark side of a society was the aim of Mao's design, the Cultural Revolution will stand as a perverse clinical experiment. It demonstrated the dark and explosive potential of self-organization without structure. Economic and social chaos followed, and it took a full five years after the Red Guard was dissolved to restore order.

Productive self-organization requires boundaries. Without them, self-organizing masses often regress into nihilism. China's Cultural Revolution destroyed all that stood out from, or above, the norm. The prolonged upheaval rent the fabric of Chinese society and spiraled toward the lowest common denominators. In this stark example, reckless and unchanneled self-organization tumbled from "the edge" into chaos itself, and set China back for decades.

It is also important to address the opposite extreme, where self-organization is sought and then throttled back through excessive control. The past thirty years' flirtation with "participative management" and "self-managed teams" is a case in point. These constructs rely, to some extent, on self-organization and emergence. But, like mushrooms, many of which look alike, reports of poisonings remind us that similarities can be dangerously deceptive.

Participative management and self-managed teams have had a disappointing thirty-year history. Too often, these techniques have been applied when management "knows the answer" but wants a little help or a superficial buy-in from the troops. In such circumstances, only limited space is allowed for contributions from the "intelligence in the nodes." The result: Three-quarters of the attempts at participative management fail. The problem rarely emanates from the workers. Usually, upper or middle management relegates these practices to the shop floor and makes sure they stay there. Participative management and self-managed teams have been hung out to dry on the hardwiring of social engineering. Self-organization and emergence will share precisely the same fate unless a living systems view is adopted as the context.[23]

Guidelines for Harnessing Self-Organization and Emergence

We have provided a half dozen organizational examples of self-organization and emergence in action. Let us summarize by distilling six general guidelines.

1. **Decide whether self-organization and emergence are really needed.** Do you face an Adaptive Challenge? Are new routes or new destinations sought? If nimbleness is required and discontinuous innovation is necessary, these dual properties can add value. Use the right tool for the right task.
2. **Analyze the health of your network.** Self-organization arises from networks that are fueled by nodes and connections. If you seek self-organization, enlarge the number of nodes and expect every organizational member to contribute (as the Army has done). Enrich the quality of the connections with simple routines and protocols that cement strong relationships (as was done at Tupperware and Alcoholics Anonymous, and in the U.S. Army).
3. **Remember the Goldilocks principle.**[24] Neither too many rules or too few rules. The key to self-organization resides in a field of tension between discipline and freedom. Nature achieves this tension through selection pressures (which impose discipline) and by upending occurrences (such as chance mutations and environmental disruptions). In organizations, rules provide discipline. They can take the form of protocols; recall Tupperware's

thick binder of party games and its tricks for identifying new recruits, or the Army's tasks, conditions, standards, and AARs. Freedom is reinforced by the power of a strange attractor (for example, Tupperware's commitment to enriching the lives of women, or the Army's challenge to recruits: "Be All That You Can Be").

4. Harness the power of requisite variety. Juxtapose people from different fields and backgrounds and let their varied work histories enrich the potential of self-organizing networks. This mixing cannot be done with abandon. But, as is evident in Silicon Valley, coevolution fosters unlikely forms of cooperation and can open the door to whole new worlds.

5. Look for the preconditions of emergence: the existence of "noise" or "heat" in the system; contradictions between words and actions; incongruencies between supply and demand; unexpressed needs. All hint at emergent possibilities and help to identify when an issue is bubbling toward the surface. "An idea whose time has come" is the conventional way we talk about emergence.

6. Self-organization and emergence should not be thought of exclusively as episodic occurrences. Self-organization can occur episodically (as it did at Sears), and emergence gives rise to periodic upwelling (for example, the global consensus to outlaw antipersonnel mines), but these properties of life have enduring power, as evidenced in Silicon Valley and the U.S. Army. When brought to the forefront of management consciousness, they can become sources of sustaining competitive advantage. They can exert a subtle influence—more akin to the way water wears away stone than to the way dynamite blasts through granite.

■ ■

Self-organization and emerging complexity are the twin engines in the evolution of all living things. But is an acquaintance with the laws of complexity required to harness them?

Our answer again is a qualified "Yes." Some challenges can be met with the management tools we have been depending on for ages. But this book is not about ordinary problems; rather, we are focusing on the adaptive challenges we encounter increasingly in the Information Age. For these challenges, familiar tools do not suffice.

In Chapter 9, we explore how managers can guide their organizations once they have tapped into their potential as living systems. The answer is not in detailed plans. One must learn to disturb an organization artfully. Avoid sledgehammers when feathers will do.

PART FOUR

CHAPTER 9

DISTURBING COMPLEXITY

Consider the war of attrition waged by ranchers and the U.S. Fish and Wildlife Service to "control" the coyote. A cumulative total of $3 billion (in 1997 dollars) has been spent over the past 100 years to underwrite bounty hunters, plant poisoned bait, field a sophisticated array of traps, and introduce tasty contraceptives to limit the fertility of females—all with the aim of protecting sheep and cattle from these wily predators.[1]

The result?

In the early 1800s, when immigrants first appeared in significant numbers west of the Mississippi, coyotes were found only in the region that now comprises eleven states West of the Mississippi, and were never seen east of the Mississippi. As a direct result of the aggressive programs to eliminate them, the modern-day coyote has migrated to all forty-nine continental states and has been seen in suburbs of New York City and Los Angeles. What's more, the coyote is physically 20 percent larger and significantly smarter than its predecessors.[2]

How the coyote came to be bigger and wiser—and everywhere—is a by-product of adversity. In response to the eradication efforts, a significant number fled to Canada where they bred with the larger Canadian wolf. Subsequently, some descendants migrated south; others went north to Alaska. Over the decades, these animals bred with the domestic survivors, increasing both coyotes' size and numbers. Humankind's persistent efforts to trap, hunt, and poison coyotes heightened the selection pressures and placed a premium on coyote intelligence. Survivors tended to be streetwise and wary of human contact. Once alerted by a few fatalities among their brethren, coyotes are usually able to sniff out and avoid our latest stratagem to do them harm.

Similar counterintuitive developments occur in business. Take, for example, recent efforts by Federal Express to optimize pilot utilization. The common denominator in both the government's effort to eradicate the coyote and FedEx's efforts to reduce pilot deadheading costs was the misapplication of linear logic to a living system. Both endeavors backfired.

Federal Express's goal was to increase pilot productivity by streamlining aircraft routing. All this seemed within reach, given more powerful computers and recent breakthroughs in scheduling algorithms. The anticipated savings (in fuel costs and in pilot hours that were wasted shuttling from one location to another) were estimated in the hundreds of millions. But FedEx made one mistake: It overlooked everything we've been discussing about living systems. Unsurprisingly, the linear game plan evoked a nonlinear response.

The fourth principle of complexity reminds us that we can't *direct* a complex adaptive system, but FedEx thought it could. "Within weeks, pilots for FedEx were screaming," wrote *Wall Street Journal* reporter Douglas Blackmon. "The system was spitting out nightmarish flight plans. Pilots found themselves blasting across the time zones of two hemispheres, pulling back-to-back trans-Pacific and trans-Atlantic flights and traveling for hours in vans and taxis to change aircraft."[3]

Complaints from pilots mounted, but FedEx management stood fast as systems analysts worked around the clock to correct the problems. But, redoubled efforts at the wrong thing produce more of the wrong thing, and that was the case here. With no relief to the scheduling nightmare in sight, FedEx's 3,500 pilots galvanized into action. They revitalized what had been, historically, a relatively compliant in-house union, and they threatened a work stoppage if their demands were not met. Their first demand was predictable: Abandon the new flight-scheduling system. But self-organization has a way of generating an emergent life of its own. Now mobilized by their protest, the pilots also demanded a 24 percent wage increase over three years, fewer required flying hours per month, and dramatically increased retirement benefits. Confronted with the first pilot strike in the company's history, FedEx management retreated. The optimization model that triggered the uproar was eviscerated, and management acceded to many of the pilots' other requests.[4]

Reflecting on this incident, let us acknowledge that FedEx management began with a reasonable objective; the strategy to implement it caused all the trouble. Reengineering an inefficient system made sense; faster computers and powerful optimization software for scheduling pilots and planes had come on the market. Management wished to exploit these breakthroughs by taking the classic "blank sheet of paper" approach advocated for reengineering efforts. The trouble is, the "blank sheet of paper" gets soiled in the execution phase. Further, in the words of evolutionary biologist Peter Schuster, we learn from evolution that "optimization does not lead to radical innovation."[5]

Tom Davenport, one of the pioneers of reengineering, observes: "Reengineering didn't start out as a code word for bloodshed. Reengineering turned ugly because it treated people inside companies as so many bits and bytes—interchangeable parts to be reengineered." (A simple example of Davenport's point is our common experience with automated menus on telephones. The branching tree of prompts looks sensible to designers, but it is invariably time-consuming and it drives customers crazy.) "When a system is reengineered top down" (as it was at FedEx), Davenport continues, "it falters because it forces those who do the work to change their behavior with no input or ownership. It becomes an automated version of Taylorism."[6]

Herding Butterflies

The FedEx and coyote experiences remind us that efforts to direct living systems beyond very general goals are counterproductive. Thus, the fourth principle of complexity: Living systems cannot be directed along a predetermined path, but, like herding the proverbial butterfly, they can be ushered forth with reasonable expectation of progress. True, through self-organization and emergence, living things tend toward order rather than randomness. But they do this in their own unique way, which seldom conforms to the straight path that we might wish. This flies at the heart of one of the most common paradoxes of organizational performance: optimization (aka control) seldom leads to radical breakthroughs.[7]

That managers, like those at FedEx, pursue optimization is logical. The problems arise not because the goals are inherently foolish, but because managers, unwittingly, try to overdirect outcomes. A quest for an optimal solution often leads to a mistaken application of Newtonian cause-and-effect logic. When the causal relationships are obscure or subject to unforeseen effects (which is almost always the case when a living system is challenged to achieve discontinuous results), optimization efforts seldom pan out as expected.

FedEx had alternatives. It could have disturbed its living system by involving its pilots in the solution. A joint project team, comprised of pilots, management, systems analysts, and accountants would have surfaced the many trade-offs that needed to be considered. Ironically, the pilots generally supported measures to improve cost competitiveness with arch rival United Parcel Service (UPS) and were aware that these competitive pressures were intensifying as E-mail and the Internet were eroding volume. A task group including the pilots would have appropriately addressed (rather than ignored) the human considerations that needed to be taken into account. Judging by previous multi-discipline team efforts at FedEx, the odds are high that a better outcome would have been generated than the one that the company lives with today.

In fitness landscape terms, it is impossible to get to a distant and higher fitness peak (discover radical breakthroughs) by climbing still higher on the peak one is already on (optimizing). Rather, one needs to descend into the unknown, disregard the proven cause-and-effect formulas, and defy the odds. One embarks on a journey of sequential disturbances and adjustments, not a lock-step march along a predetermined path. We may only be able to see as far as our headlights, but proceeding in this fashion can still bring us to our journey's destination.

Because discontinuous leaps, by their very nature, arise from unforeseen combinations, it is impossible to reverse engineer them. Extrapolation is possible when systems exhibit continuity over a wide range of conditions. In this circumstance, the relationship of the components is linear and the goal can be attained by progressing step by step. But if the system exhibits discontinuities, extrapolating "what's going to happen next" is unreliable. Something that does not lend itself to logical explanation after the fact does not respond predictably to direction beforehand. We must settle, instead, for a series of shrewd disruptions, proceeding with a reasonable degree of confidence that the outcome will tilt more in the desired direction than its opposite. When we overreach and attempt to hardwire a specific result, we almost always fail.

Nobel Laureate Francis Crick, codiscoverer of DNA, once observed that "Evolution is more clever than you are."[8] What trips us up is our inability to predict second- and third-order consequences that flow from seemingly straightforward intentions. Managers described as "street-smart" or "seasoned" have often garnered this wisdom about living systems the hard way. These veterans *expect* detailed plans to go awry. They know that the number of things that can go wrong is multiplied when a bold break with the past is attempted. If, in addition, the desired change antagonizes an organization's members (as we saw at FedEx) and they band together to "beat the system," all bets are off. "(N)othing is more difficult to carry out, nor more doubtful of success, nor more dangerous to handle," observed Machiavelli, "than achieving a new order of things."[9]

At the core of all this unpredictability are two factors. One is the inherently *indeterministic* nature of Nature. Life is shaped by probabilities, not certainties. The second is *frozen accidents,* which occur occasionally and stem from an avalanche of consequences that are difficult to alter. As in a real avalanche, little actions trigger bigger ones that become irreversible. In this chapter, we'll take a look at each of these factors.

Indeterminism

Nobel laureate Murray Gell-Mann tells us: "The universe is governed by quantum mechanical laws. This means there are probabilities for alternative histories (indeterminism). Any entity in the world around us owes its existence not only to laws of physics but to an inconceivably long sequence of indeterministic probabilistic events"[10] (frozen accidents).

For decades, paleontologists, enamored with Darwin's theories of gradual evolution, minimized evidence indicating that the long history of the planet encompassed either sudden proliferations of species, as during the Cambrian era, or avalanches of extinctions, as in an asteroid impact or the disappearance of one keystone species. As noted earlier, Stephen Jay Gould was among the first to confront this fossil discrepancy with an open mind.[11] Gould proposed that evolution was "punctuated"; it proceeded in an orderly fashion for long periods of time, then occasionally shifted in radical and unexpected ways. These points of inflection led to a reexamination of Darwin's gradualism, the prevailing paradigm of evolution.

Debates among paleontologists may be interesting, but ideas are only—well, ideas. The sequence becomes more relevant when the evolution of your industry is "punctuated." We then begin to see how extraordinarily difficult it is for managers to come to terms with indeterminism. It may be necessary to acknowledge that large endeavors to which many have dedicated their careers may amount to little, while one occurrence may have enormous repercussions.

Parents discover the importance of indeterminism in the unfolding lives of living systems called children. The unforeseen turns of destiny are also the stuff of poetry; they inspire writers as unlike each other as T.S. Eliot, Shakespeare, Emily Dickinson, and Rilke.

Gary Kildall, most likely someone you've never heard of, learned about indeterminism the hard way. The results left an indelible mark on the computer industry. In the early 1980s, Kildall headed one of the few companies that had perfected a clean and efficient operating system for personal computers. He called it CP/M.[12]

With the intention of licensing his system, executives of IBM's then-fledgling personal computer unit paid a call on Kildall at his Albuquerque headquarters. The IBM team had previously screened and tested the system and were favorably impressed. But Kildall showed up late and did not display sufficient deference toward the white-shirted executives from Armonk. Returning to the East Coast after a frustrating day, the IBM team pondered its next step in what was obviously going to be an uneasy courtship.

Interestingly, the next important figure in this story is Bill Gates's mother, who, coincidentally, sat on the United Way Board of Directors with John Opel, chief executive officer of IBM. In a side conversation, she overheard Opel describing the disappointing trip to Albuquerque. "My son, Billy," she volunteered, "has built an operating system."

Opel showed more than polite interest. Three weeks later, IBM visited Gates to examine what he jokingly called his "Dirty Old Operating System"—DOS for short. A month later, IBM made an offer, which Gates accepted. Today, his net worth is upward of $40 billion. In 1994, Kildall, bitter and disillusioned, died in a brawl in a bikers' bar in Monterey, California.

The point of this story is more than to amuse with a tale of coincidence. It is a backdrop to our inquiry into outcomes that defy explanation and otherwise confound us.

It is wise to acknowledge the numerous possibilities that may emanate from weak cause-and-effect linkages. We should anticipate the second- and third-order effects of any bold intervention we are about to undertake, but always expect several more to show up in their own good time. Indeterminism gains the upper hand in hard-to-pigeonhole ways. Seemingly unimportant circumstances can trigger a cascade of irreversible events. Indeterminism flourishes in highly volatile situations where the various factors at play exhibit "minds of their own."

Viewed through the lens of the fourth principle of complexity, unforeseen consequences in the above case flowed from, first, Kildall's tardiness and his seeming indifference toward the IBM team; next, a chance encounter between Bill Gates's mother and the IBM CEO; and, finally, the commercial leverage bequeathed to DOS once it was embedded in IBM PCs. Some of this sequence might have been anticipated; most of it came as a surprise. Microsoft was swept into the mainstream of the information industry with astonishing velocity. As economist Brian Arthur observes, "Microsoft's success is clever strategy, mediocre technology and a hell of a lot of indeterminism, and increasing returns."[13]

Indeterminism and Rewards

You may not be Bill Gates and your company may not be Microsoft, but if you understand the concept of indeterminism, you can cultivate an intuition for the weak links in many seemingly sensible plans.

Not too long ago, *The Wall Street Journal* published a thoughtful critique of contemporary reward systems. Its main finding was that, despite the current popularity of pay-for-performance, balanced scorecards, and team-based rewards, most of these schemes fail to produce the overall broad outcome desired.[14] Dogged pursuit of the perfect reward scheme, as Samuel Johnson might have said, represents the triumph of hope over experience.

That managers everywhere pursue the quest for the "perfect" reward system is a curious phenomenon, given abundant evidence that all, inevitably miss the mark. Perhaps our attachment to the notion that rewards will direct behavior is imbedded in the deeply internalized premises of social engineering. We have been "conditioned" by the belief that human behavior can be controlled if we can design the correct stimuli. But, predicated on the erroneous assumption that behavior is predictable, social engineering makes no allowance for indeterministic behavior and second and third order effects. Alternatively, if we relinquish the view of living systems as controllable and predictable, we are led to accept that rewards alone do not direct, inspire, or motivate behavior in the way we would wish.

Rewards are predicated on Skinnerian behaviorism (i.e., the stimulus–response regime that caused Pavlov's dog to perform amusing antics). At the heart of any rewards system is a deterministic model which holds that people will act in accordance with the "trainer's" desires so long as the "right" reward is offered.

Yet, in the 1950s, distinguished professor Frederick Herzberg, then at Case Western Reserve, documented that most rewards were "dissatisfiers." He observed that although they were intended as positive, the net effect of most rewards is negative. Significantly, people who are rewarded anything less than the maximum, or who compare their reward unfavorably with less deserving peers, usually focus on the gap and end up experiencing the reward as negative reinforcement. Generally, when economic incentives are at stake, the glass is usually seen as half empty rather than half full.[15]

Herzberg discerned that rewards (positive reinforcement) and punishments (negative reinforcement) are two sides of the same coin. Given that human beings are hardwired psychologically to focus on what is wrong and what is missing, we almost always concentrate on the inequities and dysfunctional aspects of rewards. Thus, extrinsic reward systems deteriorate as a source of motivation and become the source of grievances. Shortcomings are revealed, the reward system is gamed by the target community, and, despite management's best intentions, the reinforcement scheme spirals into an underworld of discontent. Eventually, its defects are acknowledged as disincentives to experimentation and risk taking; or, it becomes a source of internecine conflict or excessively short-term focus. A new reward scheme is then unveiled and the cycle begins again.

The point here, of course, is not to disregard rewards altogether, but to regard them as imperfect. They are, perhaps, necessary, but they are certainly insufficient stimuli to unleash the potential of a living system. Rewards absolutely motivate people, but only to get rewards. This backfires because it focuses attention very narrowly on "winning" rather than on the original goal for which the reward was designed. Rewards induce temporary compliance with some goals insofar as they reinforce "doing things right." But they do not, generally, encourage employees to "do the right thing." In fact, many studies have shown that rewards actually *diminish* employees' interests in larger goals and their underlying commitment to them. As they become preoccupied with "getting the reward," intrinsic meanings recede in importance.[16]

Rewards over-promise and under-deliver because organizational undertakings are always at the mercy of indeterministic effects. The terms and conditions of reward schemes fall short of anticipating the twists and turns of the unfolding world.

Foreign Aid: Trying Harder, Doing Worse

Foreign aid programs have a legacy of trying to hardwire social outcomes. Often a lightning rod for congressional and media criticism, the foibles of such programs arise because they attempt to direct living systems. Of course, the loudest critics—notably, Congress, the media, and the public—are often at fault. When Congress, for example, insists that "every AID dollar be wisely invested," the ensuing legislations impose criteria such as detailed project plans, timetables, milestones, and deliverables so that all the loose ends are "buttoned down." Much of this is problematic in a living system for the reasons we have been discussing.

Consider efforts to modernize the native Lapps, a reindeer-herding people who live in Finland, above the Arctic Circle.[17] Diffusion expert, Everett Rogers, reporting on the research of Perti Pelto, describes a new technology—snowmobiles, which were introduced in the United States in the late 1950s, as an adjunct to winter recreation. Their use spread rapidly (eventually unleashing a backlash in developed countries, because of offensive noise pollution in formerly peaceful outdoor areas). But for the Lapps, snowmobiles were regarded as much more than a plaything. In remote snowbound areas, snowmobiles were a far superior form of transportation than snowshoes and dogsleds.

Aside from an occasional government subsidy, Rogers states that "the Lapps relied on their herds of semidomesticated reindeer for their livelihood." Reindeer meat was their main source of protein, he continues, "and the hides were used for sleds, clothing, and shoes. Surplus meat was bartered at trading stores for staples such as flour, sugar, and tea. For the most part, Lapp society was egalitarian; status was determined by the quality and size of one's reindeer herd, and each family had similar numbers and types. The Lapps felt a special bond with the reindeer and treated them with respect and care."

We can conjecture, however, that the Finnish planners, in contrast, had long regarded the Lapps as a backward people. Adaptation of the snowmobile sparked interest because it could improve herding productivity and, as a means of transport that was vastly superior to dogsleds, bring the Lapps into closer contact with mainstream Finnish society—schools, health care, and commerce. The government-subsidized machines, it was hoped, would improve the tribes' standard of living, thus fostering greater self-sufficiency.

The Lapps did indeed find the snowmobiles a labor-saving device for corralling reindeer. The intervention, however, had some unforeseen consequences. Rogers explains that the herders had to stand, not sit, on their machines in order to spot obstacles and stray animals in the rocky terrain, and were often catapulted forward when they encountered snow-covered rocks and branches. Driving injuries were frequent. Moreover, the vehicles themselves frequently broke down in the rough terrain, and repairs were expensive.

For the Lapps, the snowmobile became an emergent cultural totem. By 1971, ten years after their introduction, snowmobiles were everywhere. In one major village, each of the seventy-two households had at least one snowmobile. For the reindeer herders, it completely replaced skis and sleds, and it reduced to a few hours the former three-day journey to the nearest Finnish outpost for staples.[18] The snowmobile brought the Lapps into close and frequent contact with modern consumerism and gave them proximity to the attractions and hazards of "civilization" for the first time.

The snowmobile's impact on the coevolutionary relationship between the Lapps and their reindeer held other unforeseen surprises. The reindeer were disturbed by the noise and smell of the machines. Mating, fertility, and the number of calves born each year were drastically reduced. Occasionally, the noise triggered stampedes and injuries to the animals. For all these reasons, Pelto documents that the number of reindeer per household plummeted from an average of fifty-two, prior to the introduction of snowmobiles, to only twelve in 1971. The precipitous loss of the reindeer population continued as Lapps slaughtered their animals for food or to pay for gasoline and snowmobile parts. The vehicles cost about $1,000 in 1971 dollars; gas and repairs averaged $425 per year. By 1975, about two-thirds of the Lapp households had dropped out of reindeer husbandry altogether.[19]

Most of these herdless families were unable to find an alternative source of livelihood. Ironically, they began to use their snowmobiles for trips to town to collect their unemployment benefits. There were also "winners" within the community. One family gradually increased its reindeer holdings until, by 1971, it owned 35 percent of the reindeer in the tribal area. With the accumulation of wealth, egalitarian norms deteriorated. As they reflected on the snowmobile project, "Modernization" had pushed the Lapps into a tailspin of cash dependency, debt, and unemployment, and had destroyed a thousand-year-old tribal heritage of pride and independence.[20]

Frozen Accidents

The closely related and confounding ingredient in living systems is known in science as *frozen accidents*. These are the coincidences that become locked in. Indeterminism deals the cards. Frozen accidents are what happen at the gaming table after the cards are dealt.[21]

Frozen accidents are the means by which a species acquires its destiny. Once a cell in an embryo embarks on a particular pathway, it leaves behind many other options. The number of cells it can change into from that point forward greatly diminishes. When a niche is wide open, one sees many prototypes. But as the niche is filled, extremes are weeded out. One sees this in e-commerce today.

Frozen accidents played a major role in: the development of early bicycles and automobiles; the global dominance of the English language; the standard clock design, with twelve (not twenty-four) hours, and hands moving from left to right; the acceptance of 110- and 220-volt household electricity; the adoption of VHS as the global video format; and railroad track gauges that trace their origins to the grooves left in roadbeds by Roman chariots. These ruts determined the axle width for subsequent horse-drawn carriages, and, many generations later, the same manufacturers made the first railroad axles using the same casting jigs.[22]

Why does all of this have enormous relevance to business? Knowledge-based sectors of the economy are particularly prone to frozen accidents. Once a format or technology becomes locked in as the de facto standard, it becomes a formidable barrier to entry. Brian Arthur of the Santa Fe Institute has studied the frozen-accident phenomenon in business. He calls it *lock-in*.

Lock-in runs counter to the sacrosanct economic tenet of diminishing returns. In traditional sectors such as mining, transportation, and agriculture, for example, increasing the volume of production beyond the point of diminishing returns causes costs to escalate. When capacity is added, it cannot be recovered by price increases. *Diminishing* returns occur because, beyond some point, more production means less earnings. Mining companies are stymied by increasingly inaccessible veins of ore; transportation companies, by overloaded networks; farmers, by having to use less fertile land or by the escalating cost of fertilizer which they use in an effort to squeeze multiple harvests from the same field.

In contrast, knowledge-based businesses often experience *increasing* returns. The more you produce (i.e., copies of Microsoft Windows), the more you earn. Such products often require a huge initial investment in a technology. Yet providers can manufacture and distribute additional copies for pennies and sell the copies at very high multiples of the production cost.

Frozen accidents do not obey the laws of scarcity (like diamonds); they abide by the laws of plenitude (like language). The more accepted and available something becomes, the faster it accelerates ahead of its rivals and thrives. It becomes "frozen-in" as the *de facto* standard.

Indeterminism and Frozen Accidents at Sun

Indeterminism and frozen accidents are the invisible hands behind many commercial occurrences. One illustration of both of these factors is the sequence of events that led to Sun Microsystems' highly successful programming language, Java.

When Sun programmer Patrick Naughton decided to quit and join NeXT Computer, it all could have ended before it began. But *Wired* writer, David Bank, traces an unforseen set of events. The 25-year-old employee happened to be playing ice hockey that day on the company squad, and Sun's chief executive officer, Scott McNealy, was a teammate. Relaxing over a few beers after the game, Naughton told the CEO of his decision.

"Why?" asked McNealy.

"Because they're doing things right," Naughton replied.

"Okay, but before you go," McNealy asked, "write up what you think Sun is doing wrong. Don't just lay out the problem. Give me a solution. Tell me what you would do if you were God."[23] This chance encounter would influence Sun's destiny.

Bank recounts that Naughton's response to the CEO, which was disseminated electronically, rang true. Naughton was re-recruited and asked to assemble a team of engineers (guided only by the constraint that the group be small enough in number to fit around a table in a Chinese restaurant). To protect the project from corporate "antibodies," its mission was secret and the team was housed at an offsite location. Its assignment was to invent Sun's next generation of products "the right way." McNealy invested $1 million and challenged the team to get something up and running quickly.

The team developed criteria for sifting through its list of dream projects. First among them was the principal of "user-friendly machines for normal people." Computer chips appear in many electronic appliances, which consumers hate to program. Why not develop a universal device, an all-in-one remote control, that could program most, if not all, electronic appliances? The team was gripped by the concept, but, for the device to work, a universal language was needed, one that could communicate with any kind of electronic devices: VCRs, personal computers, TV sets, home security systems, and a host of others.

As Bank describes debates within the team, it was gradually conceded that existing programming tools provided a starting point. But C++ and BASIC were as useless as fluent French in China. The team was stymied by the absence of a digital Rosetta Stone.

One night, a Sun programmer, James Gosling, attended a laser-enhanced rock concert. The colored lights that danced to the music triggered a flash of inspiration: Gosling visualized electronic messengers flowing down the wires, choreographing the lasers to the rhythm of the music. His insight clarified the programming problem. Sun needed a messenger, not a new universal language. A messenger that spoke Esperanto could communicate at a basic level with the instruction set of every electronic host. A better description is a "benign virus" that could infiltrate the hosts' programming language. The host would co-opt the viral components and assemble them like building blocks (i.e., "objects") to accomplish particular chores. The key element would be a "virus" that could coexist with every digital species—one with sufficient stealth to piggyback on the electronic neurons and synapses of host machines and evade their idiosyncratic antibodies.

This "benign virus," while representing a major conceptual breakthrough, was, of course, only an enabler for the handheld hardware—the all-in-one remote control that the team sought to invent. Because they were focused on hardware, the true soul of the new machine (i.e., Java) was undervalued. Overlooked was the fact that the "benign virus" would make it possible to set up software building blocks on networks in a very distributed manner. None of this was to become evident for a considerable period of time.

Sun embarked on a series of spurned courtships—initially, with Mitsubishi in the hope of developing a handheld device for the latter's full line of home entertainment units and household appliances. Sun then made a run at France Telecom. Neither of these proposed collaborations materialized, largely because the cost of the gadget was too high for mass-market acceptance. If Mitsubishi, for example, had elected to partner with Sun, the dice of indeterminism would have rolled differently and the "benign virus" would have had a very different destiny. Java would likely have served out an anonymous existence entombed inside an all-in-one remote control.

Two further effects of indeterminism then shaped the future of Naughton's team. Time Warner was eager to have Sun design and manufacture the set-top box for its Communications 2000 strategy.

The vision of Sun's device atop millions of TV sets as the link to the information superhighway had Naughton's team breathing pure oxygen. But when Time Warner capped the box cost at $300 per unit, exhilaration shifted to despair. Every estimate came in at double that target. In the end, the Time Warner contract went to Sun's rival, Silicon Graphics. Naughton's team lost momentum and morale plummeted.

Matters were made worse by another close encounter—this time with 3DO, a video game maker. That firm's expensive entertainment system needed to double as a set-top box to win acceptance. The deal was so close to consummation that the contracts were drafted. Then, out of the blue, the CEO of 3DO demanded exclusive rights to the technology. McNealy balked. Unknowingly, playing its cards as it did, Sun had dodged another bullet. Java came very close to being sold outright, married to a struggling product, and sinking with the failing fortunes of its manufacturer.

All these events represented encounters with indeterminism.

The entrepreneurial journey had reached its lowest ebb. Sun management mandated: "Find profits or fold." A desperate plan was concocted to entice freelance CD-ROM developers to use the code in the hope that they would carry it over into designs of visual effects for commercial online services. Unsurprisingly, this proposal received little enthusiasm from Sun's executives, who doubted the programmers would adopt it. Increasingly, Naughton's project began to look like a distraction to Sun's core hardware products. Last rites were administered. The yet-to-be-built handheld device was orphaned off into an alliance with Thompson Consumer Electronics. Naughton's team was dissolved. The "benign virus" was seemingly forgotten.

The story might have ended there. But an "avalanche" in another sector of the industry, a frozen-accident-in-the-making called the World Wide Web was about to change things. Bill Joy, a cofounder of Sun, semiretired and living in Aspen, Colorado, was among the first to perceive the importance of the Web. He was aware of Naughton's project and immediately grasped the connections between its "benign virus" and the opportunities the Web created for its use.[24]

The Internet, of course, unleashed a cascade of events that altered the fitness landscape. Joy had the savvy to see this coming. Nearly twenty years before, while at the University of California, Joy had developed the Berkeley version of the UNIX operating system. He recognized that Naughton's "benign virus" could be distributed on the Net in the form of electronic building blocks, allowing users to assemble applications for themselves with Java's modules. Here was a revolution waiting to happen.

A superstar in Sun's orbit, Joy had the credibility needed to resurrect the project. In short order, the "benign virus" was retooled for Internet use and rechristened "Java." Reincarnated Java was now recognized as a match made in heaven for the Internet, not only because it does not discriminate, as Windows does, against particular operating systems, such as Apple's Mac, but because, as a virus, it is inherently virus-proof.

However, there was a catch. Sun could not reap any commercial benefit from Java until it enjoyed wide acceptance. The only way to achieve that was to give it away, thereby luring freelance applications developers into adopting it. Bill Joy's view was: "Just screw it. Let's give it away. Let's create a franchise."[25] More financially minded executives at Sun, including prominent board members, had trouble with the idea of giving away a $300 million investment in proprietary software to all takers, including Microsoft, Hewlett-Packard, Silicon Graphics, and a host of other piranhas. All were circling the Web and looking for the best place to bite.

But indeterminism tilted the scales in favor of Java-based philanthropy. Prior to Java's formal re-release, David Bonk describes a secret line deep in the Net created to give a few potential users a peek. Netscape was among them. After its meteoric beginning—which, interestingly, was built on giving away its Mosaic browser to entice users to its server applications—Netscape was assaulted by Microsoft. All subsequent generations of Windows included a *free* Internet browser for the express purpose of freezing Netscape out of the action. These were life-and-death matters to Netscape, but they were only of peripheral interest to Sun. Nonetheless, a sequence of chance occurrences was tilting the scales in Sun's favor.

Microsoft's competitive hardball precipitated a frozen-accident. Netscape embraced Java the way a drowning man grabs a life preserver. As it played out, Microsoft was now saddled with a competitive migraine (Java) far worse than its headaches with Netscape. Java provided the means for any computer, with or without Windows, to reach into the Net and tailor its own applications. Java was preferred because it did not render customers' existing legacy systems and software obsolete. Netscape benefited because its server applications could coordinate the entire process. Threatened with losing influence over its customers and their gateways, Microsoft intensified its efforts to reestablish control. This became the final straw in provoking the Department of Justice's antitrust suit. In this sequence, we see the powerful interplay of indeterminism and frozen accidents.

During the intervening years, Java has clearly come into its own. Along with making Java available for free to programmers, Sun has created a quasi-independent board to ensure that Java is held as a community resource, not beholden only to Sun. In addition to the six million programmers who write applets in Java code today, an additional million Java programmers graduate from Chinese universities each year, reflecting that nation's belief that Java is the software of the future. Sun has reaped the benefits of this and other successes. Over the period from 1995 to 1999, the firm has matured from a scrappy underdog to a mainstream player. Revenue growth through 1999 surpassed 25 percent per year and its stock has increased nine-fold to a market capitalization of $170 billion.[26]

As time goes on and frozen accidents pile up, two things happen. First, patterns or protocols develop that are hard to reverse (the prominence of English as the global business language; the chain of events that led to an antitrust suit against Microsoft). Second, effective complexity increases. The pace of change may slacken over time, but more elaborate arrangements, once in place, tend to remain so, and new entrants must learn to cope with them as additional features of the competitive landscape.

Indeterminism and the avalanches of frozen accidents are part of life, but they need not paralyze us into inaction. The insight that we cannot direct but only artfully disturb a living system does not prevent us from taking bold action. Earlier examples from Intel, Monsanto, and the U.S. Army all demonstrate that decisive commitments are attainable. But acceptance of indeterminism and frozen accidents allows us to cope more easily with ensuing events and to herd the butterflies of chance in a fashion that improves the odds of approximating our initial intentions. It is to this matter of "herding the butterflies of chance" that we now turn.

HERDING BUTTERFLIES

"In 1994, J&J (Johnson & Johnson) sparked a revolution in the treatment of coronary artery disease with a new medical device called a *stent*," writes *Wall Street Journal* reporter, Ron Winslow. "A stent is a tiny wire mesh cylinder about the diameter of the lead in a pencil that is inserted into an artery by threading a tiny balloon into the obstructed area, inflating the balloon, pushing the stent into place, and removing the deflated balloon. Overnight, the breakthrough solved the major drawback of balloon angioplasty. The steel mesh cylinder prevented arteries from re-closing, re-clogging, or narrowing over time. (In 5 percent of cases under the former procedures, arteries would snap shut abruptly; this life-threatening occurrence required emergency coronary artery bypass surgery.)"[1]

Heart surgeons applauded the J&J breakthrough. Within three years, it captured 90 percent of a lucrative U.S. market. Revenues from the stent soared to $1 billion annually, and profits from the product accounted for 8 percent of J&J's worldwide net.[2] J&J had discovered a New Route, but, unknowingly, it was perched on the slippery slope of a fitness landscape, and traversing it would necessitate a New Destination.

Adopting classic strategic models, the J&J division, Interconnect, priced the stent at the high end of what the market would bear ($1,595)—as if it were a pharmaceutical with long-term patent protection. But, as the years ticked by, sales volume skyrocketed, and no price concessions were forthcoming, doctors and hospitals began to complain. J&J, however, steadfastly rejected requests for price reductions for its maturing products or discounts to volume customers. In addition, as imperfections in the device came to light, J&J showed little interest in surgeons' suggestions for its improvement.[3]

In a textbook maneuver to strengthen its dominant position, J&J engineered a hostile takeover of Cordis, its angioplasty-balloon maker. It did so primarily to control barriers to entry by extending its reach over the products' value chain.[4] Additionally, J&J may have been motivated by a rumor that Cordis was preparing to introduce a new, and radically improved, stent of its own.

As Cordis's new owner, J&J sought to solidify its position by imposing its top-down management style on Cordis's more organic, participatory culture. Cordis's plans to launch a rival device were scrapped—along with significant improvements to the stent that Cordis had perfected. J&J persisted with its program to release its version of an incrementally improved stent.

J&J could have learned to accelerate its product development cycle from Cordis's highly effective parallel processing development teams. But it persisted with its traditional approach, which was based on sequential handoffs. Of course, this slowed down development. J&J's next-generation stent was long in coming and only marginally better than the original. Customers grew more alienated. In large numbers, Cordis's very knowledgeable developers began to leave, taking with them valuable know-how and breakthrough ideas that J&J had ignored.

For close to three years, J&J blithely sailed along on an increasingly turbulent sea of product obsolescence and customer discontent. Then, in the fall of 1997, Guidant Corporation introduced a superior stent. "Within 45 days, we had gained a 70 percent market position," says Ronald Dollens, Guidant's president and chief executive officer.[5] A J.P. Morgan analyst describes the switch as "the most dramatic transfer of wealth between two companies in medical device history." As the annual market for stents surged toward $2 billion, Guidant and another competitor accounted for 80 percent of the market. Meanwhile, J&J was in free fall, dropping dramatically from a 91 percent share at the beginning of 1997 to an 8 percent share by the end of 1998.[6]

Robert Gussin, J&J's Corporate Vice President for Science and Technology, reflected on the experience:

> First, we misestimated the backlash of premium pricing on the medical community. Second, Interconnect, as a young company, was facing one of the largest explosions of demand in J&J history. They were so preoccupied with gearing up production that they lost peripheral vision of the disruptive challenges laying in wait in the market. Third, we did a hostile takeover of Cordis because we recognized strategically we were highly vulnerable with one product and a three-year patent. But we "Johnsonized Cordis"—something we try not to do. When the patent ran out, all these mistakes came to roost. Competition came in and they killed us. This was definitely one of our unhappy moments.[7]

From the perspective of living systems, J&J's misadventure with the stent is instructive because it ignores every principle we have discussed. *Equilibrium* best describes its business-as-usual approach toward its customers and its acquisition of Cordis. The division did not increase the number of nodes or the quality of connections with its marketplace. After acquiring Cordis, it neither tapped the collective intelligence in the ranks of that enterprise, nor encouraged cross-pollination of methods and ideas. Its sequential product development process deflected the inroads of Cordis's more agile parallel processing and innovations. Above all, J&J steadfastly rejected overtures to coevolve an improved stent and build on the distributed intelligence of surgeons, hospitals, and the Cordis team of engineers and researchers.

By so doing, it was left stranded on a suboptimal fitness peak while both a New Route (a radically improved stent) and a New Destination (an approach to the market that entailed coevolution with customers, perhaps sharing both risks and profits) allowed more agile competitors to seize the high ground.

We have previously emphasized the importance of differentiating adaptive challenges from conventional ones. J&J failed to do so. It relied on a traditional strategic model that moved through the cycle of invest, consolidate, and harvest. In hindsight, skipping the harvest stage (and partnering with surgeons to maintain leadership through a leap in technology) would have been a wiser course of action. With immature technology, obsolescence can occur rapidly; patent protection matters far less when alternative solutions abound. Substitution is further accelerated when a supplier has alienated its customer base.

A "hostage" is one with no loyalty or affinity to its host, but who is forced into the relationship by circumstances. When bonds are broken, hostages flee with a vengeance. Unwittingly, J&J made hostages of surgeons and hospitals. By ignoring the probability of technological obsolescence, J&J set up a calamity waiting to happen.

The J&J story speaks to the dangers of managerial hubris. Almost every action conveys J&J's assumption that it could *direct* a living system and impose its will on surgeons, hospitals, and its own employees. Beginning with a classic "harvest" strategy, J&J's subsequent efforts escalated to a hostile takeover of Cordis. Control of the value chain appealed to J&J as a means of increasing its power and thereby *dictating* the pace of product evolution. There was little evidence of *discovery*—J&J ignored both its customers' suggestions and the Cordis engineers' innovative and more fluid development process.

J&J deliberately engineered an approach to maximize value from its product over its life cycle. Fixed on a presupposed script of causal linkages, J&J ignored numerous warnings from customers and disaffected employees, and failed to decipher early signs of alternative technology and developmental processes. There was no design in place to facilitate a quick recovery.

■ ■

Many centuries ago, masters of the Eastern martial arts had insights into the limitations of the use of force and linear intentions. *Jujitsu* means the gentle way. *Karate* means the empty hand. Both images seem counterintuitive when confronted with an opponent hell-bent on doing harm. Both rely on deflecting or harnessing the opposing force or energy toward desired goals—a concept J&J roundly ignored early. Pioneers of Eastern martial arts discovered paths to co-opt the energy of living systems long before there were institutes in Santa Fe.

Three guidelines help us apply this wisdom to business:

1. Design, don't engineer.
2. Discover, don't dictate.
3. Decipher, don't presuppose.

We will observe the guidelines for disturbing a living system in action in two highly successful change efforts. Both entailed large numbers of people and seemingly intractable challenges: eliminating malnutrition among poor children in Vietnam, and transforming the downstream oil business at Royal Dutch/Shell. At first glance, these efforts appear to bear little, if any, resemblance to each other. One represents an adaptive challenge facing an entire society; the other is a characteristic of adaptive challenges encountered in the business world. It is not our intention to equate starving children with a corporation's competitive struggles in terms of human suffering and loss. Still, both are living systems and, interestingly, the interventions in both situations contain many common qualities. That living systems theory can be appropriately applied to such qualitatively different situations speaks to its comprehensiveness.

Positive Deviance in Vietnam[8]

Following the end of the Vietnam War, large numbers of children in that nation's poorer areas suffered from high levels of malnutrition.

Prospects for alleviating this problem were grim. A widely researched topic within the international aid community—malnutrition—when viewed under the microscope of reductionist logic, has long been regarded as unsolvable. Lack of access to clean water and sanitation, inadequate food sources, poverty, low levels of education, and scant knowledge of nutrition weave a fabric of hopelessness. If we add poor health care, unhygienic conditions, taboos against birth control, and the low status of women, the cycle seems to close in on itself with ineluctable finality.

For decades, the most common "solution" to malnutrition involved either massive infusions of supplemental food or attempts at addressing the above-noted problems simultaneously and massively (in keeping with the integrated development model). In addition to being costly and intrusive, this expert-driven approach was generally not sustainable. When outside resources were withdrawn, which always happened eventually, villages inevitably spiraled back into their original condition.

In 1990, Save the Children asked Monique and Jerry Sternin to go to Hanoi and try out a new model for helping communities alleviate pervasive malnutrition. Seeking an approach that would be both effective and sustainable, the Sternins tested a new living systems model called "Positive Deviance," which had been developed at Tufts University. Positive Deviance does not impose a nutritional solution. Rather, this model relies on "respectfully assisting evolution" by identifying children who are the "nutritionally fittest" (i.e., positively deviant) and scaling up a solution that is already working in the community.

Instead of arriving as experts with answers, the Sternins came as catalysts with questions, determined to tap into the latent wisdom and resources in each community. Choosing four of the poorest villages, the team, which included Vietnamese staff, worked alongside villagers to weigh children and record their nutritional status in order to identify the "positive deviants"—children of very poor parents who, according to economic logic, should have been malnourished but were not. The design was aimed to discover what was already working against all odds, rather than engineering a solution based on an external formula.

In this approach, each community reexamines its conventional wisdom regarding children's nutrition, health, and care. The inquiry helps the community to discover deviant (that is, unconventional or unusual) nutritional practices that are working advantageously, and to make them accessible to everyone.

The answers were there.

The exceptional families were supplementing their children's rice-based diet with freely available fresh-water shrimp and crabs, and with vitamin-rich sweet potato leaves. They were also feeding their children more frequently.

Armed with this discovery, the program sought to incorporate other villagers and induce them to reevaluate their children's eating habits. Villages sponsored workshops for mothers, and those attending were required to bring a handful of shrimp, crabs, and leaves as the price of admission. Save the Children contributed additional protein (an egg or some tofu) and some oil to each participant.

Within six months, over two-thirds of the children gained weight. Over twenty-four months, 85 percent had "graduated" to acceptable nutritional status and were no longer clinically malnourished. During this period, new patterns of collecting and consuming food were established. Because of its acceptance and success, the concept was enlarged to include sixteen more villages. The concept was scaled up consistent with its philosophy of discovering unique positive deviant solutions in each area—an approach that is very different from a socially engineered "best-practices" rollout. Within five years, the government of Vietnam embraced Positive Deviance as the national nutritional model, and it is now working countrywide.[9]

Let's consider this story in light of the three guidelines.

I. Design, Don't Engineer

Prior to the experiment in Vietnam, virtually all programs addressing malnutrition shared the common assumption that experts alone (using systems theory to identify the factors responsible for dietary deficiencies) had mapped both the problem and the answer. Accordingly, they arrived in the field with a template of prescriptions and instructions which they imposed as the remedy. Neither their analytic foundation nor their diagnosis was wrong. Economic factors, water quality, education, health care, birth control, and the role of women all contribute to the so-called "intractable problem" and need to be addressed for long-term sustainability. However, the experts' proposed interventions were often politically objectionable and/or economically unsustainable. One *can* eliminate malnutrition through a comprehensive attack on its contributing factors. But such solutions are often expensive, encounter village resistance, and, as noted, deteriorate once the intervention is scaled back.

By way of contrast, Save the Children's *design* more closely resembled an architect's rendering than an engineer's drawings marked for precise dimensions and bearing weights. The Sternins' approach left a very soft footprint on village life. Working alongside Vietnamese village women and hamlet leaders, they simply began conversations. Were some children too thin? Would mothers be interested in having their children weighed? These time-consuming conversations took many visits and many hours but were absolutely necessary because the approach required local understanding, buy-in, and support. In contrast to the expert-driven intervention, Positive Deviance has the feel of a dance and a courtship, as opposed to a march and an invasion. Essential to the approach is first, respect for, and second, alliance with the intelligence and capacities residing within the village. This model can be applied to other kinds of change. For example, the Sternins successfully applied positive deviance to increasing the educational level of girls in Egypt. Business applications of the positive deviance models have great potential for making far-reaching changes with astonishing ease. Hewlett-Packard, which will be discussed later, is one dramatic example of its successful application.

2. Discover, Don't Dictate

As discussed, the advisers did not arrive with a prescriptive template. Rather, they tapped knowledge that was already present and made it visible and socially acceptable. Such an inquiry entailed authentic learning on the part of the Sternins—a crucial underpinning of harnessing Positive Deviance.

Two years into the first three-hamlet field tests, astonishing results were confirming a breakthrough. When the project began, nearly half of the three villages' 3,000 children were malnourished. Twenty-four months later, as we have noted, 85 percent of these youngsters were within normal limits for their age group, having moved out of the "debilitating/severe" and "life threatening/very severe" categories of malnutrition.

A natural tendency in the wake of such success would have been to implement this solution nationwide. The amazing results seemed to justify imposing a diet of shrimp, crabs, and wild greens on every underweight child in the country. But such an approach denies the discovery process and is antithetical to the central tenet of Positive Deviance: *The wisdom to solve problems exists and needs to be discovered within each and every community.* Individual communities are far more likely to accept and implement *their* answer. True, an optimization approach may impose a faster solution—and sometimes even a "better" solution—but always at the cost of ownership. Dictating the answers, however well intended and sugar-coated, usurps responsibility from the community. It also assumes, erroneously, that being an "expert" gives one license to intrude on other cultures and customs. An attitude of discovery requires humility and a quest for learning about the unknown, rather than reassurance based on what is already known.

Unsurprisingly, the "positive deviant" food supplements and child-care practices differed from village to village. The very high level of local buy-in and support grew from letting each village be its own expert. Some villages did not have fresh-water crabs and wild sweet potato leaves, but relied on sesame seeds, peanuts, and dried fish. This factor, more than having the "right answer," led to the rapid cascade of malnutrition programs within sixteen additional villages and subsequently throughout all of Vietnam.

3. Decipher, Don't Presuppose

Save the Children representatives were aware that any intervention unleashes many unforeseen second- and third-order consequences. The trick is to decipher them. Nimble interpretation goes hand in hand with joint discovery; it allows—indeed, expects—that intervening in a living system will often trigger side effects that are tangential to the objective at hand. We saw this with the snowmobile and the Laplanders. One must decipher these unforeseen consequences as they *begin* to take form and, hopefully, nudge them in a positive direction before they trigger undesirable avalanches. At a minimum, by deciphering early, we can make the community aware of emerging choices it now must face. The worst strategy is to presuppose a script of expected outcomes and become blind to what is actually unfolding. The imperative is to stay alert and on your toes.

Examples of these side developments occurred in Vietnam. Many savvy, though uneducated, parents who had successfully staved off malnutrition were living in poverty on the lowest rung of the community's social order. Having their remedy adopted by the village had the tangential consequences of affecting the social status of these very poor families. In most cases, as these members found their voices and were recognized as community assets, their status and sense of self-esteem improved. In many communities, such mothers were selected as community health workers. Others, previously marginalized, were elected to local office. Another unforeseen consequence was that daily conversations with women regarding the well-being of children was a catalyst for further action. Additional issues took root alongside the agenda of nutrition. In some villages, energized women started cottage businesses or worked with the village schools to upgrade the curriculum and reduce illiteracy.

Industry has registered the success of Positive Deviance in Vietnam. When Barbara Waugh, Worldwide Change Manager for Hewlett-Packard Laboratories, came into contact with the Sternins and their ideas in 1997, she was quick to put them to use. Described at length in the concluding chapter, Waugh's goal was to enable this large, highly respected, and, at times, fragmented organization to communicate, collaborate, and innovate more. "I'm often introduced as being 'in charge' of change," she says. "I'm not in charge of anything. My role is to create mirrors that show the whole what the parts are doing."[10] Toward this end, Waugh made direct use of the project in Vietnam and, in her words, spends her days ". . . amplifying positive deviants. The '60s way of doing things was to dig into a complicated problem, pick out the worst elements and go after them. You'd attack them. Today, I take the opposite approach. I seek out the positive deviants and support them. You feed them, give them resources and visibility."[11]

Disturbing the Shell Game

Shell's attempt to transform its culture had failed utterly.[12] This fact must be understood in order to comprehend our report of its subsequent efforts to disturb the living system.

In the mid-1990s, Core Herkstroter, Chairman of Royal Dutch/Shell, took stock of this huge and historically successful enterprise. At the time, the formula that had accounted for its success for over a century was a little threadbare. Endemically cyclical, the chemicals business was losing money and seemed stuck in an eternal trough. The worldwide oil products business, known as "Downstream," which accounts for one-third of Shell's staggering $130 billion in annual revenues, was confronting the gravest competitive threats in its history. From 1992 to 1995, in France, a full 50 percent of Shell's retail revenues from fuels and lubricants fell victim to the onslaught of hypermarkets. (Hypermarkets, like Wal-Mart in the United

States, sell fuel and lubricants in the stores' parking lots at a loss. The tactic draws customers inside where they will find an eclectic mix of discounted items, including groceries, clothing, and small appliances.) A similar threat was emerging in the United Kingdom and Germany. Around the world, new competitors and new global customers were roiling the marketplace. Profits continued to flow, but fissures were forming beneath the surface. Shell faced an adaptive challenge, but doggedly approached it as though it were a conventional business situation.

Steeped in the history of Shell, Herkstroter, like Brennan at Sears, was comfortable with authority, logic, and discipline. For the most part, Shell's 105,000 predominantly long-tenured employees—its huge headquarters staff in The Hague and London, and its employees at facilities dispersed among 130 "operating companies" throughout the globe—were relatively satisfied with the status quo. Herkstroter was aware of this and, except in France, the threats felt far away. Decades of being the industry's leader allowed Shell to drift into a numbing equilibrium. Somehow this needed to change.

Herkstroter, a consummate social engineer, turned to conventional levers to address such problems. He hired McKinsey, the consulting firm, and embarked on a downsizing and streamlining of Shell Centre. In a hesitant step toward participation and involvement, he convened a meeting of Shell's top 100 business leaders (from Exploration, Downstream, Natural Gas, Chemicals, Coal, and Shell Centre) plus the chairmen of Shell's largest operating companies, in Brazil, South Africa, and Malaysia. Indicative of the lengths to which Shell had been committed to decentralization, this was the first time these representatives had gathered together since the end of World War II.

What became evident *to some* at this offsite meeting was that the source of Shell's historical strength (highly independent operating companies working closely with host governments and calling for help from the Centre when needed) was becoming a weakness. Excesses of decentralization were at the heart of the adaptive challenge. Shell had huge overcapacity in refining facilities. Yet no operating company wanted to close the plants within its national borders: Refineries were a totem of corporate—and national—virility. In addition, markets that had been xenophobically national in Asia were becoming multinational and regional. Finally, each operating company's strong national pride contributed to a not-invented-here syndrome that was approaching the formidable proportions of the Great Wall of China.

Herkstroter believed that McKinsey's restructuring, the downsizing of the Centre, and a new pay-for-performance system would correct most, if not all, of these deficiencies. He quickly reassured the organization that, given its impressive track record, "revolution" (adaptive change) was *not* called for. Instead, he advocated a measured set of improvements. All this was duly promulgated through briefings and videotapes that cascaded through the organization.

And nothing happened. A second meeting of the top 100 was convened six months later. On this occasion, more McKinsey proposals were unveiled. These were aimed at reining in the operating companies' independence by shifting more of Exploration and Downstream's overall direction to respective "business committees" in the Centre. A small team of Shell executives presented these plans in the hope that their endorsement would foster buy-in. As transparent as it was controversial, this thinly veiled gesture to disguise a top-down restructuring to alter the balance of power ignited pushback.

The operating company chairmen interrupted the presenters frequently to challenge their data and conclusions. When the dust had settled, it was evident that Herkstroter's gamble—reducing the Centre's size and power as a quid pro quo for shifting some of the field's authority to the Centre—had failed.

The question was what to do next. As a face-saving device, Herkstroter went forward with the announcement of the Business Committees for Exploration and Oil Products. What role they might play or how they were actually going to influence decisions with operating companies was left to the imagination. And there it stood. A lot of fancy footwork and very little traction.

At age 51, Steven Miller became the Managing Director of the new Oil Products Business Committee, which gave him automatic membership in Shell's top executive group—its five-person Committee of Managing Directors under Chairman Herkstroter. The "CMD," as it is called, develops objectives and long-term plans for the entire enterprise. It is a de facto corporate executive committee.

A few months into the assignment, Miller felt a bit desperate. "We were nowhere," he recalls. "We were talking to ourselves at the Centre and were an object of derision in the field."[13] In another attempt to induce buy-in, Herkstroter had embarked on a long series of extensive "cultural change workshops" for top officers. Thousands of executive hours and millions of dollars of travel expenses were sacrificed at the altar of three-day-weekend transformation workshops in Holland and Britain. The focus was on Shell's new culture, but nothing really changed. Participants were mystified by the American-inspired programs, which included Outward Bound antics and "emotional journey diagrams." Cynicism reached new heights. At the "coal face" (as Shell calls the field activities where actual work gets done), the troops saw little more than business as usual.

Miller had his hands full. In addition to Downstream's 61,000 full-time employees, Shell's 47,000 filling stations employ hundreds of thousands of attendants (mostly part-time) and cater to more than 10 million customers every day.[14] Shell's Downstream labyrinthine culture was especially worrisome. Comprising dozens of product lines, including fuels, lubricants, and asphalt, Downstream activities encompass operations such as supply and trading, and manufacturing and marketing. Altogether, these account for 37 percent of Shell's assets. Investors expected commensurate returns.[15] Miller recalls:

> Our Downstream Business transformation program had bogged down largely because of the impasse between headquarters and the operating companies. The balance of power between these two bastions of expertise, developed during a period of relative equilibrium, had ground to a stalemate. The forces for continuing in the old way were enormous and extended throughout the organization.

We were overseeing the most decentralized operation in the world with country chief executives that had, since the 1950s, enjoyed enormous autonomy. For living systems, decentralization is generally desirable but we had gone too far. But this had been part of our success formula. Now we were encountering a set of daunting competitive threats that transcended national boundaries. Global customers such as British Airways or Daimler-Benz wanted to deal with one Shell contact, not with a different Shell representative in every country in which they operate. We had huge overcapacity in refining, but each country CEO (motivated to maximize his own profit/loss ratio) resisted the consolidation of refining capacity. These problems begged for a new strategic approach in which the task at the top was to provide the framework and then unleash the regional and local levels to find a path that was best for their market and the corporation as a whole.[16]

As we have said, Herkstroter wanted to rationalize Shell's assets through well-engineered directives. From the perspective of our three guidelines, he had tried to "engineer" the transformation, "dictate" a new structure, and "predetermine" the final outcome. The Committee of Managing Directors issued directives for selling off refineries. However, the Shell country chairmen successfully thwarted consolidation. They cited objections from host countries that found the proposals "politically incendiary" and threatened retaliation if Shell closed their dedicated refining capacity. *Miller,* desperate by now, was deeply convinced that he could not *direct* this living system.

The alternative was managerial judo. Banking on "guided chance and the force of necessity," he turned to a radically different concept. As we will show, he hewed to the guidelines of disturbing a living system. By discovering a way of working with, instead of dictating to, the country chairmen, Miller introduced an initiative, deciphered reactions, amplified here and dampened there, and never imposed a predetermined plan. This design brought about gradual buy-in.

In the language of complexity, Miller tapped the emergent properties of Shell's far-flung community and shifted the locus of strategic initiative away from *both* the Centre and the too-powerful operating country chairmen, and toward employees on the front lines. Succeeding at what few imagined possible, Miller saw the system not as a resistant mass governed by obstinacy and inertia, but as a fertile organism that needed encouragement, in his words, to "send green shoots forth."

Miller engaged the members in facing Shell's challenges. He recognized that his task was to fundamentally alter the conversation that pitted headquarters against the field. (Determining which of these historical protagonists was gaining or losing power was the primary criterion by which any new policy or proposal was assessed.) Organizations are networks of conversations—via memos, E-mail, reports, procedures, talking out loud, and thinking to oneself. Miller knew that if he wanted to unleash Downstream's emergent competitive potential, he needed to change this ongoing conversation. He believed the Downstream business should be treated less like a machine to be driven and more like a living organism that needed to evolve.

Miller's solution was to cut through every layer and barrier of the organization, making sure that senior management was in direct contact with the people at the grassroots level. Working with an approach proposed by consultant Noel M. Tichy, he resolved to create a new sense of urgency, foster strategic initiatives, and, in essence, overwhelm the old order with energy and activity that could not be suppressed.

Miller began by going public with Shell's adaptive challenge: massive share losses to hypermarkets, bloated cost structures, excess refining capacity. These were considered embarrassments that were neither widely known nor discussed. Suddenly, employees at all levels were talking about these harsh realities. Predictably, this kind of candor disturbed Shell's equilibrium and evoked stress. It set the stage for subsequent self-organization and emergence. As Miller stated:

> The properties of self-organization and emergence make intuitive sense to me. The question was how to release them. The "adaptive challenge" was there alright, but it was hard going at Shell to lift the kimono and reveal how bad things really were. There is a great deal of pride at Shell. We care about how we look in public. We try to hire the best and the brightest.

But for all this pride and talent to be productive, we needed to channel it toward the challenges we faced, not internecine squabbles.

We adopted a business model to give this call to arms some structure. The model, developed by Columbia University's Larry Selden, is a practical toolkit that helps identify specific customer needs and markets, develop a value proposition, identify "key business activities" (KBAs), and rigorously track results against plan. We needed this kind of language (and an intense indoctrination in it) to shift Shell's engineering and wholesaler mindset to a commercial and retailer outlook. The model gave our troops, once mobilized, the "ammunition" to shoot with, the analytical distinctions to make the business case. But for all this to work, it had to be theirs—not mine. Powerful operating company heads had to see that they would not lose control to the Centre by sponsoring a host of local initiatives. They were so preoccupied by the Centre, in fact, that they did not recognize the revolutionary impact this would have within their own company and how it would alter how they needed to lead and how we conduct business day to day.[17]

In mid-1996, Miller began devoting more than half of his time to working directly with frontline personnel. Critical to his success was enrolling his "friends" among the chairmen of the Operating Companies to send him a team of six or eight of their guerrilla leaders. He told them:

> We're not going to tell you what to do. Pick a big-ticket business challenge you don't know how to solve. We think we've got a process that can improve our competitiveness. Give us one chance. I need your group along with five or six other groups from the other operating companies. They'll go through an intense retailing boot camp. Let's see if we can do things a little differently.[18]

Many arm-twisting days later, Miller recruited a pilot class with teams from Malaysia, Chile, Brazil, South Africa, Austria, France, and Norway.

Leaders of the first five-day workshop introduced tools for identifying and exploiting market opportunities, and exercises in grassroots leadership so that participants could enroll others back home.

Using the new tools, the teams sought breakthroughs, including doubling the net income of filling stations located on Malaysia's major north–south highways, or tripling the market share of bottled gas in South Africa.

In keeping with the discipline of the model, every market ambition was translated into a KBA (key business activity) so that progress could be tracked over time. For example, the team from Chile aimed to increase fuel margins at the pump. Closer analysis showed that lowering fuel-delivery costs was the most straightforward route to accomplish this without raising prices—and losing customers. Examining further, the team discovered that fuel delivery costs could be almost halved by delivering at night because the roads and the gas stations themselves were less congested. In addition, nighttime deliveries caused franchise filling stations to remain open. Driving up that simple KBA, "percent nighttime deliveries," contributed to a 2 percent improvement in Shell Chile's bottom line.

After the first workshop in the series, participants went home for sixty days. In their regular day jobs, they continued to press forward with their initiatives and enroll others who were essential to their success. They used the new tools to sample customers, identify segments, and develop a value proposition that would differentiate Shell from its competition. They returned to the second workshop for a "Peer Challenge"—a tough give-and-take exchange with other teams.

The next stage of the program required participants to return to the field for another sixty days to perfect a business plan. At the close of this third workshop, each team spent three hours in "the fishbowl" with Miller and his direct reports—the top executives responsible for large geographic regions, refining, finance, and marketing. The other teams observed the proceedings from the perimeter.

Miller describes how the fishbowl became the centerpiece for adaptive work at Shell:

One of the most important innovations in changing all of us was the fishbowl. The name describes what it is: I and numbers of my management team sit in the middle of a room with one of the country teams in the center with us. The other team members listen from the outer circle. Everyone is watching as the group in the hot seat talks about what they're going to do, and what they need from me and my colleagues to be able to do it. That may not sound revolutionary—but in our culture it was very unusual for anyone lower in the organization to talk this directly to a managing director and his reports.

In the fishbowl, the pressure is on to measure up. The truth is, the pressure is on me and my colleagues. The first time we're not consistent, we're dead meat. If a team brings in a plan that's really a bunch of crap, we've got to be able to call it a bunch of crap. If we cover for people or praise everyone, what do we say when someone brings in an excellent plan? That kind of straight talk is another big culture change for Shell.

The whole process creates complete transparency between the people at the coal face and me and my top management team. At the end, these folks go back home and say, "I just cut a deal with the managing director and his team to do these things." It creates a personal connection—and it changes how we talk with each other and how we work with each other. The country leaders go along because it provides support for what needed to be done anyway. After that, I can call up those folks anywhere in the world and talk in a very direct way because of this personal connectedness. It has completely changed the dynamics of our operations.[19]

At the close of each session, plans were approved, rejected, or amended. Peer pressure and learning were intense. Financial commitments were made in exchange for promised results. These projections were incorporated in the country's operating goals for the year.

Returning to the field for another sixty days, the teams put their ideas into action. This was followed by yet another workshop to analyze the experience gained—the breakdowns and breakthroughs.

The process made use of many of the concepts we have been discussing throughout this book. *Equilibrium* was disturbed as soon as Miller openly disclosed Shell's losses and loss of competitiveness (the *threat of death*). Cross-pollination of ideas was fostered as highly competitive country teams went through workshops together and engaged in peer challenges. Some teams found themselves joint-venturing with customers and host governments (the *promise of sex*).

The *edge of chaos* was palpable. When the lowest levels of an organization are being trained, coached, and evaluated by those at the very top, it both inspires and stresses everyone in the system, including the bosses who are not present. This amplified the *adaptive challenge*. Relatively junior managers logged a great deal of face time with senior executives (often nine pay grades and seven hierarchical levels removed). This provided an infusion of *amplifying feedback*. The fishbowl process put everyone on the spot—ironically, especially Miller and his reports (who needed to get their act together to come across as a respectable team). *Damping feedback* was provided by peer reviews, peer pressure, and the relentless KBAs that kept track of progress against promises. Above all, Miller's approach involved a *discovery* of the answers (not dictated from above), and a *design* with lots of room to improvise (not an engineered road map to the answer). Both the program and the teams from operating companies learned to *decipher* the needs of employees, customers, and host country governments, and to become a more agile supplier.

And it worked. Operating company chief executives, historically leery of any "help" from headquarters, were surprised as their delegates return energized and armed with solid plans to beat the competition. Old conventional schisms between headquarters and the field melted away and were replaced with multiple informal connections that served to strengthen and enrich the "conversation."

The grassroots employees who participated in the program began to create and experience the "new" Shell. Downstream was evolving into a far more informal culture than before. In the ranks of the organization, guerrilla leaders stepped forward to champion ingenious marketplace innovations. Malaysia, for example, launched the "Coca-Cola Challenge": service station customers received a free Coke if they were not offered the full menu of services. The strategy increased volume by 15 percent and, more importantly, these efforts at innovation were contagious. Employees became engaged in the marketplace in new and imaginative ways.

Looking back on the journey, Miller reflects on the mechanistic approaches that had characterized Shell's earlier endeavors:

Top-down strategies don't win many ball games today. Experimentation, rapid learning, seizing the momentum of success works better. We needed a different definition of strategy and a different way to generate it. In the past, strategy was the exclusive domain of the CMD [Shell's Chairman and his team]. But in the multi-front war Shell was engaged in, the top can't possibly have all the answers. The leaders provide the vision and are the context setters. But the actual solutions about how best to meet the challenges of the moment—those thousands of strategic challenges encountered every day—have to be made by the people closest to the action—the people at the coal face. Everyone and everything is affected.

Change your approach to strategy and you change the way a company runs. The leader becomes a context setter, the designer of a learning experience—not an authority figure with solutions. Once the folks at the grassroots realize they own the problem, they also discover that they can help create and own the answer—and they get after it very quickly, very aggressively, and very creatively, with a lot more ideas than the old-style strategic direction could ever have prescribed from headquarters. It worked because the people at the coal face usually know what's going on. They see the competitive threats and our inadequate response every day. Once you give them the context, they can do a better job of spotting opportunities and stepping up to decisions. In less than two years, we've seen astonishing progress in our retail business in some twenty-five countries. This represents around 85 percent of our retail sales volume and we have now begun to use this approach in our service organizations and lubricant business.

A program like this is a high-risk proposition, because it goes counter to the way most senior executives spend their time. When I began spending 50 to 60 percent of my time at this (with no direct guarantee that what I was doing would make something happen down the line), I raised a lot of eyebrows. People want to evaluate this against the old way which gives you the illusion of "making things happen." I encountered lots of thinly veiled skepticism: "Did your net income change from last quarter because of this change process?" These challenges create anxiety. The temptation, of course, is to reimpose your directives and controls even though we had an abundance of proof that this would not work. The grassroots approach to strategy development and implementation doesn't happen overnight. But it does happen. People always want results yesterday. But the process and behavior that drive authentic strategic change aren't like that.

It's like becoming the helmsman of a big ship when you've grown up behind the steering wheel of a car. This approach isn't about me. It's about rigorous, well-taught marketing concepts, combined with a strong design, that enable frontline employees to think like businesspeople. Top executives and frontline employees learn to work together in partnership.

There's another kind of risk to the leaders of a strategic inquiry of this kind—and that's the risk of exposure. You're working very closely and intensely with all levels of staff, and they get to assess and evaluate you directly. Before, you were remote from them; now, you're very accessible. If that evaluation comes up negative, you've got a big-time problem.

Finally, the scariest part is letting go. You don't have the same kind of control that traditional leadership is used to. What you don't realize until you do it is that you may, in fact, have more control—but in a different fashion. You get more feedback than before, you learn more than before, you know more through your own people about what's going on in the marketplace and with customers than before. But you still have to let go of the old sense of control.[20]

Miller's words testify to his own personal reconciliation with the difficulties of directing a living system. When strategic work is accomplished through a "design for emergence," it never assumes that a particular input will produce a specific output. The experimenter's design creates probabilistic occurrences that take place within the domain of focus. Period. Greater precision is not sought because it is not possible.

Today, managing bears a closer resemblance to piloting a boat than steering a car. A wise helmsman steers by course corrections. There is no constant position of the rudder to get from point A to point B. Rather, one follows a zigzag course.

By the end of 1997, Shell's operations in France had, after the earlier mentioned years of decline, achieved double-digit growth and double-digit return on capital. Market share was also increasing. Shell Austria, only months away from outright divestiture, had turned around to become highly profitable. Scandinavia, another troubled region, was in the black. In fact, all through Europe, the company gained in brand share preference, ranking first in share among the major oil companies. In Asia, despite a major downturn, Shell outperformed all of its major competition and held its own against the state-owned companies (where one never wants to win too decisively).

The overall picture as of fiscal 1997, compiled by Shell's outside auditors, attributed a $300 million net profit gain directly to Miller's initiatives. The gross impact is undoubtedly many times that figure. By the close of 1998, approximately 10,000 Downstream employees had been involved in this effort. The approach was so successful that, by 1999, it had overcome Shell's towering strategic business unit silos and been adopted by the Chemicals and Explorations businesses.[21]

In the larger business context, the above developments, arguably tactical gains in local markets, led to a much larger prize. As noted, Miller's approach quietly eroded the bulwarks of resistance among Operating Companies. There was no magic here. The process we have described fostered continuous collaborative work among teams that formerly regarded one another as rivals. As these teams chipped away at local cost problems and sought to exploit growth opportunities, there was growing consensus that refinery consolidation and regional marketing efforts presented huge opportunities for competitive gains. Whereas Herkstroter's frontal assault on the Operating Companies had failed to achieve this consensus, patience and "acting one's way into a new way of thinking" prevailed. Refineries were shuttered or sold in Europe and the U.S., an unproductive joint venture was terminated in Japan, regional marketing approaches were adopted in Southern Africa, Southeast Asia, Latin America, and Europe.

There were several other large-scale breakthroughs. Most significant among these, regarded by many as the poster child of Shell's entire transformation effort, involved its elite 600 person research, technology, and manufacturing staff. This entity, known as RTS (Research and Technology Services) had a $60 million budget and, while historically a source of Shell's competitive advantage, was widely regarded as user unfriendly, expensive, and arrogant. Under the leadership of Hans Van Luijck (a member of Miller's team and Shell's leading technology expert), this cumbersome entity reinvented itself. Sending scores of its scientists and engineers to Miller's Action Labs, the renamed "Global Solutions," sells its consulting services on the open market, has witnessed the greatest resurrection of morale since Lazarus, and earned $30 million in profits in 1999. With almost $800 million in revenues, it is the eleventh largest technical consulting firm after Arthur D. Little. Global Solutions aims to generate $300 million in earnings by 2002.[22] In a parallel success story, Shell's fragmented bottled-gas activities were consolidated into one worldwide unit and infused with focus and ambition. Today, it is the dominant global competitor.

The maintenance of vitality in a living system is never assured. When Miller moved on to his next assignment in late 1999 (turning around Shell's troubled holdings in the United States), a more traditional executive took his place. The incumbent continued Miller's process of country team initiatives and fishbowls, but he shifted the emphasis decidedly toward expense reduction. In fairness, Shell was under a great deal of shareholder pressure to do so, and its success in reducing costs has recently brought it kudos from Wall Street in recent years. But it is equally true that Shell's group leadership never really bought into Miller's transformation approach. "It was too different," "too American." In his absence, the campaign for cash served as a Trojan horse to restore Shell Downstream to a more traditional way of working. Investments in growth were applicably reduced.

Results were predictable. Within one year, France relapsed into decline as people and capital were directed to other areas. Norway, a former basket case that had turned around under Miller's tenure, was revived and poised to double profits. Now, subjected to capital rationing and starved of investment dollars, these plans were scrapped and, unsurprisingly, Norway again became a lackluster performer. Greece had gained 2 percent market share in the first of the Miller years after decades of zero growth, and it was poised to obliterate competition. Capital rationing reduced it to the old game of competitive parity.[23]

In the shift away from growth, employee morale and enthusiasm have waned. The field organization still retains vitality, but it is shackled by a short-term profit focus and, more importantly, by the return of a more traditional management approach. Some of Shell's best young managers have left the company—a highly unusual occurrence at Shell, because it pays its top performers well and affords them a prestigious association with one of the world's best known enterprises. But, having experienced the exhilaration of entrepreneurship, many have been unwilling to relinquish their newfound sense of "being able to make a difference." Shell has not regressed to the extent we saw at Sears. Its financial performance remains strong. But it teeters on the brink of equilibrium and all the risks inherent to life in the comfort zone.

■ ■

If life is indeterministic and unknowable, if we can all be killed by avalanches of both the metaphysical and physical kind, why bother? There are no wholly reassuring answers, but the distinctions and guidelines discussed here improve the odds of survival. In business, the game can be chess or roulette. It helps a great deal not to confuse the strategies appropriate for each.

With this in mind, we turn to synthesis. The objective in the next chapter is to recap what we have learned and demonstrate how all the pieces can come together in an overall "design for emergence." Subsequently, we focus on key disciplines that can sustain the vitality of a living system (specifically, corporations) over time.

CHAPTER 11

DESIGN FOR EMERGENCE

Design is the invisible hand that brings organizations to life and life to organizations.

Architects design, they don't engineer. And the architectural elements and design templates they employ, which have evolved over centuries, provide (1) structural integrity (sound buildings), (2) functionality (space appropriate for its intended use), and (3) aesthetic appeal. An architectural rendering is an evocative sketch that allows us to see what a proposed structure will look like. But equally, it is intentionally incomplete so we can engage it, infuse our values and aspirations, and, over time, generate the specific plans for the space.

Let us consider airports in this context. The lounge areas surrounding each gate do not have signs nor attendants that tell us not to talk too loudly, occupy more than one seat, or block the aisles. Yet, through the invisible hand of design, all of these objectives are broadly accomplished. Seats are arranged so that conversation takes place with those in the immediate vicinity and not with those far away. Fixed armrests between seats prevent people from lying down and occupying seats that others may need. Seats are bolted together in rows, making movement of furniture difficult. Thus, passengers are discouraged from rearranging the floor plan, blocking aisles, or inconveniencing the cleaning staff that comes late at night.

The remarkable quality of design is that it seems to just happen; it works its magic without our awareness of how it does so. From the architect's perspective, what we are experiencing is an evolved discipline at work.

The Same Old Stuff?

Let us begin with a preemptive caveat. Many readers will be familiar with terms like "alignment" and "unfreezing" as they have been used, or misused, piecemeal in corporations. Are we therefore destined to a rehash of the same old stuff?

Yes and no. *Yes* insofar as the terminology *appears* to share the same zip code with the vocabulary of emergence: "involvement," "commitment," "collective intelligence," and so forth. *No* in that a different context leads to entirely different results.

Say you inherit your grandmother's house. Unknown to you is one peculiarity: all the light fixtures have bulbs that tend toward blue rather than yellow. You find that the color of the furnishings takes on an unpleasant hue. But since you are unaware of the blue light, you spend a lot of time and money repainting walls, reupholstering furniture, and replacing carpets. Then, one day, you notice the blue bulbs and change them. But by then, what you have "fixed" is now "broken." Context is about the "color of the light" (complexity thinking or, alternatively, the machine model/social engineering), not the "objects" in the room (the techniques themselves). Context colors everything that it illuminates.[1]

Too often, fashionable techniques and terminology are like the right furnishings in the wrong light. We may hear companies recite the mantra, "People are our most important asset," but that is not how these "assets" are regarded in a crunch. Without the conceptual underpinnings of living systems, the language is empty. Traditional accounting principles provide no theoretical basis for quantifying the economic value of distributed intelligence. Notwithstanding the self-organizing capabilities and emergent potential of people, they remain marooned on income statements as an expense item. At the end of the day, the absence of an effective way of thinking about human capital causes renewal efforts to default to the conventional methods inherent in social engineering.

The distinction between "designing" and "engineering" is essential. Designing for emergence is very different from engineering for convergence. As we pointed out in Chapter 1, social engineering (like the blue light) pervades management's thinking to such an extent that it is almost invisible. As Russell Ackoff notes, "Much of the talk about business transformation is really about business reformation. Doing pretty much the same old thing but better, [such as] reengineering, TQM, team-based structures, [and] continuous improvement."[2] As we have noted, the record of success is spotty.

This shift in context is crucial. For example, if you awaken with sore muscles, how you feel depends a lot on whether you think you're getting the flu or you believe you are reaping the benefits of a good workout the day before. In the same vein, many quasi-familiar renewal techniques, when applied or viewed mechanistically, are only slightly more welcome than a case of the flu. But when they are incorporated with an understanding of living things, whole new possibilities take shape.

Traditional Refrains on Change

The rock that social engineering founders on is its incapacity to deal with the insurgent nature of social systems and their capacity to subvert programmed change. A 1995 *Fortune* article, "Making Change Stick," addressed the difficulty and opened with a series of quotations resonating with the experience of many.[3]

- GTE's Ben Powell:

It has been so aggravating. Finally, in the last six months or so, we have been getting to the point where we're really changing how we do business. But it's taken years. Not weeks. Not months. On a day-to-day basis, it feels like bowling in sand.

- Steve Knox, a union steward and member of a factory change team:

You try to keep saying, "Hey, this will work, this will be great!" And people look at you like you're an idiot, and you start to doubt yourself. It affects your home life. You get home and you don't have anything left for your family; you just want to be by yourself. Then one day you get up and you don't dread going to work, and you turn that corner, and then you hit another setback. So you think, "Is this worth it?" I've wanted to quit this job so many times in the past two or three years. Sometimes I lie awake at 2:00 or 3:00 A.M. and think, "How am I going to get these people to understand that there is no hidden bogeyman here? How am I going to do this?"

- MIT professor-turned-consultant Michael Hammer (coauthor of *Reengineering the Corporation*), on the source of all the difficulty:

Human beings' innate resistance to change is the most perplexing, annoying, distressing and confusing part of reengineering. [But] resistance to change is natural and inevitable. To think that resistance won't occur, to view those who exhibit its symptoms as difficult or intractable, is a fatal mistake. The real cause of reengineering failure is not the resistance itself, but management's failure to deal with it. Most dissenters won't stand and shout at you that they hate what you're doing to them and their comfortable old ways. Instead, they will nod, smile and agree with everything you say—and then behave as they always have. This is the kiss of "yes."[4]

Two-thirds of the reengineering efforts I have seen have crashed into flames, shot down by people's reluctance to go along, and by management's—especially top managers'—own ineptitude and fear. CEOs and senior people want to be liked, they don't want to be controversial. They see themselves as elder statesmen, not breaking legs, not going through an exhausting struggle. We have a generation of senior executives who worked hard to get to be senior executives so they wouldn't have to work so hard. That just doesn't wash anymore.[5]

Not so fast. The preceding chapters on living systems offer a different perspective. That these comments resonate with many people's change experience may suggest that we have been working against, rather than flowing with, the nature of living systems. In addition, the experiences cited and the explanations offered may say more about the backlash directed at social engineering (and reengineering) than valid evidence of innate human resistance to change.

A contrasting version of our earlier example of an airport lounge makes the point. In the former Soviet Union, some airports equipped their waiting areas with folding chairs. They were arranged in rows, and signs and announcements broadcast stern admonitions not to move the chairs or block aisles, and so forth. Security personnel on patrol occasionally enforced these policies, but passengers moved the chairs anyway to accommodate clusters of friends. The armless chairs were redeployed as beds or rearranged to make surfaces for dining or for playing cards. Children built ingenious play structures. And custodians complained of the extra work of restoring the rows before vacuuming.

One way of thinking would identify all this as the predictable fallout of social engineering. Passengers had to be controlled to compensate for design shortcomings. In contrast, the airport lounge in our earlier example achieves the desired behavior with no overt rules or commands. With the right design, people can be people without compromising the purposes of the space.

When change is driven from above and moves along a predetermined path, or when members of living systems are marched lockstep in frontal assaults on the fortress of adaptive change, these efforts will most likely fail. But a well-grounded design for emergence provides a very different experience. When properly mobilized, the so-called "resistant masses" and "permafrost of middle management" simply cease to exist as such. As we saw at Shell and Monsanto, they often exhibit as much ambition and appetite for change as their leaders.

Shifting the Conversation

Because a great deal of practical knowledge is socially acquired, influencing the social system is one of the most efficient ways to alter the knowledge system and, thus, to trigger learning.

An organization's beliefs and aspirations show up in conversation. Conversations occur on paper (strategies, white papers, vision statements), are represented by numbers (budgets, monthly and quarterly financial reports, indexes of market share, productivity, and quality), and take place in public and private discourse. They are manifest in stories of heroes, accounts of defining failures, gossip, and, of course, silently in people's heads. Conversation is the single most important business process when the goal is to shift what people believe and how they think. Lew Platt, until recently the CEO of Hewlett-Packard, frequently defined his job as "managing conversations."[6]

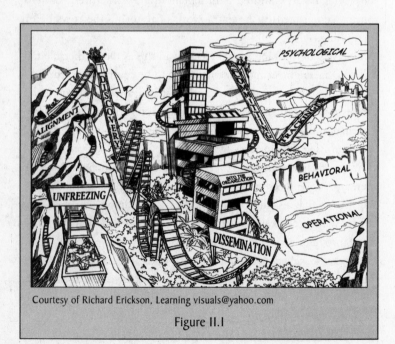

Courtesy of Richard Erickson, Learning visuals@yahoo.com

Figure 11.1

Authentic organizational transformation *always* transforms conversation. Important distinctions that we have developed throughout this book—"strange attractors" and "the adaptive challenge"—are defined in conversation. "Emergence" arises as a new theme in conversation, a theme that becomes an attractor and has galvanizing power among the members of a social system.

With this in mind, it should come as no surprise that the essential steps on the adaptive journey (described by the phases of the "roller coaster ride" in Figure 11.1)—those that generate the deepening levels of experience (the "operational," "behavioral," and "psychological" stages in the figure)—are all reflected by shifts in conversation. All the generic techniques we shall discuss are conversation-intensive; that is, they employ public events, group discussion, and social witness in a fashion that alters what people are talking about and the way they talk to each other.

■ ■

Key Stakeholders

If conversation is the source and soul of change, the first concern is: Who should be included in it? As a general rule, having many voices is better than having few. In addition, it is extremely important to include people who interact closely with customers or serve on the firing line where actual work gets done. The latter keep the conversation grounded in reality. There is no magical mix or number, and success depends to some degree on the size and nature of the business. The goal is a "flywheel effect" wherein enough of the right participants get involved and enrolled. The resulting momentum will then carry the process forward.

Most management teams can easily identify the 50 to 200 or so employees "who can really make things happen" (or keep them from happening!). One useful guideline is the no-fingerprints test: Anyone who can thwart the change effort and "leave no fingerprints" should be included. Some of these individuals may hold sway over key resources. Others are informal leaders who are central to networks of opinion. Some participants—key technologists, shop stewards, or process engineers—may fly below the radar. At Sears, the unfreezing and aligning efforts reached directly to those on the lowest level of the organizational hierarchy. At British Petroleum Exploration (BPX) and Monsanto, primarily the professional ranks were included. In each instance, the executive team gave considerable thought to where untapped intelligence, relevant to the adaptive challenge, resided. At BPX, the focus was on seismic interpretations, not efficiencies of offshore drilling platforms; at Monsanto, it was on combining unlikely technologies, not improving sales effectiveness or factory productivity. At Shell, Miller began with the professional ranks but, in time, the initiatives eventually involved union stewards, help-desk operators, truck drivers, and refinery foremen.

One thing is certain: The design to unfreeze and align should never be confined to the top eight or ten executives. Within this tight fraternity, it is deceptively easy to generate an illusion of consensus and often difficult to spark real debate and deep self-examination. And, even when these results occur, the revelations are confined to too small a circle.

The top team is only where one begins. Few executives are, or should be, willing to unleash the scary process of "unfreezing" their organization without logging many hours discussing the options with their colleagues. Exposing senior executives to the architecture of renewal should be an early step because they usually control the resources needed for the initiative's success. Their support and sponsorship are essential. Although the specific implications of the journey are rarely fathomed during the first exposure, it is best not to blindside those who feel most responsible for delivering the organization's future.

The initial session involving senior executives, which is characteristically cordial, tends to slide along on the veneer of *pseudo* alignment—not because the senior executives are ill-meaning or insincere, but because each wants to be seen as a team player. Few want to surface divisive or undiscussable issues if they don't have to.

The subsequent inclusion of many more stakeholders decreases the odds of concealing disagreement. As we observed at BPX, Sears, and Monsanto, the generic tools, such as organizational audits and learning visuals, document the adaptive challenge in a fashion that is hard to ignore. Organizational audits reveal that business-as-usual will fall short of the mark, and some sort of intervention is required. The senior team finds itself caught between (1) stark evidence of the need for discontinuous change and (2) hundreds of onlookers who are now aware of the predicament. There is no place to hide. The senior team's demonstration that it will not retreat into a comfort zone becomes a matter of public honor. In the spotlight of organizational scrutiny, the top group may step up to challenges that it avoided in the past.

In this iterative process, the top team forges ahead, occasionally stumbling upon moments of truth. At times, executives feel frightened, vulnerable, exposed, and outside of their comfort zone. No doubt there are temptations to slow down, back off, or terminate the change effort altogether. But, when top corporate officers directly confront the business issues that subordinates usually know about but don't discuss, they are sending strong signals that the change effort is real and is to be taken seriously. The leaders' attitudes and behavior can help build a sense of camaraderie, which generates momentum that may ease some tough spots later. Almost everyone, at various points throughout the process, is carried forward by others. There is a shared sense of mutual solidarity to stay the course.

Grounded Business Realities

Real work is the anvil against which the old culture is annealed and the new one is shaped. Lofty abstractions and visions (such as Shapiro's at Monsanto) can have their place in the process. But it is also easy for leaders to hide—to avoid the adaptive challenge—if they dwell too long in the thicket of platitudes and generalizations. Shapiro quickly brought those elevated ideals down to earth. Participants self-selected onto cross-functional teams to identify big ideas, and subsequently volunteered for months of hard work on growth initiatives. Sears, Shell, and the U.S. Army all plunged directly into grounded competitive issues to engage in the hard work of improving competitiveness.

The Army's National Training Center most dramatically illustrates this approach with its daily battles against a superior enemy. Businesses can also evoke productive intensity when teams, given challenging assignments (as we saw at Monsanto, Shell, and BPX), begin by documenting competitive threats or the implications of technical opportunities (through videotapes of candid employee testimony, or panels that feature critical investment analysts or unhappy customers). This "facts base" needs to be well grounded and robust. It must withstand the assault of skeptics who need to be persuaded that the challenge is authentically an adaptive one.

Manage Distress

Two factors can cause tension to mount: (1) including a larger-than-usual community of stakeholders, and (2) using a well-documented facts base to heighten clarity about the adaptive challenge. People become uncomfortable. This is the essential work of unfreezing.

When stakeholder groups roll up their sleeves to discuss and confront the issues in the marketplace, unspoken grievances, suspicions, and contentions come to the surface. This hidden conflict is a priceless resource. Like nuclear energy, it is abundant and of great value to anyone prepared to harvest its potential. Gradually, members learn to work together and to respect opinions that do not conform to their own.

What is taking place, of course, is a shift in the *relationship* among participants, an improvement in their overall emotional intelligence. As indicated by the evolving stages of learning in Figure 11.1, the goal is to move from being resigned, closed, and untrusting, to being authentic and powerful in partnership. Behavioral and psychological changes start to occur when real disagreements are expressed and worked through. As a result, mutual respect increases, and participants form a social contract around the emerging shared beliefs and values. This can be characterized as a "shift in being." When it has taken place, a new realm of possibility is available. Actions that could not have been taken previously happen quite naturally and yield surprising results. This is not easy, nor is it enough. But it is a beginning.

It is noteworthy that these significant shifts in how an organization's members are *being* with one another frequently reveal themselves to peripheral vision but are illusory to self-conscious attention and central focus. A defining moment of this nature occurred during Ford's transformation in the 1980s.

The situation was as follows. The dozen upper-level managers in charge of Engineering and Manufacturing were called into a room. Lou Ross, then senior vice president in charge of factories, got right to the point. "Here's the problem," he said. "For twenty-five years, Engineering and Manufacturing have been fighting with each other. Enough is enough. We don't care how long it takes, but we want you to answer one single question: Will Engineering report to Manufacturing, or Manufacturing to Engineering?" Then he left the room. There was hell to pay.[7]

Picture, if you will, the same meeting room and the same cast several months later. All were on hands and knees discussing the merits of the various organizational charts that covered the floor. The conversation was noticeably infused with give-and-take. With an edge of frustration, someone asked, "Which of these organizational charts is best?" Someone answered, "Maybe *this* is?"—referring to the *process* they were engaged in. A hush fell on the room as they realized that how they were relating to each other was the "best organizational chart." Who they were *being* was the answer—not the boxes or the solid and dotted lines on the paper.[8]

Collaboration cannot remedy all of an organization's structural defects. But, in Ford's case, a desperately needed reinvention occurred because people learned to relate to each other in new ways. They created a different conversation rooted in shared purposes instead of one based in competitive quarrels over turf and suboptimal goals. The team persuaded Lou Ross to give them three months to test their new ideas (which involved shortening the time it takes Ford to develop a model from scratch). Progress was encouraging and, after eighteen months with no radical restructuring, they laid the groundwork for reducing Ford's cycle time from eight years to five.

Igniting the potential of a complex adaptive system is—on purpose—not a smooth process. The journey's ups and downs are all necessary for the unfreezing and resocialization experience. The large group process encounters peaks and troughs in morale as initial euphoria is dampened by conflict and dogged task force work. Morale rises again as alignment among stakeholders occurs—then recedes in the long and demanding task of enrolling the ranks below. It is a rollercoaster experience, an adventure to be sure, and it is supposed to be that way. The experience, the emotions, and the achievements alter a company like no bumpless highway could.

■ ■

Revitalizing a business requires three essential steps: (1) unfreezing and aligning, (2) discovering and disseminating, and (3) committing and tracking. Performance of each step, in sequence, is necessary. It is a "Do-not-pass-go, do-not-collect-$200" proposition. As people progress through these steps, they experience a predictable cycle of operational, behavioral, and psychological changes. Let's take a look at each.

- *Operationally,* it is essential that participants accept that "something needs to happen that wouldn't happen otherwise." The design must convey the urgency of the business situation so that a consensus for a discontinuous shift is generated.
- *Behaviorally,* this requires an alteration in "the way we do things around here."

- *Psychologically,* the journey to self-organization and emergence alters who people are being, the way they relate to each other, what they talk about, and how they think and feel about crucial subjects.

"Revitalization is all in the setup," says organizational architect Bill Broussard, who spearheaded many of the remarkable accomplishments achieved at Ford in the 1980s.[9] The simplicity of the quote belies its wisdom.

It has taken considerable buildup to get to this point—and that *is* the point. So far, we have discussed the following considerations: (1) selecting and including key stakeholders, (2) building-in an iterative process to chip away at hidden misalignment, (3) grounding work in concrete business realities to frame the adaptive challenge, (4) orchestrating all these elements to generate enough stress to unfreeze the organization, and (5) regulating distress. All are cornerstones of an effective design for emergence. The generic techniques allow us to build a new structure, but only after the foundation is in place.

Unfreezing and Aligning

The central premise in a design for emergence is that mature adults are "more likely to *act* their way into a new way of thinking than *think* their way into a new way of acting."[10]

All the design considerations we've discussed thus far—inclusion, alignment, use of grounded business realities, and management of distress—leverage real-time experience. More is accomplished by "getting on the court"—jumping into the middle of things and learning from the breakdowns and breakthroughs. Over the course of experience, deeply entrenched beliefs tend to reverse-engineer themselves to conform to new realities. Importantly, you cannot start with a blank sheet of paper and design a "brave new world" from scratch. Instead, you jump in, disturb things enough to allow for new possibilities, and figure the rest out as it unfolds.

For the better part of the twentieth century, ecologists attempted to recreate tracts of the tallgrass prairie that once undulated across the Great Plains. Their first attempts resembled the way a business might approach changing something: figure out where you want to go, commit resources, eliminate obstacles, and execute with single-minded intensity. Accordingly, ecologists cleansed the acreage that was designated to be restored to "virgin prairie"; they cleared away the Asian and European migrants and sowed original species in the freshly tilled and sanitized earth. For a while, the protected vegetation (insulated from incursions of more aggressive contemporary stock) did well. But once it was left untended, the plots regressed. Nonprairie vegetation, alien species, and farm weeds invaded via mammals, insects, and wind-borne spores. The tracts hosted a hybrid ecosystem that was neither prehistoric nor contemporary.[11]

Writes author Kevin Kelly:

> Something was missing, a key species, perhaps. In the mid 1970s, that species was identified. It was a wary animal, once ubiquitous on the tallgrass prairie, that roamed widely and interacted with every plant, insect and bird making a home over sod. The missing member was fire. Fire made the prairie work. It hatched certain fire-triggered seeds, it eliminated intruding tree saplings, it kept fire-intolerant urban competitors down.[12]

What ecologists have learned since is that it is impossible to recreate a prairie from pristine conditions and assemble it in what seems like a "logical" way. You have to begin with what's already there.

Surprisingly, ecologists were more successful when they recreated an authentic tallgrass prairie by planting in destabilized weedy fields rather than in sanitized plowed fields, and then allowing fire (an unfreezing event) to do its work. Although it may seem counterintuitive (surely aggressive, established weeds would suffocate the newcomers) it turns out that a fallow field, "unfrozen" by fire, is far more conducive to regenerating the prairie than a plowed field. Some weeds in a fallow field are original prairie members. Their early presence quickens the assembly of the prairie system. "The weeds that immediately sprout in a plowed, naked field," continues Kevin Kelly, "are very aggressive. The beneficial late-arriving weeds come into the mix too late to gain a foothold. It's like having the concrete reinforcement bars arrive after you've poured the cement foundation for your house."[13] The new species must carve out a niche among preexisting competitors. Whether it can survive the struggle will determine its ultimate sustainability.

Ecologists also learned that even this process cannot succeed in isolation. The surrounding islands of trees and savanna that dotted the original prairie remain essential because they house symbiotic species. Kelly notes, it is not by wind, but by animals and birds that most prairie seeds are dispersed.[14] The prairie coevolves through interlocking organisms.

What fire does for the savanna, unfreezing does for organizations: It disrupts and regenerates. In the prairie, fire moves the system to the edge of chaos. Within organizations, as with prairies, one cannot get very far with pristine and hermetically sealed experiments. "Acting your way into a new way of thinking" entails coping with reality and using a design that stacks the deck in favor of learning and change. In fact, this is one reason for reaching out to a broad cross-section of key stakeholders. In addition to contributing skills and strengths, they bring awareness of the limitations and organizational constraints that any successful change effort must transcend.

How Xerox Got It Wrong

The lessons outlined in the previous section have been lost on many companies, including some of the world's most famous think tanks: Bell Labs, IBM's Research Center, and Xerox PARC. Among these, Xerox will surely enjoy a dubious notoriety. Although it has been relatively successful as a competitor in the copier industry, Xerox acknowledges a long legacy of lost opportunities. It ignored or bungled a good number of the greatest wealth-creating opportunities of the past thirty years. The reason, metaphorically, is that the company failed to heed the lessons of the prairie.

Researchers at Xerox PARC (Palo Alto Research Center) developed Alto, the first personal computer (which served as the inspiration for companies subsequently founded by Steve Jobs and Bill Gates). They also developed the first commercial mouse, flat screen displays, the laser printer, Ethernet (progenitor of the Internet), and most of the operating protocols that launched the Internet.[15] The list goes on.

What did Xerox do wrong? It cultivated promising young shoots in the greenhouse but mismanaged the transplant to the jungle. The Xerox PARC experiments were sheltered—indeed, they were so protected from the politics and realities of Xerox's mainstream business that any real prospect of coevolution and cross-pollination was thwarted. Large workshops were never convened (as they were at Monsanto); mainstream Xerox stakeholders were not enrolled (as they were by Shapiro at Monsanto) to reinvent whole new businesses through the intersection of new technologies and market knowledge. Xerox leaders did not generate a strange attractor to pull the enterprise from its comfortable fitness peak. No effort was made to generate (let alone regulate) the employee distress that would have been necessary for Xerox to exploit the vast treasure of discoveries within its grasp. Never was there authentic alignment within the Xerox power structure to provide a welcoming climate to the green shoots of innovation sprouting in Xerox PARC. In summary, there was no "design for emergence" to disturb equilibrium and unfreeze the myopic fixation that Xerox was a mainstream copier company.

Unfreezing and Aligning at BPX

As we described earlier, British Petroleum's Exploration unit faced an adaptive challenge. The division needed to pool technical know-how, from centers of excellence in Britain and the United States, to interpret geological profiles of the earth's crust. Use of the Seven-S

Framework permitted BPX's 100 most senior managers and professional staff to examine how the new "end game" strategy fit with the way the organization worked. The size of the gap was intimidating, and the challenge spawned disequilibrium. This dislodged old patterns and generated alignment around essential new priorities. Participants saw:

1. The dysfunction within the feudal regional *structure;*
2. Tightly wired financial systems and controls that fostered myopia and incompatible information platforms;
3. A style of working characterized as "warring tribes";
4. Incompatible staffing policies that inhibited career paths across regions and functions;
5. A general absence of shared values across the Exploration unit;
6. Mediocre skills at discovering and recovering oil.

Juxtaposition of this profile of BPX alongside its ambitious strategy served to remind people of the unit's potential. It also provided a powerful wake-up call to realize it. At the *operational* level, participants grasped the stark incongruity between desired ends and organizational means. At the *behavioral* level, these problems brought conflicts to the surface, evoked debate, and, in time, led to collaborative interactions across regions. At the *psychological* level, the process unfroze old beliefs and began to alter deep-seated attitudes about "the way it is."

Unfreezing and Aligning Through Learning Visuals at Sears

The learning visuals at Sears enabled literally hundreds of thousands of employees to grasp the competitive forces that had been successfully siphoning off Sears' customers and revenue. Two learning visuals—"New Day on Retail Street" and "Sears Money Map"—and the discussions they evoked, allowed participants to see the connection between their everyday activities and larger corporate results. This unleashed thousands of new ideas. Employees committed themselves to team efforts to alter the customers' shopping experience throughout the stores.

- *Operationally,* the learning map furthered understanding of competitive cause and effect.
- *Behaviorally,* it fostered teamwork and strengthened employees' identification with the goals of the store and the company as a whole.
- *Psychologically,* it paved the way for participants to feel differently about their work, to be a part of something bigger. Employee satisfaction surveys, administered both before and after Town Hall meetings, indicated that self-esteem and commitment increased.

Learning visuals contribute to adaptive change by enabling a company to tap its collective intelligence, wherever that intelligence resides within the organization. Adaptive challenges, by their very nature, benefit from cross-pollination, self-organization, and the emergence of new ideas and approaches. Massive levels of participation cause redundancy and seem chaotic, but nature teaches us to live with that messiness. All the nodes of a network can't be coordinated by optimizing and assembling one perfect coordination system. Nature employs multiple systems that run in parallel—sometimes converging, sometimes colliding. That's why Sears gave each store its own head, why Monsanto allowed fifty-eight Big Idea teams, why Shell sponsored thousands of initiatives in its operating companies, why BPX ran parallel efforts to tackle its "Nine Big Problems."

Discovering and Disseminating

The first task for any group that is immersed in an adaptive challenge is to *discover* for itself that change is necessary (i.e., "We can't get there from here"). Improving on preexisting skills and the old repertoire, while staying in the comfort zone, comes to be acknowledged as insufficient to bring about the desired outcome. Once awareness shifts and a consensus for action is achieved, the task is to *generate and disseminate* ideas that result in discontinuous change.

The United States Agricultural Extension Service stands out as a model program of discovery and dissemination.[16] The Service's program—exerting extraordinary influence on America's fiercely independent farmers; discovering and introducing new methods and technology—is credited with spurring the dramatic increase in farm productivity that gave the United States a competitive advantage in agriculture throughout the twentieth century.

Political adversity actually helped the Service get it right. In 1900, as now, there was strong sentiment that the federal government should relinquish as much authority as possible to state and county governments. Policies to impact agriculture and the farmer were particularly sensitive on this point. As a result, atypical of most federally sponsored programs, the Agricultural Extension Service was not socially engineered. To obtain congressional approval, land grant colleges were established as a Trojan horse: States were given federal grants to start their own universities—with the proviso that they would teach and promote agriculture. This gambit proved important in two respects: (1) it sparked initiative on the local level, and (2) it provided a platform for investment in agriculture. It all may have ended there were it not for a third innovation that advanced the frontier of diffusion.

Parallel research efforts at numerous land grant colleges spawned new hybrid seeds for crops, harvest mechanization technology, and soil-conservation practices. However, as one might expect, conventional attempts to disseminate these innovations were met by a great deal of skepticism from farmers. Unsurprisingly, faculty field trips and the distribution of the resulting research papers did not bridge the gap. Most farmers couldn't read, and those who could were rarely willing to abandon their hard-earned experience in favor of "academic experiments."

These difficulties, in fact, sparked the Agricultural Extension Service's most significant innovation: local Farm Bureaus, county-level extension agents, and Bureau-sponsored 4-H Clubs specializing in agriculture and home economics. By subtly infiltrating the farming communities, these diffusion vehicles went right to the heart of the living systems they were trying to change. In their capacity as legislative pressure groups, they were seen as the farmers' friends. As members of the community, the Farm Bureau agents had relationships with farmers and could coevolve workable solutions. Rather than try to persuade farmers that a new hybrid crop or harvesting technique was superior because research had proven it so, they were able to demonstrate the approach in a test plot that all could see, and seeing was believing.

Cast in the theory of this chapter, the U.S. Department of Agriculture pioneered a design for emergence. The nodes (Farm Bureaus, Agricultural Extension Agents, 4-H Clubs) reached into every corner of the farm community, and those ties were powerful conduits for diffusion. They included kicking the soil at test plot sites, conversing around a cast-iron stove at the town hardware store, seeding new ideas among the younger generation at 4-H Club meetings, benchmarking crop yields and quality at county fairs, and working together on legislation. Community events like county fairs and 4-H Club meetings were the yeast for fertile dialogue in which early adapters could debate traditionalists. Distress could be managed.

Earlier, we noted the profound importance of changing the "conversation." Within the American farm community, it gradually shifted from one of caution and of resistance to change (which is still witnessed among many farm constituencies around the world) to a more forward-looking conversation about the possibilities of new technology and methods. To this day, a distinguishing characteristic of American farmers is their openness to innovation. Many experts regard this as a sustaining source of global competitive advantage.

The Agricultural Extension Service models the concept of incubating new ideas in a protected environment, then shepherding these innovations from the greenhouse into the jungle. Another such illustration occurred hundreds of years earlier. Before the genocidal colonization of the Americas, native tribes evolved migratory patterns that were optimal for diffusion. Tribal migration and intertribal trading patterns resulted in long periods of isolation interrupted by occasional meetings. That isolation allowed one tribe to perfect a technology, or, in genetic terms, disseminate a fortuitous mutation that provided, say, resistance to a particular disease. In isolation, technology—or an antibody—could spread without excessive dilution. Subsequent encounters with other tribes led to an exchange of ideas and technology and promoted intermarriage among members of isolated communities. Nature does best when a positive mutation is cultivated within a small population until it becomes robust enough to withstand being diluted by a crossover from a wider community. These practices are relevant to corporations. We saw it at work in the design of initiatives at Shell and Monsanto.

Discovery and dissemination can take many forms. For illustrative purposes, we will use a device employed widely at Shell and Monsanto: the "Action Lab," with which many readers are generally familiar. What differentiates it from most task-force-type activities is the comprehensive design that gives it legs. This is important because, to an increasing degree, projects and initiatives are the *primary* means by which mainstream organizations reform themselves. Such devices can give shape and voice to less powerful individuals. They provide a launching pad for latent ideas that have lain buried in the organization or the marketplace. Given the right sponsorship and visibility, these changes can catalyze larger ones.

Successful Action Labs are grounded in several essential design principles.

1. The Lab's charter needs to be explicit. It should be challenging and aspirational, but too much blue sky (e.g., "Grow the business") leads to confusion. Avoid topics with too many uncertain externalities, such as chaotic technological change or legislative/ regulatory reform. Project teams work best with solid, cornerstone "givens."

2. Sponsorship is a key factor in determining ultimate success. Sponsors should be executives with "skin in the game," but not with so great a vested interest that they hijack the project. They need their authority to provide air cover and make key resources available (usually, time, money, and people). They should be mature enough to allow a lab to do its work without micromanaging the process. Nothing deflates a project faster than a presumptuous sponsor who "knows" the answer before the team begins.

3. A discontinuity in how a team is "led" is a prerequisite for achieving a discontinuity in performance. Executive sponsors need to "lead" the Action Labs by reinforcing the adaptive challenge. Leaders' conventional repertoire—which often relies on authority, having "the answers," or exercising detailed levels of control—typically fails in the lab. Executives often feel uncomfortable "leading" the lab with a living systems approach, but it is incumbent on them to do so. Merck's Sir James T. Block, a Nobel laureate in medicine and leader of one of the world's most prolific R&D labs, extols the necessary philosophy: "We work in groups of twenty young scientists. They team up as they see fit to follow the flow of the problem and inquiry. When the problem defines the team, my job as a leader is to help them get the problem right—and to cheer them on when we fail. They have less experience in failure than I do."[17]

4. Create an environment that is safe enough to promote experimentation and learning but intense enough to foster breakthroughs. For the leader, the trick involves keeping the group's attention focused on the challenge, particularly if participants avoid doing so by scapegoating others or looking to authority for the answers. The leader should regulate distress so that it does not become dysfunctional. This experience triggers both behavioral change and psychological shifts. The group becomes more cohesive and committed. At the individual level, people feel more hopeful about the possibility of change, and are more ready to work toward it. Facilitate the required tension and the learning.

5. Uncover the "ground truth"—the issues and expectations that remain when all the obfuscating layers are peeled away.

The aim of the Action Labs is to provoke new thoughts and behavior patterns by confronting the team with a business issue that will both stress and challenge them. The situation—which must be relevant, prolonged, and intense—should be daunting enough to force members outside of their comfort zones and into ambiguous and uncharted territory. Radical innovation seldom occurs unless these conditions are met.

Discovering and Disseminating Through Trade Shows at Shell

Shell's discovery and dissemination effort made extensive use of trade shows. Managing Director Steve Miller had launched his change programs on very tentative ground. Cajoling allies from among the more friendly Operating Company chairmen, he (barely) managed to recruit seven teams for the pilot program. Afterward, participants were highly enthusiastic. But one big challenge remained for Miller: How could he overcome Shell's notorious not-invented-here syndrome and entice other operating companies into the effort?

Miller turned to the trade show. At the next annual meeting of Downstream's leadership group (which included headquarters staff and the chairmen of the fifty largest operating companies), each pilot team was asked to design and staff a booth, which, typically, has a three-paneled display. Each floor-to-ceiling panel contains pictures or charts that identify customer segments, size up business opportunities, and display competitive benchmarks. Booths often use videos or photographs to convey a message in as real a manner as possible. The third panel usually summarizes the team's business case, its plan for action, and the deliverables and milestones that will track its results.

At the *operational* level, the key activity is information transfer. As participants rotate through each booth, they are briefed, ask questions, and engage in informal conversation about data, questionable assumptions, or how a particular proposal might be applied to their situations.

"The compelling advantage of the trade show format," says Steve Miller, "is that you can learn at your own pace, stop, ask close questions, tailor the information transfer to your needs. Stick those same enthusiastic booth presenters behind a podium and a PowerPoint presentation and you end up with the usual stilted, sanitized stuff. With the trade show, people feel they get behind the press release, access the gritty details about land mines and politics, and leave with an authentic understanding of what has transpired."[18]

Miller identifies shifts at the *behavioral* and *psychological* levels. One of the most reliable findings of social psychology is that when you say something out loud, you tend to believe what you're saying. *Presenters* become *champions;* one actually sees the shift from agnostic to advocate. All this whets the appetite for more challenging work.

Miller's trade show sparked a great deal of curiosity. Other operating companies stepped forward to involve their teams in the process. "The rocket had finally left the launch pad," Miller reflects. "The trade show created exactly the kind of grass-roots buy-in we needed."

Shell utilized this format many times. In 1999, a major initiative was undertaken to slim down headquarters activities and devolve most of the staff work to centers of excellence in the field. This was Miller's overall desire, but he made it clear that, case by case, he wanted to do what was best for the business. Joint headquarters/field teams were assigned to sort it out.

Over 100 of Downstream's most knowledgeable professionals from Shell Centre and the operating companies descended on London for an intensive one-week workshop. For the first four days, respective teams analyzed specific lines of business: Lubricants, Natural Gas (LNG),

Bitumen, Distribution, New Ventures, Brand Management, and Retailing. Drawing on experience and hard-earned competitive successes and failures in the field, the teams addressed the central question: How could Shell retain, or regain, significant competitive advantage if turf and a legacy of field–HQ power struggles were set aside? Teams were encouraged to think unconventionally about acquisitions, reducing costs, or finding alliances to widen the customer base. The secondary question was: How should all this be organized so that Shell could become as agile and aggressive as possible?

Working late into the final preshow night, the teams readied their booths. The panels outlined deliberations, highlighted the sharpest debates, displayed customer data and competitive benchmarks (unusual for Shell!), and outlined the underlying logic that led to strategic and organizational proposals. Each team posted its next steps and its requests for resources.

As a claxon sounded, Steve Miller and his executive team entered the first booth. Participants who were not staffing booths were invited to rotate through booths during the morning schedule. In this fashion, not only were the executives briefed on each proposal, but most of the workshop participants were able to see one another's work product and receive a helicopter view of the overall process.

In the final afternoon session, the executive team sat in the center of the room and was joined by each of the teams in succession. As the others looked on, the executives asked further questions, suggested amendments to proposals, and made commitments. Booth members and onlookers at the perimeter were invited to clarify, challenge, and surface fudges. In most instances, meaningful closure was achieved.

Steve Miller states:

> I wasn't sure if we could carry this off. The entrenched suspicion between field and headquarters is so charged and historically deep that polarization could easily obscure the business issues. But they raised above it. Not all teams achieved the same level of progress, of course, but we got further in five days than in the five preceding years of consultant studies and

top-down reorganizations. That's the real payoff. Combining Action Labs with the trade show and the fishbowl accelerates change to warp speed. When you do it the traditional top-down way, you get backsliding. Everyone is looking for the conspiracy: headquarters retaining control or hints of favoritism or private deals. When you do it the new way, it's all out there on the table. The inmates are in charge of the asylum. The merits of the case are presented in the booths for all to see. Buy-in and implementation go much easier.[19]

Discovering and Disseminating Through Positive Deviance in Vietnam

Discovery and dissemination are central to the Positive Deviance approach. Studying the habits of poor but well-nourished Vietnamese children led to *discovery* of freely available sources of nutrition and better nutritional routines. Positive Deviance, the methodology used to identify why some children were faring so much better than others, illuminated desirable, but formerly obscure, practices. It provided a design wherein all could benefit from the local wisdom.

Dissemination was accomplished over a month-long program in which mothers acquired new habits. They were asked to collect ingredients, acclimate their children to new tastes, and establish different eating routines. The children's challenge was to adjust to the unfamiliar texture and flavor of such "oddities" as sweet potato greens and fresh-water shrimp.

- *Operationally,* Positive Deviance is an exquisitely simply idea: Look for unusual behavior that is working and that a community wants more of, and give it sufficient visibility to foster replication.
- *Behaviorally,* the community grows more cohesive. Mothers and children, in this instance, altered lifelong habits. Low-status community members rose in stature and influence.
- *Psychologically,* the approach fostered a significant shift in the self-esteem of poor women who could now see themselves as

capable of raising healthier and happier children. It also gave rise to greater solidarity and influence among women in the village.

Committing and Tracking

We turn now to the final task: committing and tracking. As illustrations, we use two generic tools: the fishbowl process and the valentines exercise. Each provides an effective means of ensuring that commitments are made and promises are kept.

Operationally, the success of any implementation effort requires authentic handshakes and contracts. To achieve the necessary authenticity, the techniques we describe tap the underlying force of social witness. They harness the power of peer pressure to shape behavior by staging "a theater of commitment": verbal contracts are made in a public realm. With a hundred or more witnesses, the signatories think twice about failing to deliver what they have promised.

The Fishbowl at Shell (redux)

As we have previously implied, subtle dynamics in the fishbowl process evoke *psychological* stress and *behavioral* change. Among these dynamics are:

- The "at stake-ness" of the presenting team.
- Resocializing senior executives by putting them on the spot publicly.
- Involving both participants and onlookers in a new conversation that launches well-founded business initiatives.
- Managing stress. Many intermediate echelons are *not* present during these negotiations and, understandably, fear being left out of the loop as important deals are struck between the top executives and representatives from the front lines. This distress is managed by videotaping all the discussions and making these visual transcripts widely available.

- ■ Tapping the energy and optimism of less jaded members of the organization, to help get the organization to believe in itself again.

When the fishbowl commences, the physical layout is a table and chairs in the center of a room, and dozens of additional chairs around the periphery. Seated at one end of the table are the reviewers. (At Shell, these were Steve Miller and his direct reports.) At the other end is a team of relatively junior-level participants from an operating company. Seated in the peripheral chairs, in a typical Shell session, are dozens of team members from other countries. These peers are observing the fishbowl.

Staged for dramatic effect, the fishbowl is designed at the *operational* level to accomplish work and syndicate commitment. And, as we noted earlier, the proceedings are videotaped so that when teams return to their operating companies, stakeholders from middle and upper management who were not present at the workshop can watch and learn from the visual record. (These inexpensive videos had a huge multiplier effect on the transformation of Shell's Downstream business.)

The fishbowl and similar public conversations ensure that commitments are taken seriously. They exploit a specific protocol in which requests are made and promises are given. *Psychologically,* there are numerous advantages to this public forum. People feel that they are on the line to deliver. They also experience solidarity and excitement from witnessing a critical mass of agreements that, if kept, could alter the nature of the company.

The architecture of these events includes a *process design* and an *accountability design*. Without a protocol—such as the public witness to the contracts in the fishbowl—good intentions may not reach fruition. Commitments need to be specific and personal. In the example of Shell, the KBAs gave an edge to all this. Not only did participants personally agree in principle, they accepted yardsticks to monitor progress toward completion. There is a big difference between being accountable for one's actions ("I tried hard") and being accountable for the consequences of one's actions (hard evidence of progress against KBAs).

The Valentines Exercise at Shell Malaysia

Borrowed from Ford, the valentines exercise is a useful technique when initiatives have interdependencies across organizational silos.[20] It helps to ferret out all that can go wrong in a major change effort. The valentines hammer out interlocking agreements and save new initiatives from "a death of a thousand cuts."

One of Shell Malaysia's Action Labs created a Customer Service Center. Its aim was to improve Shell's relationship with its franchised service stations, which were often frustrated in their efforts to get responses from headquarters—for example, for expediting fuel deliveries. The early goals were: (1) to give customers a single point of contact with Shell via a toll-free number, and (2) to give the Customer Service Center the authority to break logjams and satisfy customer needs. It is easy enough to recruit a staff of operators to cover a toll-free number around the clock; it is quite another matter to transfer organizational power so that Customer Service Center representatives will be able to break deadlocks and redeploy resources. This is the stuff over which organizational blood is spilled. This challenge did not play to the strengths nor the historical patterns of Shell Malaysia's silos.

In these matters, the commitments that count are those made laterally between people who are accountable for business outcomes. The problem is that organizations usually only measure and acknowledge commitments made vertically. That is where we see the importance of social leverage. Commitments made publicly (and then periodically reviewed among one's peers) tend to be taken as seriously as the more conventional vertical commitments.

The valentines exercise is a vehicle for conflict resolution. Each functional team is required to write a succinct description of its "grievances" against any of the other functions in the room. The team must pinpoint how the identified group inhibits productivity, and how it is likely to interfere with the success of a proposed initiative—in this example, the Customer Service Center. When each group receives, say, half a dozen of these valentines, its members sift through them, then select two issues that are particularly important to resolve. The group is allotted two hours to formulate: (1) a detailed plan for corrective action that can be implemented within sixty days; (2) the name of an individual from this team who will be accountable for delivering the plan; and (3) the name of a committed partner from the team that sent the valentine, who will share responsibility for making the new solution work.

In plenary session, each person who has been assigned an action must stand and explain the grievance, the proposed solution, and the team's nominee for a committed partner—often, the individual on the other team who is viewed as most likely to sabotage the proposal, and, therefore, the person most essential to its success. When the committed partner stands, the large room grows tense, very quiet, and very small. With coaching from the facilitator, the two principals often bring conflicts to the surface or express underlying distrust of one another's motives. Usually, they are able to get past these differences and a robust solution is the result.

Taking advantage of these and other techniques, Shell Malaysia reversed its ten-year drift. It fostered a new level of individual power, an increased sense of identity with the enterprise as a whole, an improved capacity to deal openly and productively with conflict, and a new appetite for learning that still persists to this day. Power, identity, conflict management, and learning might be thought of as the vital signs of a living system.

■　■

Having provided guidelines for a design for emergence that restores vitality to an organization, we turn next to what may appear to be an opposing concept: discipline. This domain brings us squarely to grips with the paradox of structure and freedom, and it defines the heartbeat of all living things. The chapters that follow investigate this in detail.

CHAPTER 12

THE EXTREME
SPORT OF "DISCIPLINE"

Having breathed new life into organizations, how do we sustain it? Paradoxically, the answer lies in "disciplines." These fractal-like routines have many variations and can take many different forms, but all evoke vitality. Specifically, the disciplines help organizations sustain disequilibrium, thrive in near-chaos conditions, and foster self-organization. If taken to heart, they can also foster changes at the individual level. Indeed, they must be internalized if their far-reaching benefits are to be tapped at an organizational level.

The seven disciplines are:

1. Infuse an intricate understanding of what drives business success.
2. Insist on uncompromising straight talk.
3. Manage from the future.
4. Reward inventive accountability.
5. Harness adversity by learning from prior mistakes.
6. Foster relentless discomfort.
7. Cultivate reciprocity between the individual and the organization.

At first blush, the list is oxymoronic. How can disequilibrium, the edge of chaos, and all those wonder-inspiring properties of life coexist in partnership with disciplines? The paradox dissolves as we come to understand disequilibrium's Janus-like nature. The disciplines do establish a strong foundation of repetition and continuity. But, as we shall see, there is another face that is ambivalent toward structure. One side gazes fondly upon replication and routine; the other delights in messing up anything that is too neat. The disciplines embrace structure as both a necessity and a danger. Practices that undergird excellence can also hold it back.

Three Stages of Mastery

Mastery of the disciplines is a three-stage process. The first stage is superficial understanding. ("These disciplines seem logical enough. I get the concept. Let's give them a try.") The next stage commences when protocols and routines are put in place to establish a backbone of practice. All this can evoke stress and apprehension. ("I didn't recognize the full implications of this. I'm not sure we're up to it.") The third stage triggers introspection, personal distress, and, if persistent, inner change. ("This discipline is not just about the organization; it's about me.") The third level is the most difficult because the focus is on a facet of life called "you." This arena is taxing, but it also holds the greatest promise. When an organization (or a relationship) faces a challenge and you're a part of it, you are always the part that's easiest to change—as hard as that is!

Disciplines as Fractals

Understanding how the disciplines spur generativity in organizations brings us full circle to Chris Langton's beehive simulations, described in Chapter 2. Recall that one set of hard-to-pigeonhole "rules" moved the hive to the edge of chaos. Mathematicians call these "rules" fractals. As it turns out, fractals have far-reaching importance in bringing both order and variety to life.

Fractals are the Legos of life—simple building blocks that can be assembled into more complicated things. The discovery of fractals has been traced to unlikely origins. In 1977, Benoit Mandelbrot, a Yale professor and a Fellow at IBM Laboratories, was manipulating a simple formula, which, like a dog chasing its tail, generated an output from the first iteration which became the input to the next. With access to powerful computers, Mandelbrot ran millions of iterations in search of generalizable patterns. To visualize possible symmetries in the cascading printout of numbers, he assigned colors to differing values, thereby creating a visual display.

The result was astonishing. A kaleidoscopic amoeba, shifting into ever-changing patterns, formed on the computer screen. Most remarkable, all the evolving shapes were derivative of the original form. Telescoping back or magnifying down revealed infinite precision at any level of detail. "I was staring at the DNA of God," Mandelbrot later said.[1] He was awarded the Wolf Prize in Physics and the Steinmetz Medal for his discoveries.

From a purely geometrical standpoint, fractal structures are those in which the nested parts of the system have the same pattern as the whole. This repetition turns out to be highly relevant in the life sciences because fractal properties are exhibited in almost all living things. Broccoli, human lungs, a zebra's stripes, and the architecture of our circulatory system are examples. Computerized fractal simulations have shown that a three-pronged "crow's foot" pattern, combined in novel ways, perfectly replicates the foliage patterns of every fern on earth.[2]

Fractals are important to this discussion of disciplines because they direct our attention to singling out fundamental symmetries from superficial differences and distracting details. The disciplines we are about to describe involve core routines and protocols that can take dozens of forms and can be applied or combined in a near-infinite number of imaginative ways. But it is important to not lose sight of the core constructs. The disciplines have yet to be expressed as fractal algorithms, but the seven we will describe here share the common quality of channeling distributed intelligence in the ranks, both to ensure threshold levels of reliability, and to provide an invigorating stimulus for creative new arrangements and novel applications.

As noted above, whether the pattern is an abstract shape (such as the three-branch motif that combines to form the leaves of ferns) or a social repertoire (such as fishbowls or quality circles), the fractal nature of the disciplines reveals how simple patterns can spawn intricate and complex forms. When Ford sponsored volunteer quality initiatives in its assembly plants during the dark days of 1980, it could have been described as introducing a fractal concept.[3] What was proven as a good idea in one plant was adapted by a second, multiplied to four, and proliferated in exponential fashion—each time with a slightly different manifestation. Miller at Shell harnessed the power of fractals through the widespread replication of fishbowls and Action Labs. Together with a rigorous business model, this spawned diverse marketplace innovations that shared a common framework for fostering growth and operational excellence.

■   ■

Let us now explore the first six disciplines in detail. (The seventh discipline is the subject of the next chapter.) The following sections describe the specific practices that translate intentions into sustainable patterns of behavior. Examples will illustrate how businesses have used the disciplines to ensure replicability, innovate continuously, and sustain organizational attention. The disciplines are important because they reinforce the four principles of living systems described in previous chapters. The chart in Figure 12.1 captures these relationships.

1. Infuse an Intricate Understanding of What Drives Business Success

Intricate understanding is an important discipline for disturbing equilibrium and promoting self-organization in the ranks. It is based on establishing clear connections between a firm's overall strategy

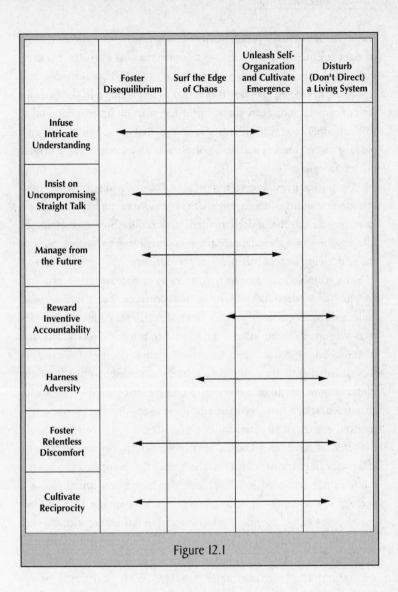

	Foster Disequilibrium	Surf the Edge of Chaos	Unleash Self-Organization and Cultivate Emergence	Disturb (Don't Direct) a Living System
Infuse Intricate Understanding	←		→	
Insist on Uncompromising Straight Talk	←		→	
Manage from the Future	←		→	
Reward Inventive Accountability			←	→
Harness Adversity		←		→
Foster Relentless Discomfort	←			→
Cultivate Reciprocity	←			→

Figure 12.1

and each individual's performance. Colloquially, this is called "line of sight": Employees see the direct connection between their contributions and their company's commercial success. This is harder than it looks. Burying employees in raw data won't achieve it, nor will abstract financial indicators such as profit, return on investment, and so forth. Rather, one must identify activities that are tangible, that employees can influence, and that correlate with an overview of strategic intentions.

"Deep indicators" are an important facet of the discipline of intricate understanding. Identifying them requires moving beyond the surface scorecard to the underlying drivers of results. Surface metrics are like a game score; they capture the outcome. Deep indicators monitor the underlying factors that produce the outcome.

Sears stumbled over these trip wires as it endeavored to establish an intricate understanding within its workforce. For decades, Sears collected reams of data on every facet of retailing: employee satisfaction, customer retention, and the impact of pricing, promotions, and merchandising programs. As described earlier, this raw information was distilled into meaningful insight by a research spin off of the University of Michigan. Assuming relative price parity, one factor correlated, more strongly than all others, with driving customer retention: employee satisfaction.

Retailers have long known that customer retention significantly affects profit margins. Astute analysis has now quantified the precise relationship. As noted in Chapter 4, the researchers found that a 5 percent improvement in employee satisfaction in the first quarter correlates with a 1.3 percent improvement in customer satisfaction in the second quarter, and translates into a 0.5 percent improvement in store revenue by the third quarter.[4] This is a crisp illustration of what we mean by an *intricate understanding*. With Sears' mall stores barely breaking even, margin improvements were essential, and improving the relationships with customers offered the quickest route to higher margins. To achieve this shift, Sears needed to dramatically improve its employees' satisfaction and gain support from nearly 300,000 frontline workers.

Using Town Hall meetings, Arthur Martinez shared the research with the entire organization. His aims were: (1) to give employees insight as to the sources of Sears' profitability, and (2) to highlight the importance of improving the organizational climate (to impact employee satisfaction, increase customer retention, and so on).

As noted, learning visuals were used to clarify the relationship between an individual worker's performance and the company's overall strategy. The first mural traced changes in demographics, lifestyles, and competitive dynamics. At a second series, six months later, employees studied the "Sears Money Map" and then estimated the amount and sources of money flowing in, and where it was subsequently spent. Employees, on average, believed the company made 45 cents per dollar of sales. The accurate amount was 4 cents. So far, so good. An open-and-shut example of infusing an intricate understanding of what drives business success.

Sears executives were unprepared for the second- and third-order consequences that arose from this new perspective. Initially, employees directed their efforts toward improving customer service on the sales floor, generating efficiency in the warehouse, and reducing stockouts. But, the more knowledgeable employees became, the more questions they asked. For example, at one Town Hall meeting, a forklift operator asked his store manager: "If visits to shopping malls are declining, why is Sears investing $4 billion in refurbishing our mall stores? Wouldn't it be wise to improve the hiring, pay, and training of sales clerks to improve customer retention?"

At another session, a supervisor of the housewares department asked: "The research on sales margins that you shared last quarter tells us that *our* attitudes are very important in bringing customers back. It helps Sears make more money. Why have you cut back on part-time sales floor coverage during the coming three-day weekend? Maybe we're doing it to meet quarterly profit goals, but it frustrates us. It rubs off on our customers and can't be good for the long-term health of the business."

Shared understanding of the business redistributes power within a company. Managers accustomed to edicts from the top, or those who cut corners to achieve short-term financial goals, find themselves victims of their own prior testimony. They must face the jury of an informed workforce. This exemplifies the second-order consequences of an intricate understanding.

Harvard's Chris Argyris has coined the term *skilled incompetence* to characterize the ingenious ways in which organizations waltz around adaptive challenges. Such patterns of work avoidance are often smoked out by this discipline—and herein lies its third-order consequences. As employees assemble a composite picture of what is *really* happening to the business, they often ferret out the issues that no one wants to discuss and the difficult work that everyone wants to avoid.

At Sears, the discrepancy came to light when employees noticed that Sears had reported retailing profits three times higher than the 1.5 cents per dollar that the stores earned on their merchandise. When queried, management acknowledged that Sears' credit card had earned $480 million in the past year on sales of $6.8 billion. (By way of contrast, the "dominant" merchandising activities earned $220 million on sales of $30 billion.)[5] As employees grappled with the Money Maps at Town Hall meetings, it became impossible to ignore that the underappreciated credit card business was delivering two-thirds of Sears' retail earnings. Indeed, it could be argued that the mall stores were a large, expensive, and geographically dispersed *credit card distribution system*. They were selling marginally profitable merchandise to attract marginally creditworthy customers. The customers, in turn, used their cards, rolled over their balances, and provided Sears with the bulk of its profits. (Seventy million Americans own Sears credit cards; 50 million are used regularly, and 70 percent of these pay off their principal in installments.[6])

Martinez opened Pandora's box through the Money Maps and Town Hall meetings. The retail organization now confronted an adaptive challenge—and it was there for all to see. Martinez was courageous in permitting his organization to face the huge "credit card subsidy" that had kept the mall stores afloat. Inequities in status, influence, and compensation (all anchored in the past, but no longer relevant) were revealed. Martinez was personifying the changes he wanted to see in others. As noted earlier, his willingness to confront these issues was not shared by his lieutenants. By refocusing attention on pricing, promotion, and the merchandising mix, they deftly retreated into their comfort zone as soon as Martinez became distracted by other priorities.

2. Insist on Uncompromising Straight Talk

Straight talk fosters disequilibrium and is a particularly important discipline for organizations that are operating near the edge of chaos.

Put two human beings together and, in time, you get competing truths. *Conflict* arises over the correctness and prioritization of these truths. Conflict evokes images of turf battles, injured egos, wounded relationships, and all manner of sundry unpleasantness. Small wonder that most of us who survive long enough to accumulate organizational experience often sidestep such unexploded land mines.

It happens, albeit infrequently, that there is sufficient mutual trust and respect, that cards can be laid on the table, and a creative solution can be discovered. In these instances, the outcome is often better than if either side had gotten its own way. But such instances are rare. Notwithstanding brave efforts to deal with conflict—from T-Groups to facilitated sessions, from climate surveys to 360 degree appraisals—most organizations have not bridged the chasm of making straight talk the norm. "Telling it like it is" remains an extreme sport for career-aspiring employees.

Straight talk fuels disequilibrium and is essential to navigating near the edge of chaos. The key to this discipline is to view contention in a different context. Conflict, reframed as "fuel for organizational learning," can contribute to an organization's long-term vitality.[7] Peter

Senge has written that "learning disabilities are tragic in children, but they are fatal in organizations. Because of them, few corporations live even half as long as a person—most die before they reach the age of forty."[8] What Senge doesn't say is that most organizational learning disabilities stem from the avoidance of conflict.

Making straight talk a "discipline" requires objective data. The data then point the finger, not you. The U.S. Army provides an excellent example of how to do this. The National Training Command (NTC) is built on facts: still photos, videos, tape recordings of radio communications, maps showing the actual movement of troops and the places where shots were fired. These facts make short work of second guessing and subjective interpretations. The data fuel frank exchanges among soldiers as they sort through the confusion of battle and figure out where things went wrong. This cannot occur in a climate of excessive deference to superiors, or of team members' holding back for fear of hurting someone's feelings. The Army's observer/controllers are skilled at using objective data to bring an issue to the surface, foster healthy give-and-take, and create a safe environment for candor. Soldiers learn to disagree without being disagreeable.

Extensive surveys have shown that, in slightly more than half of the instances in which conflict appears, it is glossed over and avoided. Another 30 percent of the time, it precipitates heated clashes with no productive result. Only one time in five is conflict surfaced, debated, and authentically resolved.[9]

Straight talk occurs when "Yes" is the answer to a simple question: "Are the benefits of talking straight worth the risk?" The discipline element of straight talk is in the protocols, which lower the risks of putting an issue squarely on the table. Protocols make doing the right thing for the business the right thing to do.

At Intel, the protocol for straight talk consists of blunt verbal exchanges that may appear brutal to the uninitiated. Several years ago, a number of Intel's most senior executives traveled to Tokyo to assess Intel's competitiveness against Japanese quality and service standards. Near the end of the weeklong trip, the entire team was polarized in a fierce debate. Underlying the finger pointing were long-smoldering resentments on the part of those representing internal Intel customers who could not get the quality and service they desired from manufacturing. Craig Barrett, then the head of manufacturing (and now the CEO of Intel), was one of the protagonists in the melee. "Four-letter epithets flew back and forth like ping-pong balls in a Beijing masters tournament," stated one attendee.[10] "One outsider was in tears, having never experienced such heat and intensity." But, a week later, back in their Santa Clara headquarters, the same team sat down with chief executive officer Andy Grove, sorted out their differences, and put ideas into motion that would enable Intel to match or surpass its Japanese rivals.

Craig Barrett recalls: "I've got pretty thick skin. Sometimes it takes a lot to penetrate my strongly held convictions. But this kind of hard-hitting session was precisely what we all needed, to strip us of our illusions. It brought us all face-to-face with one another—the games we were playing, and how this prevented us from facing Japanese competitive realities."[11] Another participant warns: "If you're used to tennis, Intel plays rugby. Without the psychological padding, you walk away with a lot of bruises. Andy has created an attitude toward contention that regards direct, hard-hitting disagreement as a sign of fitness. After it's out on the table, you put it all behind you in the locker room. It's forgotten before the next day's scrimmage."[12]

Experiences at Intel and within the U.S. Army reveal the several levels of mastery that unfold as this discipline takes root. The first level of mastery focuses on the *past* conflict. Revisiting old disputes that are no longer highly charged is the safest place to begin.

At the second level of mastery, there is sufficient confidence in dealing with conflict that the protagonists can do so in real time. This is, of course, preferable; contention dealt with quickly has less time to fester into lasting wounds and entrenched positions.

The third level of mastery, evidenced at Intel, is emotional reconciliation with the tenet: Conflict fuels productive disequilibrium. However difficult, conflict is embraced as a source of learning. When conflict is taken to this level of proficiency, people actually *design* it into the way they operate. The particular composition of the senior Intel team that visited Japan guaranteed conflict because of their differing functional perspectives, and the force of their personalities. Most importantly, none of the protagonists believed that the conflict would be terminal.

3. Manage from the Future

Managing from the future—establishing a compelling goal that draws organizations out of their comfort zone—is a key discipline that moves us to the edge of chaos.

The term means literally standing in the new future and undertaking a series of steps, not in order to get there some day, but as if you are there already (or almost there *now*). The task, therefore, involves removing whatever obstacles remain in the way to being there fully. The discipline of managing from the future begins with this mental shift. It whets an organization's appetite for disequilibrium and provides the compelling goal that draws organizations toward the edge of chaos.

The Olympics and Atlanta's Stand for the Future

In 1987, inspired by a church service, a real estate lawyer, Billy Payne, set his sights on a very distant fitness peak: he wanted to bring the 1996 Olympics to his hometown, Atlanta. As it turned out, he would receive no direct financial support from the city or the state. Atlanta had few facilities suitable for Olympic competition. Public debate and media criticism constituted a skeptical chorus during the start-up years. But, piece by piece, Payne stitched the Atlantic games together like a patchwork quilt. He succeeded, in part, because his goal of bringing the Olympics to Atlanta was tangible. In addition, it resonated with a strange attractor—Southern pride and hospitality.[13]

With Coca-Cola's commitment to sponsorship in 1992, Payne secured his first seed money—$540 million. He solved the problem of too few facilities by spreading events as far north as Washington, DC, and as far south as Orlando, Florida. He had to create a $1.7 billion temporary corporation, oversee projects involving 82,500 workers and 42,000 volunteers, and host five-and-a-half million visitors. After the Games ended, he turned $250 million in assets (a new baseball stadium and swimming complex) over to the city of Atlanta.[14]

Payne understands what it means to manage from the future:

> I've always thought the way to engage life—in business or personally—is to set enormously high goals that seem absolutely unattainable, and work from the conviction that you're going to pull it off. By doing that, I'm convinced you are going to reach half of them. As to the others, you're going to go further than you would have otherwise. My approach with the talented people on my team was: "When you hit a roadblock, come in here and talk to me and we'll go around the roadblock." Whether we turn right or left or we look back and say, "We should have gone the other way," we're getting around the roadblock.[15]

Standing in the future doesn't eliminate obstacles; they just change form. In the middle of the process, Payne, with neither city nor state financial backing, was forced to sell the Olympics media rights to NBC for $456 million and was later criticized for not achieving the market price of $600 million.[16] True to his word, he stood in the future, maneuvered around the roadblock, and was not deterred by the criticism he knew would come.

In this context, Payne demonstrated an explicit awareness of the strange attractor.

> There's a sense of ownership that comes from focus, dedication, and commitment. The more people worked, the more fired they became, the more they loved their jobs. Few, if any, of us on the Olympic effort would have referred to what we were doing as our job. It was the reason we were put on this earth. Life's greatest rewards are reserved for those who bring joy to the lives of others.[17]

The Future from the Ancient Past

Kendo, the ancient tradition of Japanese fencing, was used to train Samurai warriors. Wooden swords, brandished by combatants, are employed in fierce clashes punctuated by screams, cunning feints, and powerful blows. It's all orchestrated to unsettle one's opponent as a prelude to the coup de grâce.

As with all Japanese martial arts, the teachings are concerned less with victory than with inner calm. Kendo masters require beginners to memorize these verses that are as instructive in life as in fencing:

> When you focus on winning, you will lose.
> When you focus on not losing, you will lose.
> Pay attention to your inner balance.
> Then perhaps you have a chance to win.

At first blush, these guidelines seem inconsistent with our theme. Isn't managing from the future all about winning? It is not. It is about being open to what unfolds, while feeling confident that the goal you are striving toward is inevitable. You believe that either you or someone else will succeed.

Trapeze artists understand the wisdom of the Kendo masters. When one concentrates too intently on getting safely across the chasm, the risk of falling increases. Likewise, concentrating on *not* falling increases the risks exponentially. High-wire artists train themselves to be "in the present" and feel sublimely confident that reaching the other side is a foregone conclusion. At stake is the capacity to exhibit poise during the crossing. None of this alters the laws of gravity or the physics of the human body in free fall. But approaching the wire with the right frame of mind vastly increases the odds of traversing the abyss without mishap.

We can translate this imagery into the constructs of living systems. The towers to which the high wire is attached are akin to fitness peaks, and the chasm in between is the valley of the fitness landscape. The force that draws the performer forward on the high

You're Only as Big as Your Future:
A Tale of Two Companies

In 1981, a relatively unknown executive, John F. Welch, Jr., was promoted up from the ranks and became the CEO of General Electric. Jack Welch followed on the heels of a widely respected chairman, Reginald Jones. His predecessor had generated a decade-long stream of reliable earnings. He was also widely visible as a corporate statesman at the Business Roundtable and other public platforms.

Welch did not like the looks of what he inherited. Many of GE's large oligopolistic businesses—Lighting, Turbine, Switch Gear, Aircraft Engine, and Nuclear—had been harvested aggressively and had lost their competitive edge. Other businesses—Factory Automation, Small Appliances, and Electronics and Mobile Communication—were having serious problems. Wall Street regarded GE as a conglomerate and discounted its stock accordingly. A growing chorus of opinion urged GE to spin off its businesses into single-focus companies. Separate CEOs could then give each business full concentration.

Welch did not do this. Instead, he expressed his wholehearted faith in GE's future and did what was necessary to make it work. He dedicated himself to performance excellence; he downsized GE, sold off nonperforming businesses, and unleashed the set of programs we discussed earlier—Workout, Change Acceleration, Total Quality—to reinvigorate GE's competitiveness. In addition, he shifted resources to GE Capital, which drew on the company's financial acumen and mastery at financial controls. GE Capital (which started as a financing subsidiary for purchasers of GE's expensive items, such as aircraft engines) set its sights on underserved customers, the captives of a comfortable fraternity called *merchant bankers.* Once in the fray, GE Capital gobbled up huge chunks of market share before the merchant banks woke up from a sound sleep. Today, it contributes nearly two-thirds of GE's total earnings. Its success makes the less impressive performance of the rest of GE's portfolio of secondary importance.

Jack Welch allows us to believe in GE's future. It remains unclear what will happen when Welch retires, but, as of now, GE's future carries an enormous cachet. Welch envisioned it, enrolled people in it, and manages from it.

In contrast, Sears failed to manage from the future. Ed Brennan pursued a strategy to get Sears to the future, but he failed to make that future real enough to motivate employees and investors.

Brennan faced a predicament similar to Welch's. Like GE, Sears had been a reliable performer until the early 1980s. But, as we described earlier, Brennan took many of the right steps but he did not engage in adaptive work and he did not create a compelling future. Patient investors gave him fifteen years, but, ultimately, they forced him to divest his financial businesses. At that point, Sears lost one of its top executives, Phillip Purcell, who took with him, in addition to the Dean Witter and Discover Card assets, a vision of how powerful these assets could be if merged with Morgan Stanley. Thanks in part to the longest bull market in American history (small investors flocked to Dean Witter in droves, and credit card usage and debt hit record highs), Brennan's concept of the future was ultimately realized, although in a different context than he would have wished.

Sears' unrealized future did not end with Brennan. Arthur Martinez might have exploited opportunities that lay within his grasp. One possibility would have been to dominate the home improvement segment—a category since captured by Home Depot. In 1992, Martinez's first year as CEO, Home Depot, then only one-quarter Sears' size, approached Sears for a merger.[a] Admittedly, Sears' mall stores had lost considerable ground to Wal-Mart and Kmart, but Sears' large appliances, paints, power tools, hand tools, and automobile products were the national leaders in these categories. Martinez did not take Home Depot seriously—nor create a new format for his organization to capitalize on these assets.

Another missed opportunity was the discontinuation of Sears' catalog business in 1996—a $2 billion write-off. This occurred a year and a half after e-commerce had made its appearance as a viable channel of distribution. Sears' traditional catalog format was unquestionably dated, but it occupied a niche in the American psyche as "vendor of damned near everything" (a position that Amazon.com now strives to establish). Martinez viewed the catalog in conventional terms rather than as a platform from which to establish a radically different business model.

Managing from the future is an essential act of adaptive leadership. The importance of generating a compelling future is clear when we see the consequences of its absence.

---

[a] Bernie Marcus and Arthur Blank, *Built from Scratch*, (New York: Times Book, 1999), p. 173.

wire is analogous to a strange attractor. What the trapeze artist "controls" is the psychological context for the undertaking. As this image suggests, three elements—(1) past and future fitness peaks, (2) strange attractors, and (3) a mental map for the journey—are the keys to managing from the future.

Expeditions on the Fitness Landscape

Managing from the future can shift how people see the world. They come to believe that they are playing in a larger context that has revolutionary potential. The vision of the future (i.e., the attractor), like a magnetic or gravitational field, draws many small day-to-day contributions of collective intelligence into a constellation of concerted action. "Being it now" causes belief in the future to fuel daily activity. A good way to achieve this is through "back casting."[18] Imagine a highly ambitious goal, such as turning Sears' catalog sales into an e-commerce leader. Make the goal as tangible and concrete as possible. Then describe "how it all came about" as if it had already happened. This is managing from the future.

The aspirational fitness peak must meet two criteria: (1) it must be an audacious and worthwhile goal—something not easily achieved without extraordinary effort, but worth a try; (2) it must be concrete and plausible. The goal should be compelling enough to attract followers to view the present from that vantage point. Goals that work best can be imagined visually (bringing the Olympics to Atlanta), or can be exceptionally simple (Toyota's goal of manufacturing perfection). Powerful beliefs about the future, akin to a runner's commitment to finish a marathon, recontextualize the pain one experiences in pursuing the goal. The beliefs keep you going. Also, as we have noted, the goal must resonate in people as a strange attractor. It has to tap into deep yearnings as a means of giving expression to a life purpose.

Winston Churchill's "finest hour" speech meets these two criteria and is an engaging example. Churchill did not overplay the

German threat or the theme of fear by dwelling at length on Hitler's imminent invasion of England. Nor did he waste rhetoric on the remote prospect of Hitler's unconditional surrender. Instead, he painted a picture that was both aspirational and concrete, defining not only the challenge of enduring the onslaught but who the British people would *be* as they did so. It resonated with a strange attractor in the British psyche—pride and a deep sense of history:[19]

> Hitler knows he will have to break us on this island or lose the war. If we can stand up to him, all Europe will be free, and the life of the world may move forward into broad, sunlit uplands. But if we fail, the whole world, including the United States, including all we have known and cared for, will sink into the abyss of a new Dark Age, made more sinister and perhaps more protracted by the lights of perverted science. Let us therefore brace ourselves to our duties and so bear ourselves that if the British Empire and its Commonwealth last for a thousand years, men will still say, "This was their finest hour."

Ironic, isn't it: You can't get there from here but you can get here from there. It all works because the fitness peak is a destination worth striving for. The strange attractor derives its power from feelings, passions, and aspirations, and these factors combine to alter how the present occurs. Managing from the future helps us to discover that which is latent within us and which seeks fuller expression.

Doing and Being

As the examples of the Atlanta Olympics and Churchill's speech suggest, managing from the future provides a framework for *doing* and *being*. This draws us into understanding the deeper level of mastery of this discipline. In pursuing the Olympics in Atlanta, the aspect we are calling *doing* was hosting the games. But who Payne and his team were *being* along the way was essential to their ultimate success. It echoes the earlier teachings of Kendo.

Ralph S. Larson, CEO of Johnson & Johnson, appears to run his business with this in mind: "The core values embodied in our credo might be a competitive advantage, but that is not *why* we have them. We have them because they define for us what we stand for, and we would hold them even if they became a competitive *dis*advantage in certain situations."[20]

A credo often comes from a founder or leader. But it is usually shared widely by a community and awakened when articulated in a particularly evocative manner. The acid test is that it shapes who people are *being* with one another despite the hassles and headaches of difficult undertakings. It is usually important that the credo or "future" not be localized in one person who acts as "the group's conscience." Rather, it must be continuously regenerated and shared by all members.

4. Reward Inventive Accountability

Inventive accountability is an essential discipline for self-organization and emergence. It also contributes to the productive means by which we disturb, but not direct, a living system.

On January 2–3, 1999, a blizzard closed Detroit Airport, canceling many outbound flights. Snowplows kept runways open and a good number of inbound planes were able to land throughout the evening. Most carriers—United, TWA, and American—were able to bring their planes to the gates and offload passengers with modest delays. But that is not what happened with Northwest Airlines.

In perhaps one of the greatest public relations debacles in airline history, Northwest's overwhelmed ground staff at Detroit Airport seemed paralyzed in a freeze-frame photo of inaction and indecision. Eight thousand passengers (many of whom had already spent five or six hours in the air) were literally imprisoned on thirty Northwest flights for as long as eight and a half hours without food, water, or working toilets. One passenger went into diabetic shock. Mothers ran out of formula and diapers for their babies. An irate executive used his cell phone to track down Northwest's CEO (waking him in the middle of the night) to appeal for help. Fights broke out. Passengers threatened to blow open emergency exit doors. Northwest pilots screamed at ground staff over the radio to tow the planes to the gates before all control of the situation was lost.[21]

A congressional investigation, extremely critical reports issued by the Department of Transportation, and four lawsuits all found Northwest Airlines guilty of many acts of omission. By inflexibly adhering to "procedures" for ground operations and "rules" for passenger safety, those in charge overlooked many possible solutions. They could have brought the planes near the gates and let passengers off on the tarmac; or they could have disembarked them on the airfield and bused them to the terminal. Alternatively, they could have brought service vehicles out to the planes to deliver food, water, videos, baby formula, and diapers; or, the planes could have left Detroit for nearby airfields.[22]

The Northwest story is interesting because it lacks any sign of a living system's capacity to self-organize. The principal reason was that the machine model and social engineering had squeezed all intelligence out of the "nodes" that needed to respond in an unscripted manner. Northwest's rigidity proved toxic to intelligent life.

We have all witnessed smaller versions of the Northwest incident. In the film *Five Easy Pieces,* actor Jack Nicholson orders toast from a grumpy waitress. She replies: "We don't serve toast here." Nicholson then orders a "chicken salad sandwich on toast, hold the chicken salad."[23]

From a living systems vantage point, these infuriating events are caused by a very narrow interpretation of accountability, taken to illogical extremes. Rules and procedures, unfiltered by human common sense, become as frustrating as some of the telephone menus we encounter. These incidents are enraging because all room for discretion and judgment has been leached away.

Inventive accountability was missing that night in Detroit. Had it been present, one would have seen (1) an understanding of the larger context, and (2) threshold levels of mastery permitting Northwest's Operations Center to delegate with confidence that the echelons below would do the right thing. These ingredients would have shifted Northwest from the mode of "listen and comply" to "anticipate and preempt, interpret and improvise."

Employees at Northwest Airlines lacked both the context and the mastery to do what was needed. Ironically, the system behaved like a stereotypical army—unthinking and slavish in its adherence to doctrine and the chain of command. In contrast, as we have noted, the U.S. Army has taken the managerial high ground. Facing conditions infinitely more dangerous and unpredictable than those encountered that night at Detroit Airport, the Army trains soldiers to exploit unforeseen situations for competitive advantage.

The discipline of inventive accountability is deeply ingrained in the Army's After Action Review (AAR). As is true with other disciplines, the operating context is never left to chance. Each engagement is preceded by communicating the Commander's Intent. Imagine how Northwest's employees might have coped with the events at Detroit Airport if their company's CEO, John Dasburg, had clarified his "intent" during the blizzard as an opportunity to earn customer loyalty.

As we have noted, the U.S. Army takes pains to translate every essential battle skill into a concrete task, to test it under various conditions, and to define threshold standards. Long before soldiers appear for live action at the NTC, they have been drilled to proficiency on these tasks, conditions, and standards.

In establishing inventive accountability, the first questions are:

- Where lies the greatest benefit to discretionary energy?
- Where is the need for baseline reliability?

The answers are determined by how a business elects to differentiate itself. At Federal Express, the value proposition is: "Guaranteed next-day delivery by 10:30 A.M." Improvisational skills and discretionary judgment are encouraged among the route delivery staff, but not among the information technology unit that runs Cosmos, FedEx's automatic tracking system. Neither is it encouraged among the pilots or within the logistics system at the Memphis hub. Likewise, at Sears, discretion is sought among the sales personnel who respond to customers' requests, but it is not desired in warehousing or replenishment. Shell seeks improvisation in the marketing of its downstream oil products and in discovering untapped growth opportunities, but seeks high reliability in its management of refinery productivity and safety, offshore drilling, and operation of its $6 billion natural gas liquefaction facilities.

Inventive accountability begins with philosophical acceptance that both accountability and improvisation are essential. The second level of mastery entails the work of creating and disseminating the Commander's Intent, and implementing detailed programs that ensure threshold levels of competence. The third level involves letting go— allowing the discipline to inform self-organization and to unleash the distributed intelligence that is now possible.

5. Harness Adversity by Learning from Prior Mistakes

Harnessing adversity is a discipline tailored to a world of unpredictable outcomes—a world where one can disturb, but not wholly direct, a living system. Because the unexpected—adversity—is guaranteed, this discipline is about routinely making lemons into lemon meringue pie.

Airline safety employs the discipline of harnessing adversity. Each and every airline accident, or near accident, is exhaustively analyzed, and the cause (mechanical failure or human error) is determined. The result is a worldwide air-safety record far in excess of six sigma—that is, less than three errors per million.[24] This example illustrates how combining human intention and an organizational design can help us learn from mistakes. Harnessing adversity is an essential skill in the domain near chaos. It is the means by which self-organizing units can learn from errors, curtail wheel spinning, and arrest the degenerative tendencies toward denial that can prevail in groups.

Harnessing adversity is harder than it looks. The trouble begins with the nature of human nature. Mistakes and failure can easily blow the fuses of our all-too-human psychological wiring. In the face of setbacks, it is an unfortunate truth that we tend to blame someone or something: ourselves (guilt or shame); other people (finger pointing); or the situation itself (resignation and fatalism). Conscious discipline is required to overcome these propensities. Without a concerted effort to transcend our small self, it is hard not to retreat into defensive routines. There, as we have noted, we may experience fear, denial, or other feelings that are counterproductive to the challenge we face or avoid. In this psychological Bermuda Triangle, evidence goes in but productive learning rarely comes out.

The discipline of harnessing adversity is not a way of calling a screw-up by another name. True, repositioning "failure" sounds suspiciously like letting people off the hook. But, interestingly, if it becomes safe for people to be accountable for breakdowns, that is enough. When a climate is created that allows people to face failure squarely, they almost always take appropriate corrective action. The "discipline" part deals with establishing such a climate.

Soldiers at the Army's National Training Command (NTC) know from the beginning that they are fighting an enemy far tougher than any they are likely to meet in a real battle. The 2,600-person force against which they do battle has spent at least a year on the terrain and knows every inch of it. Observer/controllers consistently remind the visiting units that their maneuvers are about learning, not winning. They harness adversity when they recontextualize failure and treat breakdowns as a source of breakthroughs. Through defeat, they have an opportunity to learn. Day after day, the Army's observer/controllers talk about the benefits of "controlled failure" until soldiers learn to embrace setbacks as a window to learning.

Harnessing Adversity:
The After Action Review[a]

The After Action Review (AAR) constitutes the heart of the National Training Command (NTC) experience. Each afternoon, the commander of the brigade that is undergoing training receives an assignment such as "Penetrate enemy defenses" or "Defend your sector against a superior force." Inside crowded command tents, thirty to forty staff officers and senior fighting unit commanders study the situation and endeavor to hammer out a winning strategy. By late afternoon, this strategy begins to filter out to 3,000 soldiers who are dispersed across many square miles of rugged terrain. Tank crews and platoons are briefed, minefields are laid, artillery and helicopters are coordinated, reconnaissance is initiated. Commencing at midnight, both friendly and "enemy" probes get under way.

By dawn, the day's battle is in full swing. The "enemy" (the 11th Armored Cavalry Regiment) is permanently stationed at Fort Irwin. It knows the terrain, behaves unpredictably, and almost always devastates the unit in training. Every aspect is recorded. Perched on mountain tops, powerful video cameras zoom in on the hot spots. An elaborate laser-based technology precisely tracks when and where each weapon is fired, and electronically disables any fighting unit that is hit. Audiotapes record communication and confusion over the voice net. By 11:00 A.M., the outcome has been decided. Within ninety minutes, the observer/controllers converge their combat team near terrain that was pivotal in their piece of the battle.

Let us take a closer look at an AAR in progress. A company team of two platoons—plus two tanks, four armored personnel carriers, and a HMMV (the modern version of a jeep)—has been pulled into a tight circle in the shade of a desert outcropping. The crews lean back against tank treads, and a flip chart hangs over the HMMV's antenna. The fighting is in its fifth day and everyone is exhausted. The observer/controller, using rocks and twigs, has recreated the units' movements on the ground. The makeshift reenactment of the maneuvers indicates that this unit was annihilated in today's battle. He asks a gunnery sergeant to come forward, position the company's armor on the sand table, and explain the unit's mission.[b]

SERGEANT: Our overall mission was to destroy the enemy at objective K-2.

OBSERVER/CONTROLLER: Why was this important? What was your tank's particular role in all this?

SERGEANT: I'm not sure.

OBSERVER/CONTROLLER: Can anyone help?

A trickle of comments gradually builds into a flood of discussion. It begins to appear that only the lieutenant in charge understood the mission. No coordination of individual tanks and vehicles had occurred, and no one had been assigned a particular sector for concentrated fire. Nor had they understood that their unit's main task was to drive the enemy column away from a weak point in the defenses and into a zone where it would be within range of more numerous tanks and artillery.

Key lessons for the next day are recorded on the flip chart. The soldiers come away with a picture of what they were involved in but could not see at the time. All have contributed to their composite grasp of the engagement, which was supplemented by video clips and hard data from the observer/controller. Day after day, particular themes are reinforced; for example, trainees are indoctrinated in the importance of understanding the big picture. They are encouraged to use their own intelligence and always place themselves in the shoes of an uncooperative enemy. They are drilled to prepare to a point where surprise will no longer surprise them. To achieve this, they must set aside hierarchy, be receptive to criticism, and work as a team.

Brigadier General W. Scott Wallace, former commander of the NTC, explains: "The After Action Review has democratized the Army. It has instilled a discipline of relentlessly questioning everything we do. Above all, it has resocialized many generations of officers to move away from a command-and-control style of leadership to one that takes advantage of distributed intelligence. It has [taught us never to] become too wedded to our script for combat and to remain versatile enough to exploit the broken plays that inevitably develop in the confusion of battle."[c]

The success of the NTC experience and the After Action Review is the result of harnessing adversity. Here is how this protocol can be applied in any organization or corporation:

253

1. Take a team of people who must work together across function and hierarchy, and immerse them in a prolonged, intense, action learning experience. Assign them a very tough project or a very tough competitor. The right conditions will unfreeze old patterns of behavior and create an opening for new understanding and behavior to take root.
2. To eliminate subjectivity and debate, collect hard data on what transpires. Let the data, not the trainers, point the finger.
3. Utilize highly skilled facilitators (the observer/controllers) who are knowledgeable about what they are observing. Use the Socratic method of questioning to evoke self-discovery. It delivers far better learning than criticism.
4. Do not make the learning experience about success or failure. Focus on how much each individual can learn. Make it safe to learn.

---

[a] R. Pascale, field notes at the National Training Command, Fort Irwin, California, Spring, 1996.
[b] Ibid.
[c] Ibid.

Learning from adversity is not confined to the Army. Albert Yu is the senior vice president of Intel's microprocessor group, the unit that delivers the continuous stream of breakthroughs that feed Intel's insatiable appetite for "the next big idea." As we know, Intel's competitive advantage stems from developing more powerful microprocessors at an extremely fast rate. Yu, who creates the climate in which this occurs, is often asked for the key to Intel's extraordinary string of successes. His answers surprise listeners. He doesn't talk about recruiting brilliant minds, stock options to retain them, or clever techniques to spark creativity. He talks about failure.

There is power in glorious failure. Failure is part of the culture of innovation. Accept it and you become stronger. The infamous Pentium flaw in 1994 was devastating and we went through all the stages of grief: denial, anger, depression, acceptance. It was incredibly painful to the company and to me personally. But we managed to become better as a result. We've beefed up the ways we validate our technology before it goes out the door. We went from having a product-engineered orientation to a consumer orientation. The emergency broke down barriers and generated superb teamwork. We can now respond to any crisis ten times faster than before.[25]

Wal-Mart's legendary Sam Walton had a similar philosophy. When briefed on the Army's After Action Review, he noted that Wal-Mart had been involved in a similar process for years. Executives and store managers fly into Bentonville, Arkansas, every Saturday to sift through results of real-time data collected from stores throughout the country. These intensely real and hands-on sessions explore what's working and what isn't. Asked why Wal-Mart was so successful, Sam Walton answered, "We learned from failure faster than the other guy."[26]

Harnessing adversity has something in common with kayaking in white-water rapids. The most counterintuitive part of navigating through rapids is to resist a tendency to go slowly to avoid mistakes. When you go slowly, you sacrifice your capacity to maneuver. Your velocity must match the current. The key is to keep paddling, right yourself when you capsize (hopefully, you'll be wiser the next time), and continue. In the white water of today's competition, moving on and learning as you go is the best strategy. Learning doesn't require enormous amounts of time.

From "Fail-Safe" to "Safe to Fail"

Despite the professed desire, in many companies, for "discontinuous" improvements in growth rate, quality, cost, or cycle time, these aims are usually compromised by an unspoken precondition: no breakdowns. Goals should be reached by secure means with no untoward surprises. The problem with such preconditions is that authentic breakthroughs rarely occur without setbacks along the way. In seeking an authentic breakthrough, it is essential to strip away the "fail-safe" mechanisms and make it "safe to fail."

The word *breakdown* is used here, instead of *problem,* to signal the need for a particular understanding of the unsettling developments that accompany discontinuous change. When problems emerge, people attempt to eliminate them quickly. Often, as noted earlier, they look for someone to blame. Significantly, organizations often gain more insight from the *process* of reaching a goal than from achieving it. This is the learning-through-adversity model. Rather than suppressing and avoiding breakdowns, it is important to regard them as a desirable means of revealing previously hidden assumptions or patterns of behavior that must be altered to facilitate the quantum change sought.

"Breakdowns" by Design

Let's look at some situations in which breakdowns are part of established practice. Japanese manufacturing plants employ several devices that generate breakdowns—for example, they will stop an entire assembly line when any operator spots any defect. This practice, of course, ensures that there is no way to hide from mistakes, and that is precisely the point. From one vantage point, it seems extreme: one defect can cost thousands of units of lost production as an entire assembly line grinds to a halt. Why not keep the line moving and address deficiencies later? The answer in the Japanese plants confirms what we have been saying: Dramatizing breakdowns is the best way to eradicate the underlying cause.

Performance "Wedgies"

Any discipline worthy of the name evokes mindfulness, attention, and learning. The discipline of harnessing adversity benefits from protocols that bring adversity to our immediate attention. We call them "Performance Wedgies."[27]

When Cemex, the Mexican cement company described earlier, offers a 10 percent discount on each cubic meter of cement not delivered within twenty minutes of its scheduled time slot, it is not only standing behind its standard of service but inviting customers to monitor that standard. When Domino's Pizza offered a free pizza if an order was not delivered within thirty minutes, it was doing the same.

Keeping an organization true to its customer commitments is a great way to evoke learning. Bain and Company, a consulting firm, has documented that U.S. corporations, on average, lose half of their customers every five years. This statistic shocks most people. Yet, hard data on customer defections, like hard data on employee attrition, are readily available to anyone who chooses to research them. That so few organizations do so calls attention to the pervasive mechanisms of denial, which effectively suppress adversity. That is why this discipline is so necessary.

The first level of harnessing adversity recontextualizes failure as a source of learning. This usually leads us to examine old norms and procedures that have unreasonably punished mistakes and foreclosed access to their instructive kernel.

The second level of mastery arises when mechanisms are put in place that amplify mistakes into "show stoppers" and establish protocols (like AAR) to harvest learning. The U.S. Army, Toyota, Domino's Pizza, Cemex, and Intel are examples. All exploit adversity and create a constructive climate for learning.

The third level of mastery—most evident at Toyota, Intel, and the Army's National Training Center—builds in failure as part of the design. Accepting the premise of "Adversity is life's best teacher" prepares us to welcome difficult challenges *because* of the failures that will be experienced.

6. Foster Relentless Discomfort

Relentless discomfort supports all four of the bedrock principles of living systems. Yet it evokes troubling connotations: reengineering, which strips away 50 percent of the headcount and leaves one survivor to do the work of two; stretch targets, which allow managers to impose impossible goals with a straight face; and, at its worst, relentless discomfort, which gives tyranny a respectable face. Sunbeam's former CEO, Al Dunlop, browbeat, humiliated, and exploited an organization's members in the name of "tough love."

The efforts by Sears, Shell, and the U.S. Army to interject relentless discomfort into their organizations are very different from these examples. They are not designed to induce fear. Relentless discomfort occurs as a gnawing question within each employee: "Can I help us do better?" It is a quest, not an admonition.

Relentless discomfort is a discipline that arrests the drift of living systems toward self-confirmation and homeostasis. In this respect, it supports all of the four bedrock principles we have discussed. It entails much more than setting unrealistic targets that drive employees to despair, cynicism, and burnout. At the core of the matter, relentless discomfort is the aspiration for peak performance. It is most readily seen among Olympic athletes who have an internalized passion for self improvement. Nike ads once phrased it well: There is no finish line.

The After Action Review (AAR) is based on the notion that people can improve—and, in most cases, improve dramatically—in everything they do. Practices continually stretch an organization's capabilities and focus attention on unresolved questions rather than comforting answers. The Army's observer/controllers continually reinforce the transferability of After Action Reviews to life beyond the NTC. After a while, the protocol tends to get under the skin. Soldiers carry it back to their home bases—and their homes. The AAR helps every level of the organization see that just "meeting acceptable levels of performance" is insufficient for sustained vitality. Those who internalize this discipline live with high levels of creative tension and relish it.

Review *Fortune*'s list of America's most admired companies and you will find a strong correspondence with the discipline of relentless discomfort. Johnson & Johnson (notwithstanding its earlier mentioned stumbles with the stent) and General Electric are two examples. Their products and customers are dissimilar, but both organizations employ teams of traveling auditors who visit and study a business unit for several months at a time. They ask penetrating questions, go far beyond the predictable matters of financial records and controls, and evoke deep-seated self-questioning at all levels. Recipients of these visits testify to the intensity of the experience—and the importance of the process to their performance culture. Striving becomes an internalized frame of mind.

Relentless Innovation at Capital One

Capital One is one of the great success stories of recent years. Originally the financial services division of a small Virginia bank, it spun off as a public company in the early 1990s. Focusing its energies on credit cards, it expanded from 1.5 million to 17 million cardholders and established a presence in 11 percent of American households between 1992 and 1998. Along the way, it has accrued $17 billion in managed assets; it ranks among the top ten credit card issuers in the United States; and it achieves returns of close to 25 percent on equity.[28]

Capital One is a story of self-organization. It also takes the discipline of relentless discomfort very seriously. The firm has carved out its niche by using powerful information technology and highly agile teams of professionals to identify and mass-market credit offers to customers in a sophisticated way. At the cutting edge of this strategy is its ability to try, on a daily basis, dozens of what it calls "experiments."

An "experiment" is a market probe, defined by demographics, pricing, and initial interest rates. It is limited in extent and expense. Using complex algorithms, Capital One quickly determines the winners and eliminates the rest.

Dartmouth's Phillip Anderson, associate professor at the Amos Tuck School of Business, describes the competition among ideas at Capital One as "Darwinian." He writes: "The five thousand credit card offers (and other financing packages) that Capital One markets today prevailed in the intense competition for attention and resources. Capital One is poised at the edge of chaos in the sweet spot where the proliferation of experiments produces 99 failures in 100, some modest winners, a few large wins, and the occasional stupendous revenue-generating concept."[29] One such success was the company's foray into wireless communications. It has become the largest direct marketer of cellular phone service in the United States.

At the foundation of Capital One's success is its system of relentless discomfort:

- Associates are given mandates or "charters to innovate." Their jobs are to champion ideas. In fact, they are encouraged to ignore everyone and everything that will distract them from their current project.

- Everyone is responsible if an error occurs or a problem arises. No one is allowed to blame anyone else (i.e., the usual complaint— "So and so dropped the ball"—is unacceptable). An important aspect of job performance is the shared responsibility when mistakes are made or something goes wrong.

- Organization members see themselves more as entrepreneurs working to identify or satisfy customers than as workers within a chain of command. George Overholser, vice president of new business, notes: "It's scary. Senior managers have little idea of what people are doing day to day. They report to the marketplace."[30]

- Capital One combines Action Labs with musical chairs. Teams focus on projects, and management continuously shuffles the teams. Members are rotated to foster cross-pollination. Shuffling is certain when one group generates too many look-alike proposals.

- Requisite Variety is made explicit through arrangements that bring the outside in and the inside out. A network of venture capital firms has been cultivated to spot business ideas that

Capital One's direct marketing skills can take to market. Internal employees may move outside for temporary assignment on such ventures.

- The most important performance measure is the predicted and realized net present value of a customer over his or her lifetime. But in addition, twice each year, individuals are assessed on their social competencies—enrollment skills, recruiting success rate, project management. Bonuses are tied to ratings on what management calls the "behavioral anchors."

- Capital One invests at least 20 percent of senior management's time in recruiting. The firm is nakedly elitist. Recruiting targets the top-ranked MBAs from the best business schools, and undergraduates with near 4.0 averages and SAT scores over 700 in math (out of a possible 800).[31]

- Capital One navigates close to the shadow side of this discipline. Like others (e.g., Intel, Toyota, General Electric, Goldman Sachs, and Honda), the intensity is not for everyone. Relentless discomfort can use people up.

The Big Square

The most important symbol of Capital One's pursuit of relentless discomfort is its visual image. "Our senior managers have spent years popularizing something called the 'big square,'" states Overholser. "It is an antidote to the evils of 'monovariabilitus.' People walk around with 'big square' buttons pinned to their shirts."[32]

The "big square" is the icon of relentless discomfort. Its sides are defined by four competing desires: *economics, customer satisfaction, internal people satisfaction,* and *growth.* Emphasis on each dimension is depicted as the distance of each of the quadrilateral's respective corners from the center. "At any given time," says Overholser, "we want to make sure we see a square. If it stops being shaped like a square, we're willing to retreat on one dimension in order to restore the balance."[33]

■ ■

The first step in a journey toward relentless discomfort begins with ambitious goals. The idea is: Run a marathon in half-mile sprints and the sprints can be exhilarating. The second level of mastery embraces the "big square"—a system of protocols and rewards that pushes the boundaries but also allows the center to hold. As with each of the disciplines, the third level of mastery is personal in nature. Relentless discomfort occurs as an internalized state of alertness, a quest for learning and excellence.

The six disciplines described thus far have the advantage of face validity; they resonate with common sense. ("Managing from the Future" is perhaps the biggest stretch and the most taxing to the executive imagination.) We have saved the hardest for last. Establishing an authentic basis for reciprocity between an organization and its members is the most demanding discipline of all.

CHAPTER 13

RECIPROCITY: BRINGING LIFE TO ORGANIZATIONS AND ORGANIZATIONS TO LIFE

Reciprocity is the most important discipline, the hardest to codify, and the most difficult to establish. It is essential to sustained collaborative work. Reciprocity provides the bonds that enable the distributed intelligence within a living system to cleave together for the common good. The stronger the linkages, the more capable the organism of adaptive work.

In nature, reciprocal relationships are common. Chapter 5 noted the manner in which "new destinations" arise through surprising symbiotic arrangements between species. Reciprocity is also an essential requirement within species that collaborate to live or hunt (ants, bees, termites, lions, hyenas, and so forth). The Capuchin "organ grinder" monkey of South America occasionally hunts for smaller mammals and does so in groups. Only one monkey typically captures the prey, but all in the troop share the meat together. Particularly relevant to our topic, recent studies have shown that reciprocity is situationally determined—influenced by whether the monkeys have to work together to obtain food. Nature's rule seems to be: What is gained as a group must be shared by the group. Capuchins that obtained food on their own did not share it with their comrades.[1]

The Dilemma of Reciprocity

The aim of reciprocity is to ensure that an organization's members receive benefits commensurate with their contributions. Without this quid pro quo, it is difficult to sustain members' commitment over time. Reciprocal arrangements must be robust enough to thrive during periods of stress and disequilibrium. This is especially relevant to businesses that face a turbulent environment and, as a result, encounter expectations of employer and employee that are very much in flux. These stresses arise from the convergence of at least five competing considerations.

1. Companies must be agile to survive. The ideal employment arrangement must be flexible enough to avoid being saddled with inappropriate skills or an onerous cost structure.
2. Notwithstanding their reluctance to make long-term commitments, companies today are asking more of the employees on their payrolls. The philosophy parallels that of professional sports teams: "We may trade you tomorrow, but we expect you to play your heart out today."
3. Following two decades of downsizing, workers are wary. They are less willing to entrust their fate to the vagaries of any single enterprise.
4. The nature of knowledge-work rebalances power. Employees are increasingly the source of competitiveness in knowledge-intensive

fields. When they leave a company, they can take hard-to-replace expertise and intellectual property with them.

5. Ownership is extending into the ranks. Employee stock ownership plans (ESOPs), 401(k)s, stock options, and union pension funds are increasingly available to a wide cross-section of employees. Such measures redistribute wealth to some degree, but, most importantly, they motivate employees to more closely scrutinize management's actions.

This chapter explores these aspects of reciprocity. Organizations must craft their own unique arrangements. With examples from five very different organizations—Southwest Airlines, United Airlines, Toyota, Intel, and Hewlett-Packard—we will demonstrate how a different yet disciplined approach to reciprocity reconciles high levels of employee contribution and commitment with the organizational demands for adaptive work.

The Unfolding Drama

The drama of reciprocity involves three protagonists: (1) the organization, (2) the individual, and (3) society. Corporations see themselves as doing what they must to survive and thrive. They juggle their need for a flexible cost structure (payroll) with the opposing requirement that they tap into, and reward, the commitment, intelligence, and loyalty of employees.

At the same time, survivors of corporate downsizing have gradually come to terms with their newfound independence and freedom. They have personally experienced (or observed) that trusting any organization too much can result in betrayal, separation, disorientation, and loss of self-esteem and social identity. Consequently, a large percentage of today's workforce defines a "career" as a string of jobs with different employers.

The starting point for crafting an authentic code of reciprocity is to not leave employees' expectations to chance. From the employees' vantage point, reciprocity must address five issues. According to former Stanford Business School lecturer, James C. Collins, these are: "freedom and self-direction *in* your work, purpose and contribution *through* your work, and wealth creation *by* your work."[2] Reciprocity must, as well, provide organizations with the flexibility they need. The dynamic models of living systems are useful here because Nature is a master at the juggling act.

As in most compelling dramas, the protagonists are entangled with one another in complicated ways. This makes the task of evolving a workable code of reciprocity more difficult. Organizations need to powerfully knit people together to achieve excellence. In an era of downsizing, these collective activities are more intense than ever: tight deadlines, significant competitive consequences from failure, heightened aspirations for performance. The modern corporation must master the art of "marrying" individuals to accomplish common goals. Consistent with this matrimonial imagery, a great deal of interpersonal trust, investment of self, shared meaning, and commitment is needed to pull it off. Society provides a backdrop in which these challenges are contextualized.

The orchestration of serial "marriages" to accomplish work does not spare the contemporary corporation from other kinds of competitive threats. For example, even the most flexible workforce arrangements and dedicated collective effort cannot overcome some disadvantages in technology or cost position. Periodically, this necessitates placing corporate survival ahead of individual employment continuity. The successful business must, therefore, master the art of arranging marriages of talent for the purpose of accomplishing complex tasks, but also muster the will to decree mass "divorces" (layoffs).

The role of the third element, society, is an essential piece of the puzzle. It sets the context for appropriate levels of reciprocity. Cultural norms suppress or dignify human expectations and organizational ambitions. To date, societal awareness does not acknowledge the grief and loss associated with work life as among the most painful of human experiences, ranking alongside divorce and the death of a loved one.

These issues are exacerbated in the United States. Ray Oldenburg, author of *The Great Good Place,* asserts that a healthy and balanced social identity has historically relied on three factors: family, work, and "a Third Place." The Third Place is the pub in England, the sidewalk café and bistro in France, the *tapas* bar in Spain, the coffee bar in Italy and Austria, and the *biergarten* in Germany. In Japan, it is a private after-hours bar or a cocktail club.[3]

The essential requirements of the Third Place are: (1) it is neutral ground, (2) rank is forgotten, (3) conversation with everyone is the central source of entertainment (not music or video games), (4) it is frequented by a core group of regulars, and (5) it fosters playful interpersonal exchanges.[4] (The U.S. television series "Cheers" depicted just such an institution.) The Third Place provides novelty, perspective on life, a "spiritual tonic" (in Oldenburg's words), and friends by the "set," which emphasizes socializing with an open and inclusive group instead of the clique one walks in with.

The problem in the United States is that the Third Place—once provided by the church, community groups, and the local tavern—has largely vanished. Indeed, this is often what Europeans residing in the United States miss most in their new surroundings. Oldenburg concludes: "Without the Third Place, a society fails to nourish the kinds of relationships and the diversity of human contact that are essential to a psychologically balanced life."[5] And here is the rub: For most North Americans, not only is there no Third Place, but family and community have lost potency as counterweights to life during the past four decades. Meanwhile, work consumes more of us than ever before. The result: a void. This exacerbates the dilemmas confronted by the corporation and the individual, and intensifies the quest for reciprocity.

Complicating matters, wherever societal norms do exist, they are unsupportive. When disaster strikes, we are apt to be told (or recite to ourselves) unhelpful clichés such as: "Hey, it's only a job," or "It happens to everyone," or "Work should not have become so impor- tant to your life." Such self-talk is better at repressing feelings than at permitting a grieving process that creates emotional space for subsequent healing. Societal awareness must shift, as it has in recent years around such previously silenced subjects as alcoholism and child abuse, so that the struggle to deal with disruptions in work is legitimized. Such a shift might serve to facilitate our quest for inner reciprocity, the ultimate source of spiritual and emotional development.

Tapping the Volunteer in Each of Us

We have noted that reciprocity is widespread in Nature. It has been a central factor in every civilization, and it occurs routinely among mammals, especially primates such as monkeys, baboons, chimpanzees, and gorillas. Reciprocity ensures that favors get returned and social ob- ligations are repaid.

Reciprocity is especially important when what is exchanged is intangible or hard to quantify—trust, diligence, commitment, cre- ativity. We can take our pound of flesh. But an ounce of commit- ment or original thinking is hard to extract by coercion. It must be volunteered.

Peter Drucker observed first that most dedicated people are ulti- mately "volunteers," even when they are paid for their labors.[6] Most of us exercise some choice over where we work and what direction our life will take. But we also determine how much of us shows up each day. In this respect, we are all "volunteers." As intelligent nodes in a living system, we alone determine how much of ourselves we will invest in the task at hand. Reciprocity, first among all other dis- ciplines, is important because it defines the conditions under which we are willing to give an organization our best.

Xerox PARC's John Sealy Brown has observed that enthusiasm and commitment cannot be compelled. The employee, he states, "chooses to opt in—to voluntarily commit to his job and colleagues."[7] Stan- ford's Jeff Pfeffer has documented that high-performing organizations have sophisticated strategies of reciprocity that reward commitment, excellence, integrity, and teamwork. These enterprises do so because they understand that the retention of good people and their contributions is a key success factor.[8] The organizations named in *Fortune*'s annual survey of the "100 Best Companies to Work For" have all evolved a code of reciprocity, and, not coincidentally, all surpass their peer companies by 10 percent in earnings: 27 percent as compared to the norm of 17 percent.[9]

To summarize, effective collective work requires selecting talent (which is expensive and time-consuming), binding individuals to the corporation and to one another (which requires socialization), and linking of individuals and teams into a network that knows "what to do and how to make things happen." Almost all teamwork worthy of the name requires shared purpose and the evolution of effective group norms. Without these essential ingredients, it is difficult to smooth the rough edges of individuality to achieve a common purpose. This is not an "add water and mix" proposition.

Reciprocity of the Past and Future

Once upon a time, corporations were like ocean liners. Anyone fortunate enough to secure a berth cruised through a career and disembarked at retirement age. In return for loyalty, sacrifice, and tolerating the idiosyncrasies of a difficult boss, employees at Sears, Shell, and the U.S. Army, among other organizations, enjoyed implicit, if not explicit, job security.

That was then. Today, organizations and their members are reluctant to take vows for life. William H. Whyte's best-seller, *The Organization Man* (1956), reminds us of just how much things have changed. Describing the code of reciprocity in the 1950s, Whyte portrays arrangements so quaint as to evoke incredulity in today's context:[10]

> The fundamental premise of the new model executive is . . . simply, that the goals of the individual and the goals of the organization will work out to be one and the same. The young men have no cynicism about the "system," and very little skepticism. . . . They have an implicit faith that

The Organization will be as interested in making use of their best qualities as they are themselves, and thus, with equanimity, they can trust the
resolution of their destiny to The Organization. . . . The average young
man cherishes the idea that his relationship with The Organization is to
be for keeps.

Times have indeed changed, but the data are mixed as to precisely
how. True, a wave of restructurings and downsizings starting in the
1980s displaced tens of millions of U.S. employees. The financial
community applauded the streamlining, but not for long. Media coverage brought more scrutiny to management's decisions and results—
increasingly, the topic of front-page news. A *Wall Street Journal* study
of downsized companies found that, within three years, two-thirds
lagged their peers in market valuation by 20 to 50 percent. Only
slightly more than half realized improvement in the bottom line.[11] In
retrospect, for many firms, downsizing turned out to be a short-term
solution at best.

Sears provides a case in point. In the vanguard of the downsizers,
Brennan laid off 50,000 workers. Afterward, return on equity actually declined and further momentum was lost.[12] AT&T's downsizing, from 1986 to 1996, eliminated 120,000 jobs—along with
$15 billion in earnings.[13] Kodak implemented six downsizing ini-
tiatives between 1982 and 1996. Its cumulative loss was 15,000
jobs and $2.5 billion in write-offs. During this time, Kodak's rev-
enues remained unchanged, its profits were halved, and its stock
languished.[14]

These results were not lost on an increasingly aware—and wary—
workforce. Corporate America seemed to be enacting a "New Deal,"
the tenets of which seemed to be:[15]

- We don't know how long we'll be in business.
- We can't promise we will not be bought by another company.
- We can't promise you promotions or regular salary increases.
- We can't promise you employment until retirement age.
- We can't promise you a pension.

- We know we can't expect your unwavering loyalty, and we aren't sure we want it.

Insofar as there ever was an employment contract, the downsizing by blue-chip companies, together with such implied terms and conditions, signaled all bets were off. It was every person for himself or herself. No longer would savvy employees be as likely to trust their fate to the potentially fickle loyalties and errant judgments of industry leaders.

For many persons displaced from the traditional workforce, the answer was self-employment. Since 1980, the number of self-employed workers in the United States has increased tenfold to 16 percent of the U.S. workforce, or 25 million people.[16] Many so-called "temporary employees" work continuously, but are characterized as "temps" so that the employer can avoid the moral and financial responsibility of full-time hires. A sizable number of these individuals work from their home or car and are tied to the workplace by telephone and modem. The number of nontraditional workers has increased 240 percent in the past ten years. Manpower (the nation's largest temporary agency) has an army of 600,000 persons on its rolls.[17] Outsourcing constitutes a staggering $100 billion industry today. Over 90 percent of corporations outsource at least one service.[18] However describing oneself as "a temp" or "self-employed" is generally not greeted with the reverence that is encountered from association with an established institution.

Alongside these rather sobering trends is some good news. Over the past two decades, the United States has experienced its longest economic boom in history, and the net effect of these changes is, for the most part, positive. Between 1980 and 1995, the United States, with a smaller employment pool than the European Union (EU), created 26 million new jobs versus the EU's 9 million. As of this writing, unemployment in the United States is 4.5 percent; in Europe, it's 11 percent.

These findings suggest that the new flexibility of both employers and employees, while it has taken a social and psychological toll, has fostered competitiveness, low unemployment rates, and economic resilience. Unnecessary hardship may have wreaked havoc when the

pendulum swung too far. But the statistics do not suggest an apoca-
lypse. The challenge of reciprocity is therefore not so much one of re-
dressing massive social dislocations as it is one of tailoring specific
relationships to balance both employers' and employees' needs.

"Reciprocity": A Solution
Looking for a Problem?

If the majority are better off, if employers are more agile and workers are appropriately wary, why not leave well enough alone? This
question turns on how much we expect from the nodes of intelligence. If most of the challenges to be faced are operational in nature
(that is, improving an already known formula), we could stop here.
But, as we have noted, a great many of the challenges facing organizations are adaptive. In this arena, the bonds between company and
employee need to be strengthened considerably to unleash the collective, untapped intelligence, and to marshal the determination necessary to shift performance to the next level.

When Peter Drucker coined the term "knowledge worker," he
was referring to an elite cadre of professionals: engineers, managers,
software programmers, and so forth.[19] Even within this narrow definition, knowledge workers, who deal primarily with the generation
and dissemination of ideas and information, constitute between 35
and 40 percent of all employees.[20] Furthermore, these workers, while
not the upper class, are increasingly becoming the most influential
"class" (although paychecks do not always reflect their dispropor-
tionate contribution to wealth creation!). It is probably safe to assert
that knowledge workers generated roughly two-thirds of the wealth
created over the past ten years, and this percentage is increasing.

From a living systems perspective, *all* workers are knowledge workers—a concept well understood at Nissan and Toyota.[21] And if we do
not think of soldiers as knowledge workers, the Army believes otherwise. Most modern-day warriors operate expensive and technically

sophisticated equipment, and they do so in life-threatening circumstances. As described earlier, they are expected to self-organize to use their tools and talents. That's why the Army invests in building strong reciprocal relationships, not just technical training. The Army learned in Vietnam that loving relations (not patriotism) evoke trust, courage, and commitment.[22]

Sears learned to regard its sales personnel (many are part-timers and only half have high school diplomas) as knowledge workers. Their capacity to please and to improvise on-the-spot was essential for reversing the tide of customer defections. And when *Industry Week* tracked the best manufacturing plants in the United States for the period from 1991 to 1996, it confirmed: "An open, nurturing trust-based relationship is necessary to light the motivational fire and unleash the long-stifled knowledge and potential of the manufacturing workforce."[23]

There is a delicious irony here. Karl Marx advocated that workers should own the means of production. His prophecy has come to pass. And it all has occurred under the blazing endorsement of knowledge-based capitalism in which the means of production is between our ears.

Reciprocity in the Skies

If we think of knowledge-intensive businesses, the airline industry is not one that immediately comes to mind. Yet, for decades, upstart Southwest Airlines has adapted the opposite view: It regards all of its employees—not just pilots and machinists—as knowledge workers, and it challenges them to contribute to its unique form of differentiation. For ramp-service personnel and flight attendants, that contribution ranges from pitching in to clean an aircraft—or handling baggage during tight turnarounds—to having fun.

Treating work as play is one of the foundational tenets of the enterprise. Southwest is renowned for flight attendants who surprise passengers by popping out of overhead storage bins, singing the flight safety announcement to the tune of the William Tell Overture, making outrageous in-flight announcements such as asking that all plastic cups be passed toward the aisle so they can be reused for the next passengers, or requesting those who wish to smoke to use the lounge on the starboard wing where they will be entertained by "Gone With the Wind."[24]

Beneath the hijinks is, of course, a highly disciplined operating system that gives Southwest a cost structure 25 percent below the industry standard (7.0 cents/seat mile vs. 9.5 cents industry average). Southwest flies 2,443 passengers per employee each year; the industry norm is just over 1,000.

Southwest realizes that it must compensate for what it chooses *not* to offer (including meals and advance seat reservations). It does so through its low-cost airfares and its committed, friendly service. Southwest screens 150,000 applications a year to hire 5,000 employees. (Statistically, it is easier to get into Harvard!). Applicants must submit ten references, perform impromptu skits, and dazzle a dozen interviewers. The firm looks for extroverts, good team players, and individuals with flexibility and resilience. Believing that honesty and commitment are, figuratively speaking, "in the genes," Southwest hires couples and family members. All employees own stock.[25]

Executives—particularly CEO Herb Kelleher—are down-to-earth and wholly accessible. Kelleher actually tries to know each employee by name. Steve Lewins, a security analyst who has been following Kelleher since Southwest began flying in 1971, states: "I think Herb is brilliant, charming, cunning, and tough. He is the sort of manager who will stay out with a mechanic in some bar until four o'clock in the morning to find out what is going on. And then he will fix whatever is wrong."[26]

All this begins to capture how Southwest enacts reciprocity: accessible executives, careful selection of staff, expectations that each employee will contribute in unique ways above and beyond the job description, shared ownership, and an unambiguous message to people that they matter. Unlike most companies, Southwest puts employees first, customers second, and shareholders third; its argument is: If the employees are happy, everything else follows. This is the reverse order of most other companies' priorities.

Friendlier Skies

United Airlines has paid close attention to the Southwest model. In 1994, after years of strikes, turmoil, losses, and customer dissatisfaction, United's employees bought their company for $4.9 billion. Wall Street analysts, union leaders, and many rank-and-file workers were skeptical about the deal. It was predicated on the exit of unpopular Chairman and CEO Stephen Wolfe and the willingness of a former Chrysler Vice Chairman, Gerald Greenwald, to become the new CEO.[27]

Employees traded an average of 15 percent in pay cuts for 55 percent of the company and three of its board seats. With these new terms, a foundation was in place that could incent union members to abandon their adversarial stance and to identify with the success of the company.[28]

For a variety of reasons, a new spirit took hold. The productivity of United's 83,000 employees soared, grievances plunged, and the airline began to carve out big bites of market share from its number-two rival, American, and its number-three rival, Delta. Today, United is indisputably the nation's largest, and frequently its most profitable, airline. It outperforms the majors in almost all areas, including earnings per employee, growth, and stock valuation.[29]

It took much more than the deal structure to revitalize this living system. Gerald Greenwald was the quintessential "adaptive leader." He immediately turned to employees to help pilot the way forward. He created dozens of Action Labs, with staff from every tier of the organization. These teams addressed everything from cash management to reducing sick leave. The common denominators of these and other actions were: collaboration, shared gains, and give-and-take. These are cornerstones of reciprocity.[30]

Investors feared that the United employees would not step up to the hard decisions. Not so. In 1995, United implemented electronic ticketing without a hitch, beating American to the punch despite that airline's history of leadership in information technology. When a pilot shortage developed, the pilots' union agreed to fly longer hours rather than cancel flights. "If we openly talk about our interests and try to solve problems, we're going to have an advantage over other companies," says one Boeing 727 captain. One Action Lab, studying United's Salt Lake City base, recommended hiring extra workers to help unload skis in the winter. With union ramp workers paid $38 an hour for overtime, the team recommended "temps" at $7 per hour.[31]

For years, aircraft cleaners had been asking that ashtrays be soldered shut. (Smoking is no longer allowed.) Susan Chandler reports that, one day, as part of the new reciprocity, "James Goodwin, then United's president [and CEO since Greenwald's retirement], was working alongside baggage handlers and cleaning crews—an activity he engages in once a month. On this occasion, he had to dig a big hunk of wet chewing tobacco out of an ashtray with his fingers. The lids got soldered pronto."[32]

An Action Lab chartered to increase "employee dependability" sought to reduce no-shows and sick time. One recommendation was that pilots and flight attendants be able to swap job assignments with colleagues. In addition, they proposed that, twice a year, twenty-five employees (picked at random from the pool of those with six months of perfect attendance) win $25,000 or a Jeep Cherokee. Result: From March to December in the first year of the program, 32,000 employees—40 percent of the workforce—had perfect attendance. Sick time and absenteeism were down 17 percent.[33]

In keeping with the new reciprocity, Greenwald astonished observers when he involved employees in all deliberations concerning a proposed acquisition of USAir. "Instead of the usual secrecy surrounding merger talks," states one industry observer, "Greenwald, who sports his company ID on a chain around his neck like everybody else, sought union leaders' input. They recounted the disastrous record of most airline mergers, mostly due to combining union seniority lists. Greenwald listened intently—and killed the bid."[34] Union members were impressed by their inclusion as well as the result. With Greenwald's retirement, the question remained—as it does with all fragile systems—whether top management would continue to listen to the rank and file with the same level of commitment.

Both United and Southwest raise the issue of employee ownership as an essential component of the new reciprocity. In this context, "ownership" needs to be reconsidered in fresh ways. Even traditional forms of ownership are changing. Microsoft, worth $88 billion, has been entirely self-financing throughout its history. Bill Gates formed the corporation for the primary purpose of giving employees stock.[35] As of December 1999, more than $2 trillion of union retirement funds were invested in America's corporations.[36] Increasingly, pension-fund managers assert their authority when companies chronically underperform. In between these two examples, we find the widespread use of 401(k)s and other employee stock programs that extend the notion of ownership.

Regarding organizations as living entities helps us think about less conventional definitions of "ownership." We don't ignore the fact that corporations also have financial responsibilities and shareholders who formally own the economic assets of the enterprise. But *all* living things also seek to perpetuate their own survival. It is well documented that organizational members, routinely and in a self-interested fashion, interpret management's directives in an attempt to exercise more influence over matters that concern them directly. Employees, as "owners in residence," are the bees in the hive of complexity. They simultaneously pay their dues to keep the beekeeper happy, and dedicate energy to matters that affect their own interests. Profits and returns are the by-products of how well (or how poorly) the organization mediates among *all* its stakeholders, including the "owners-in-residence."

Reciprocity and the Factory of the Future

Dave Marsing—plant manager of Intel's $2 billion fabrication plant ("the Fab") near Albuquerque—resides at the epicenter of one of the most intense jobs in American industry and the largest semiconductor facility on earth. Characterizing himself as a "transforming virus," Marsing's calm demeanor seems, at first, incongruous, given the business risks his organization faces each day.[37] A single mistake on just one eight-inch silicon wafer (covered with hundreds of microprocessors) costs Intel a quarter of a million dollars, and thousands flow down the line every day. Fail to install a component on an automotive assembly line and you pick up the discrepancy at the final repair station. In the Fab, one fleck of dust, one machine slightly out of kilter, one moment of worker inattention, and you toss out the wafer. If a car is ruined on the assembly line (which never happens), it costs about $15,000; a wafer costs fifteen times that! Yet Marsing goes through routine production and stressful new-product launches with barely a raised voice.[38]

Intel's Fab (and similar operations in this and other industries) is a magnet for knowledge workers. Marsing is a master at tapping their potential. On the art and science of reciprocity, he reflects:

> If the goal is to maximize profits, it seems obvious to me that the best way to get there is to have happy people who are motivated to work. And the way you do that is to bring together different types of people, allow them to be themselves, get them behind the larger corporate vision, and then give them room to create. Above all, if you want breakthrough thinking and innovation—and you definitely do in this business, to survive—then you have to cultivate those aspects of each employee's personality. Imagine if you could build a company that was capable of learning from all its experiences, as well as from other companies' experiences. What you'd get is a new kind of asset: corporate wisdom. Now, combine that with the kind of compassion that accepts employees for who they really are, that motivates them to reach their potential, and you'd have something truly extraordinary. Just think what a company like Intel, with 35,000 highly intelligent people, could do if it ever reached that combination.[39]

As we noted earlier, when employees join your enterprise, they volunteer to work for you. They volunteer *again* (each day) to give that extra ounce of energy and commitment that provides your company with a competitive edge. Marsing's brand of reciprocity is based on his conviction that what causes employees to "volunteer" is that the work generates intrinsic satisfaction. He also grasps that part of the deal is that employees understand where the enterprise is going, and they have some say in shaping its destiny.

World's Best Industrial Research Lab

Few examples better illustrate the linkage between reciprocity and the renewal of a living system than the transformation of Hewlett-Packard Laboratories (HP Labs). Headquartered in Palo Alto, California, this institution arguably resides in one of the world's most taxing environments in terms of employee retention and motivation. Hewlett-Packard competes for talent in a region with a voracious appetite for IQ points. Add to this a siren call of abundant venture capital chasing ideas and would-be entrepreneurs, and one begins to fathom why a robust code of reciprocity is essential to sustained success.

Joel Birnbaum, the director of HP Labs and Senior Vice President of R&D, surveyed his operations in 1993 and was troubled by what he saw. Birnbaum was no stranger to high-powered research facilities.[40] In the 1980s, he had been a leading light at IBM's laboratories and was widely regarded as the pioneer of R.I.S.C. architecture. At HP, his remarkable vision had, with Lew Platt, turned HP's computer business into a powerhouse. But, based on a recent employee survey, very little collaboration was occurring across the technology divisions of HP Labs, and communication within the silos was primarily vertical. There were no consistent or shared measures of output across the silos. This made the allocation of resources and the promotions and rewards process highly subjective. Finally, members of the HP Labs felt little pride in the quality produced, and few ranked it favorably alongside its industrial peers.

HP Labs was staffed with the best and the brightest—an elite cadre of knowledge workers. But the usual inducements of above-average salaries and stock ownership could not keep HP's scientists and engineers down on the farm. In Birnbaum's view, the ship wasn't making much innovative headway, and it was leaking precious talent. Three Rs—redirection, resocialization, and reciprocity—were required to regain momentum.

Birnbaum recognized that he faced an adaptive challenge. He turned to Barbara Waugh, a former public-sector activist, as his partner in the transformation process. He gave her the title of Worldwide Change Manager. Harder to figure out was what the job really entailed and the means to make change happen.

Over the ensuing months, and with the help of many of the lab professionals, Waugh and Birnbaum generated a design for emergence. The architecture of these efforts represents a tour de force for how an organization can employ the ideas of living systems in highly imaginative ways. Among the highlights was the orchestration of a conversation with the lab's 1,200 professionals (300 support personnel and 900 scientists and engineers) to generate a commitment to become the "World's Best Industrial Research Lab."[41] Dozens of bottom-up initiatives and ingeniously designed events provided authenticity and momentum.

Four years into the process, HP Labs was a teeming web of communication in all directions. The vision (or future) of the Labs had inspired five new business platforms with significant financial benefits. Within the Labs themselves, robust criteria and measures had been adapted across the technology divisions and had created first-ever peer comparisons and friendly competition. HP Labs' journey is a landmark in demonstrating the efficacy of the living systems approach and the role of reciprocity in the transformation process.

Barbara Waugh reflected on some of the surprising lessons of that experience:[42]

There were things we did intuitively that proved extraordinarily important. *First,* we learned to keep a low profile, fly below the radar and generally value minimalism. Help happen what wants to happen. Assume resistance and legitimize it as a valid response. Don't try to change it. Go with the innovators and early adopters. Small-scale, short-term efforts, fueled by the passion of people, result in large-scale, long-term transformation. Everett Rogers' work on the diffusion of innovation tells us that when 3 percent of a total population accept an innovation, it won't go away. When that number rises to 15–20 percent, it cannot be stopped. HP's experience reinforces these findings.

Second, circumvent resistance by reframing. Help people see things in fresh ways by setting everything you're working on in its next larger context.

Third, "Be the change you want to see." If we want to see more risk-taking, we must ourselves take more risks. If we want to see more generosity toward others and their ideas, be generous. If we want people to dream bigger dreams, we must dream ourselves. If we want the whole person to come to work, we must bring all of ourselves to work.

Fourth, listening and questioning are more important than speaking and advocating. When we got too hooked on our own agenda, we missed the boat. Not knowing what should happen can be more important than knowing. It gives others the room to create and generate new ideas.

Birnbaum's first move was unusual: He did not share his vision as a statement. He raised the issue of the HP Labs' ambitions as a question. Rather than proselytize, he gathered scientists and support staff together—cynics and believers alike—and asked: "Does anyone want to be 'the best?' What does it mean to be 'the best?'" He hosted these conversations with employees at Town Hall meetings (at which he interacted with almost all employees personally) in California, England, and Japan. A Web site was created to further the dialogue. The comments poured in—all told, 800 single-spaced pages of feedback.[43]

The challenge now became: How do we use this feedback to inform the emergent conversation? Drawing from her previous experience as a social activist, Waugh dusted off a concept called "Readers Theater." In April 1994, the inaugural performance took place. "I selected quotes that represented the major points and passion and character of our folks and wove them into a play about HP Labs," she recalls. "Then I recruited managers to read engineers' lines, engineers to read support staffs', and vice versa. We invited our top three

282 SURFING THE EDGE OF CHAOS

echelons of managers (about forty) to preview the performance. At the end, they were very quiet. Then they began to clap. At the break, their excitement was clear: 'I really got it.' 'I really see what is going on now.'"[44]

The Readers Theater led to, among other things, a radical new approach to the HP Labs' strategic plan. The earlier Town Hall discussions and subsequent feedback had generated a consensus that the level of ambition was too low. Instead of existing solely as a think tank, why not use its diverse disciplines, collective imagination, and intelligence to define a number of new business platforms for Hewlett-Packard? This galvanized the organization. It resulted in hundreds of ideas and initiatives that "came out of the woodwork." The next challenge was to focus them.

As we have seen in earlier examples, coincidences sometimes have startling consequences. The HP Labs had a regularly scheduled meeting of its managerial cadre. Its organizers made a predictable request for an "inspiring speaker." Waugh recounts:[45]

"What if, instead of a great speaker, we had a great listener who could "hear them into speech" about their visions for HP's future driven by the integration of HPL's technologies? I try the idea out. Joel [Birnbaum] doubts the listener idea will be well received, but agrees to preview one.

My partner in the most "out of the box" schemes is our strategic planner. He deeply understands HPL's technologies and the future they could enable. He is totally with me on my latest cockamamy idea. We spend eight hours preparing our Listener-candidate for a half-hour dress rehearsal with Birnbaum's staff. He has them on the edge of their seats in fifteen minutes. He is invited to the offsite.

We go forward and use the inspiring listener at the big event. Senior management sees connections they've never seen before. There are clearly core technologies that span alternative futures. These must be invested in, no matter which future the company pursues. The research agenda is getting clearer.

Following this session, Birnbaum and Waugh considered how to enroll HP's line executives (i.e., the individuals who run HP's businesses) in the "Five Futures." Could the material be presented in a more engaging way than the usual scripted monologue? Waugh narrates how events unfolded:[46]

> At the end of each year, the Labs has its Annual Review. The Lab Directors prepare the standard reports, for the CEO and his staff, on what happened last year and will happen next year. The strategic planner and I remind Joel that our CEO once chided us that "HPL is Disneyland for grownups." Why not play that out? Involve the whole person. Hook the kid inside each of them and pull that energy and perspective into strategic discussions. Joel is skeptical but keeps listening, and agrees to a compromise. We'll do both; in the morning, an abbreviated traditional approach; in the afternoon, Disneyland (i.e., each of the Five Futures given its own room and staged as a theme exhibit). Previewing the Disney-like theme rooms the night before, Joel asks, "Are you sure this will work? It's not too late to cancel . . . ." We try to reassure him it's going to be great, and then stay up three more hours obsessing before we surrender to the possibility that this may be a disaster. (At least we've modeled risk-taking!)
>
> The next day, I shadow the CEO, Lew Platt, as he walks into "HP the medical company," a future driven by HP's potential in medical technologies. He looks around at the skeleton hanging in the back of the room, at the two lab directors in lab coats with stethoscopes, takes a seat, removes his jacket, loosens his tie, stretches his legs. Fifteen minutes later, he is engaged in heated debate about HP's future in medical technology. Not traditional Annual Review behavior! He later tells Joel that this is the best review he's ever attended, and that HPL is giving him the information he and his staff need to really do their jobs—figure out what kind of company HP should be in five years. He and his staff take slides from the presentations and debate the futures for the next six months. All three visions turn into major businesses for HP within the next three years. All this drives more collaborative work across the divisions within the Labs. Lab workload and collaboration increase by 40 percent.
>
> Engaging the whole person, both among line executives and lab staff, we seem to have tapped into much greater creativity for strategic decision making. We wonder: What is lost when individuals at work come only from that subset of themselves we know as "the professional"? Transforming a living system requires tapping the whole person.

As this narrative suggests, by late 1996, the pace of cultural change and innovation at HP Labs had markedly quickened. Many dozens of engineers on cross-functional teams were addressing thorny technological problems. One of Birnbaum's objectives was to fire up junior talent to take more initiative. Waugh, having been exposed to the notion of Positive Deviance through Jerry Sternin's earlier-cited success in Vietnam, decided to introduce the idea to HP Labs:[47]

> Exploit Positive Deviance. Don't begin with imported ideas from the outside or even from above. Try to find what's cooking within the system.
>
> Chandrakant Patel is an engineer in HP Labs. He formed one of the original thirty-six groups that self-organized in the first six months of our vision effort to make HP Labs "the world's best." Noticing that people didn't talk to each other at the coffee machine, he and another engineer decided to create "Chalk Talks"—informal gatherings on Friday afternoons on any preannounced technical or social–technical problem. Over a two-year period, thirty-five talks took place, on everything from how big is the universe to the future of silicon. Some of these topics led to weekly cross-divisional conference calls.
>
> Having introduced a stellar program for the entire division as an entry-level engineer (with no budget and no formal position of authority), Chandra decided to take on the subject nearest to his engineer's heart: thermal transfer inside the computer. No one else in HP Labs cared much for the topic, so Chandra depended on those scattered in other divisions that cared as well. He and six folks, and then others whom they knew, showed up for a two-day conversation. Suddenly there were over 100 people self-organizing on the topic of thermal transfer!
>
> Chandra is one of many great examples of Positive Deviance—how someone in the system can create change despite the system and become a positive deviant for others. As a lone engineer in HP Labs interested in thermal cooling, Chandra sought and found a few others who cared. When they put out the call for a two-day conversation on the topic through E-mail and a Web page, they enabled people all over the system to self-identify as "Positive Deviants" (e.g., people unlike those surrounding them, who were interested in this topic). Once the weak arrows aggregated, they became a strong vector for change. Through phone calls, a newsletter, and an annual conference, they became a powerful agent within the system. No senior manager was involved in driving this change—though quite a few joined the group along the way!

Self-organizing transformation requires a disconcerting break from a more traditional approach. Traditionally, a consultant and leader know a lot and do a lot. They design and facilitate off-sites, charter reengineering teams, develop plans that cascade down through the organization, install systems to make sure all goes as planned. Scorecards report results against commitments. We did very little of this.

We began with not knowing what "the World's Best Industrial Research Lab" might be or how HPL might get there or even if it should. This created a huge empty field on which others were invited to play at any level they chose. Joel and his staff brought the organization into the conversation. The change agent's job is listening, mirroring, making the whole visible to the parts.

Back up a step. What did the initial HP-wide Chalk Talks allow for? Well, everybody present wanted to continue talking at the close of the session, so a small group took responsibility for hosting conference calls every week. What did the conference calls allow for? The core group became the Cool Team. Through constant communication, they created a new model of technology transfer: technology co-creation! All this moved much faster than developing things and throwing them over the wall. Chandra's small group developed proprietary cutting-edge thermal cooling technology. What did this technology allow for? Differentiation in HP's high-end servers that resulted in millions of dollars to the bottom line.

If you ask Chandra, "Did the Chalk Talks deliver millions to the bottom line?" the answer is a resounding "No." On the other hand, if you ask him if the millions would have happened without the Chalk Talks, his answer is, "Probably not!" The paradigm of living systems allows for things to happen. It is not predicated on causality. Paying attention to peripheral activities allows us to nurture activities that might otherwise seem trivial or at best remain sidebars to the main story.

Four years into the journey, HP Labs appeared to have taken an organizational dose of Viagra. There was a vibrant web of communication in all directions. The Labs had inspired a vision for Hewlett-Packard. As noted earlier, significant new business platforms had been launched—digital imaging, automotive, and so on. Cumulatively, these new businesses have contributed in excess of $1 billion in revenues.[48]

HP Labs serves as an appropriate finale for this book. We have echoed earlier refrains here—disturbing equilibrium, surfing near chaos, fostering self-organization and emergence, and, above all, having the wisdom to artfully disturb—but not expect to rationally direct—a living system.

■   ■

Knowledge-based competition demands more of us, not less, and, ironically, the requirements for committed involvement in work will increase in parallel with the insecurity associated with it. Although you may hang your hat at Intel, Sears, Hewlett-Packard, or Shell, where do you hang your heart and your passion to make a difference? What form of reciprocity is necessary to motivate you to go the extra mile to make challenging ambitions possible? There are no shortcuts or easy outs. Just "living fully and contributing generously," in this context, is the ultimate challenge—and it is a dangerous sport.

Each of the seven disciplines can stand alone, but enormous power exists in the relationship among them.

- *Intricate understanding* creates the basis for urgency and evokes action.
- *Uncompromising straight talk* becomes essential both to spur disequilibrium and to cope with a world near chaos.
- *A powerful future* creates an overarching purpose that calls people forth.
- *Inventive accountability* (the blend of reliable performance and improvisation) informs the ways in which self-organization is expressed.
- *Harnessing adversity* helps us learn from the rough spots.
- *Relentless discomfort* sharpens the edge of action and reveals further possibilities.
- *Reciprocity* keeps the living system together in the midst of competing tensions.

Remaining attentive to all these factors at the same time is a draining task. Once practices are in place, however, much is self-sustaining.

Keeping the life in a living system may be hard work, but it is exhilarating, rewarding, and crucial.

ENDNOTES

CHAPTER I

1. Alex Trisoglio, "The Strategy and Complexity Seminar," unpublished, London School of Economics, July 1995, p. 3. This paper is a tour de force on the relationship of complexity to management. It is the best treatment on this subject encountered in the research.
2. See, for example, Mitchell Waldrop, *Complexity* (New York: Simon & Schuster, 1992). For a concise overview, see M. Gell-Mann, *The Quark and the Jaguar* (New York: Freeman, 1994); also, J. Cleveland, J. Neuroth, and P. Plastrik, *Welcome to the Edge of Chaos* (Lansing, MI: On Purpose Associates, 1996).
3. S. Kauffman, *At Home in the Universe* (Oxford, England: Oxford University Press, 1995), p. 37.
4. *Ibid.*, pp. 38–65.
5. For an overview of this issue, see J. Petzinger, "A New Model for the Nature of Business," *The Wall Street Journal*, February 26, 1999, pp. 81–82.
6. There is a considerable literature on these remarkable insects. See Edward O. Wilson, *The Insect Societies* (Cambridge, MA: Belknap Press of Harvard University Press, 1971); also, Edward O. Wilson, *Sociobiology* (Cambridge, MA: Harvard University Press, 1975), pp. 33–37; Richard Conniff, "The Enemy Within," *Smithsonian*, October 1998, pp. 82–96.
7. Conniff, *ibid.*, pp. 92–94.
8. *Id.*, p. 96.
9. *Id.*, p. 92.
10. See Gell-Mann, *supra* note 2, pp. 16–24; also, Waldrop, *supra* note 2, pp. 294–299.
11. H. Sherman and R. Schultz, *Open Boundaries* (Reading, MA: Perseus, 1998), pp. 16, 67; Michael McMaster, *The Intelligence Advantage* (London: Knowledge Based Development, 1995), p. 19; Danah Zohar and Ian Marshall, *Who's Afraid of Schrödinger's Cat?* (New York: Morrow, 1997), p. 103; Trisoglio, *supra* note 1, p. 20.

12. Richard Pascale, conversations with Stuart Kauffman, Santa Fe, NM, July 1998.

13. Peter Katel, "Bordering on Chaos," *Wired,* July 1997, pp. 98–107. Also see Thomas Petzinger, Jr., *The New Pioneers* (New York: Simon & Schuster, 1999), pp. 91–93; Anonymous, "How the Mexican Corporation Cemex Turned into an Industrial Giant," *Le Temps,* October 26, 1999, p. 31.

14. Richard Pascale, notes from Bios Fellows meetings, Santa Fe, NM, July 1998.

15. *Ibid.*

16. Richard Pascale, conversations at Monsanto with Robert Shapiro, Pierre Huchuli, and other senior executives, St. Louis, MO, Fontainebleau, France, and Frankfurt, Germany, September 4, 1997–October 18, 1999.

17. See, e.g., David Stipp, "The Voice of Reason in the Global Food Fights," *Fortune,* February 21, 2000, pp. 164–172; David Stipp, "Is Monsanto Worth a Hill of Beans?" *Fortune,* February 21, 2000, pp. 157–160; Michael Pollon, "Potato 3.0," *The New York Times Magazine,* October 29, 1998, pp. 46–47.

18. T. Petzinger, *supra* note 13, pp. 18–19.

19. Walter Isaacson, "Who Mattered—And Why," *Time,* December 31, 1999, p. 60.

20. Richard Pascale, conversations with change practice consulting teams of Price Waterhouse Coopers and Andersen Consulting, Oxford, England, and Colorado Springs, CO, 1997–1999.

21. Richard Pascale, conversations with David Schneider, Partner, North American Change Practice, Price Waterhouse Coopers, Santa Fe, NM, March 1998; Richard Pascale, Bios Fellows meetings, *supra* note 14; R. Eccles and N. Nohira, *Beyond the Hype* (Cambridge, MA: Harvard Business School Press, 1992), pp. 3–21; Darrel Rigby, "What's Today's Special at the Consultant Café?" *Fortune,* September 7, 1988, p. 162.

22. J. Petzinger, *supra* note 5.

CHAPTER 2

1. Yvonne Baskin, "Yellowstone Fires a Decade Later," *Bioscience,* February 1999, p. 93; Edwin Klester, Jr., "A Town Buries the Axe," July 1999, p. 78.

2. For the Law of Requisite Variety, see W. Ross Ashby, *An Introduction to Cybernetics* (New York: John Wiley & Sons, 1956). On the dangers of equilibrium to a living system, see John Holland, *Hidden Order* (Reading, MA: Addison-Wesley, 1995).

3. Bert Hölldobler and Edward O. Wilson, *The Ants* (Cambridge: The Belknap Press of Harvard University, 1990), p. 179; also Jane Goodall, *Through a Window, My Thirty Years with the Chimpanzees of Gombe* (Boston: Houghton Mifflin, 1990), pp. 211–213.

4. Anonymous, "Dodo," *Microsoft Encarta Encyclopedia 1993–1997;* also see Joel Swerdlow, "Biodiversity: Taking Stock of Life," and Virginia Moreli, "The Variety of Life," joint article in *National Geographic,* February 1999, pp. 27–28.

5. Moreli, *ibid.*, p. 26.

6. D. Depew and B. Weber, *Darwinism Evolving* (Cambridge, MA: MIT Press, 1996), pp. 12–15.

7. Thomas Peters and Robert Waterman, *In Search of Excellence* (New York: Harper & Row, 1982).

8. R. Pascale, *Managing on the Edge* (New York: Simon & Schuster, 1990), pp. 16–17.

9. R. Pascale, conversations with James Cannavino, Dallas, TX, May 1996.

10. Mitchell Waldrop, *Complexity* (New York: Simon & Schuster, 1992), pp. 220, 225–226.

11. Jim Rohwer, "Japan's Debt Bomb Is Scarier Than You Think," *Fortune,* November 9, 1998, pp. 124–126.

12. For a general treatment on Darwinism, see Depew and Weber, *supra* note 6.

13. *Ibid.*, p. 79.

14. Hölldobler and Wilson, *supra* note 3, p. 179; also Goodall, *supra* note 3, pp. 211–213.

15. Richard Pascale, conversations with John F. Welch, Jr., Fairfield, CT, September 16 and October 8, 1983; July 17, August 15, and September 29, 1984; August 28, 1985; June 1 and 13, 1988.

16. *Ibid.*

17. Richard Pascale, conversations with Steve Kerr, Chief Learning Officer, General Electric, Crotonville, CT, Fall 1996.

18. Richard Wolkomir, "Racing to Revive Our Embattled Elms," *Smithsonian,* June 1998, pp. 40–48.

19. David Stipp, "Biotech's Real Power Lies in Reading the Book of Life," *Fortune,* March 31, 1997, p. 55.

20. Barbara Tuchman, *The Distant Mirror* (New York: Knopf, 1978), pp. 94, 196.

21. Alex Trisoglio, "The Strategy and Complexity Seminar," unpublished, London School of Economics, July 1995, p. 24.

22. *Ibid.*, p. 23.

23. *Id.*

24. Michael Hiltzig, *Dealers of Lighting* (New York: Harper, 1999).

25. Danah Zohar, *Rewiring the Corporate Brain* (San Francisco: Berrett-Koehler, 1997), p. 77.

26. Richard Pascale, Interview with Tony Rucci, Vice President of Human Resources, Sears Headquarters, Hoffman Estates, Spring 1995.

27. Gary Hamel, "Strategy as Revolution," *Harvard Business Review,* July–August 1996, pp. 69–82.

28. Depew and Weber, *supra* note 6, p. 6.

29. As quoted by Professor John Sterman, MIT, Cambridge, MA, September 29, 1999, based on Irving Kotz, "Bending Perception, Book Review," *Nature,* 1996, p. 412.

30. Mark Roudebusch, unpublished research on attrition rates of the Fortune 500, San Francisco, CA, 1976–1996.

31. Are de Geus, *The Living Company* (Boston: Harvard Business School Press, 1999), pp. 2–3.

32. Ronald B. Heifetz, *Leadership Without Easy Answers* (Cambridge: Belknap Press of Harvard University Press, 1999), pp. x–xi.

33. *Ibid.*, pp. 2–9, 26–27.

34. Winston Churchill, *History of World War II: The Second World War, the Gathering Storm* (Boston: Houghton Mifflin, 1948), pp. 322–339.

35. *Ibid.*, pp. 549–585.

36. Heifetz, *supra* note 32, pp. 250–276.

37. *Ibid.*

CHAPTER 3

1. Anonymous, "The 25 Top Managers of the Year," *Business Week,* January 8, 1996, p. 54.

2. Richard Pascale, Conversations with Dan Laughlin, V.P. Strategic Marketing, Sears, Hoffman Estates, Illinois, October 1996.

3. Donald R. Katz, *The Big Store: Inside the Crisis and Revolution at Sears* (New York: Viking, 1989), Chapters 1–12; also James C. Warthy, *Sharing an American Institution: Robert E. Wood and Sears, Roebuck* (Urbana, IL: University of Illinois Press, 1989); also Boris Emmet and John E. Jevek, *Catalogues and Counters: A History of Sears, Roebuck and Company* (Chicago: University of Chicago Press, 1950).

4. Katz, *ibid.*, Chapters 13–22; also, Richard Pascale, conversations with Anthony Rucci, Senior V.P., Human Resources, Hoffman Estates, Illinois, October 1996; also, interviews at Sears facilities in California, September 1996. Mark Millemann, conversations with Arthur Martinez, Chicago, Illinois and Phoenix, Arizona, 1993–1995.

5. Patricia Sellers, "Sears: In With the New, Out With the Old," an interview with Ed Brennan and Arthur Martinez, *Fortune,* October 1995, p. 97; also see John Greenwald, "Reinventing Sears," *Time,* December 23, 1996, pp. 53–55.

6. Conversations with Rucci, *supra* note 4.

7. *Ibid.*

8. Richard Pascale interviews at Sears, *supra* note 4.

9. *Ibid.*

10. *Ibid.*

11. *Ibid.*

12. Conversations with Rucci, *supra* note 4.

13. *Ibid.*; also, Millemann, *supra* note 4.

14. *Ibid.*

15. *Id.*

16. Conversations with Rucci, *supra* note 4; also interviews at Sears, *supra* note 4.

17. *Ibid.*, Millemann; conversations with Martinez, *supra* note 5.

18. *Ibid.*

19. *Ibid.*
20. A. Rucci, S. Kirn, and R. Quinn, "The Employee-Customer-Profit Chain of Sears," *Harvard Business Review,* January–February 1998, pp. 68–79.
21. Greenwald, *supra* note 5, p. 54.
22. Millemann, conversations with executives at Sears, Summer 1999.
23. *Ibid.*
24. See for example, Joseph B. Cahill, "Sears Agrees to Plead Guilty to Charges of Criminal Fraud," *Wall Street Journal,* February 19, 1999.

CHAPTER 4

1. See Patricia Shaw, "Intervening in the Shadow Systems of Organizations," *Journal of Organizational Change Management,* Vol. 10, No. 3, 1997, p. 238. For scientific underpinnings to this principle, see discussion of Chris Langton's work in Roger Lewin, *Life at the Edge of Chaos* (New York: MacMillan, 1992), p. 50; also see M. Waldrop, *Complexity* (New York: Simon & Schuster, 1992), pp. 146–147, 222–240; also Murray Gell-Mann, *The Quark and the Jaguar* (New York: Freeman, 1994).
2. Richard Conniff, *Spineless Wonders* (New York: Henry Holt, 1996), pp. 38–56.
3. *Ibid.,* p. 40.
4. D.R. Hofstadler, *Godel, Escher, Bach: An Eternal Golden Braid* (New York: Basic Books, 1979).
5. *Ibid.*
6. R. Conniff, *supra* note 2, p. 42.
7. *Ibid.,* p. 42.
8. *Ibid.,* pp. 46–48.
9. *Ibid.,* p. 46.
10. Quoted in Conniff, *ibid.,* p. 47.
11. *Ibid.,* p. 52–54.
12. Andy Grove, "Managing Segment Zero," *Leader to Leader,* Winter 1995, pp. 15–18. Interestingly, Grove's successor, Craig Barrett, has moved toward the edge early in his tenure with a number of risky bets. See Anonymous, "The New Intel," *Business Week,* March 13, 2000, pp. 110–129.
13. W. Broecker, et al., "20th Century Showdown of Ocean Currents," *Science,* Vol. 286, No. 5442, November 9, 1999, pp. 1132–1135.
14. Lewin, *supra* note 1, pp. 52–54.
15. R. Eccles and N. Nohira, *Beyond the Hype* (Cambridge, MA: Harvard Business School Press, 1992), pp. 3–21.
16. D. Depew and B. Weber, *Darwinism Evolving* (Cambridge, MA: MIT Press, 1996), pp. 12–15.
17. Stuart Kauffman, "Antichaos and Adaptation," *Scientific American,* August 1991, p. 82.
18. *Ibid.,* p. 82.

19. H. Sherman and R. Schultz, *Open Boundaries* (Reading, MA: Perseus, 1998), pp. 16, 67.

20. Tests show humans do best psychologically in an environment that is poised between too much and too little order. See Danah Zohar and Ian Marshall, *Who's Afraid of Schrödinger's Cat?* (New York: Morrow, 1997), p. 103.

21. For a good overview on attractors, see Lewin, *supra* note 1, pp. 19–22. Also see Gell-Mann, *supra* note 1, and Depew and Weber, *supra* note 16, pp. 438–440, on the three types of attractors.

22. See Yahoo Finance, http/biz.Yahoo.com, Profile, Vulcan Materials, NYSE.

23. Strange attractors have a fractal dimension. See Zohar and Marshall, *supra* note 20, p. 158.

24. Whirlpool's vision and objectives is a component of its "Worldwide Excellence System," published 1991.

25. Richard Pascale, conversations with Anthony Athos, Boston, Massachusetts, Fall 1992.

26. T. J. Larkin and Sander Larkin, "Communicating Change," a self-published pamphlet, undated, p. 14; see also R. Pascale, "Crisis and Transformation at Ford," *Managing on the Edge* (New York: Simon & Schuster, 1990), pp. 116–141.

CHAPTER 5

1. See Robert Shapiro's Letter to Shareholders, "Delivering on the Life Sciences Strategy," Monsanto Annual Report, 1998, pp. 2–5. In 1992 when Shapiro embarked on this strategy, they were virtually alone. Also see R. Melcher and A. Barrett, "Fields of Genes," *Business Week,* April 12, 1999, p. 68.

2. As reported by Mike Vinitsky, Director of Organizational Development, Nutrasweet Division of Monsanto, September 1, 1997.

3. Monsanto grabbed large segments of market share from rivals. See Capelli, Kerry, "Healing Novartis," *Business Week,* November 8, 1999, p. 48.

4. R. Pascale, conversations with Robert Shapiro and interviews with Monsanto executives, September 1997, St. Louis, Missouri; also Pascale notes of Shapiro Town Hall Presentation, Big Cedar, Missouri, January 1997.

5. R. Pascale, *ibid.* Also, Pascale notes of video transcript of Shapiro's first Town Hall meeting, Big Cedar, Missouri, January 1997.

6. *Ibid.*

7. *Id.*

8. R. Pascale, conversation with Pierre Hochuli, Director of Research, Monsanto, Frankfort, Germany, October 1999. Also, R. Pascale, notes of Hochuli presentation at INSEAD, May 1999, Fontainebleau, France.

9. *Ibid.*

10. *Ibid.* See especially Hochuli time line for the reinvention process as presented at INSEAD, Fontainebleau, France, May 1999, and at McKinsey University, September 1999.

11. Scott Kilman, "Once Quick Converts, Farmers Begin to Lose Faith in Biotech Crops," *The Wall Street Journal,* November 19, 1999, pp. A1–A8; also John Barry, et al., "Frankenstein Foods," *Newsweek,* September 13, 1999, pp. 33–35; also Amy Barrett, "Fields of Genes," *supra* note 1, p. 65.

12. *Ibid.* Also, see David Stipp, "Less Than A Hill of Beans?" *Fortune,* February 21, 2000, p. 160.

13. Michael Specter, "The Phasmageddon Riddle," *The New Yorker,* April 10, 2000, pp. 64–65.

14. Pascale interviews with Hochuli, *supra* note 8.

15. Michael Pollan, "Potato 3.0," *The New York Times Magazine,* October 25, 1998, p. 51.

16. "Why Ford Came Clean," *Newsweek,* May 22, 2000, p. 50.

CHAPTER 6

1. For general background on Amplifying and Damping Feedback, see Danah Zohar and Ian Marshall, *Who's Afraid of Schrödinger's Cat?* (New York: Morrow, 1997), pp. 93, 145–147.

2. R. Pascale, conversations with John Browne and interviews at British Petroleum Exploration, November 1989–April 1999.

3. *Ibid.*

4. *Id.*

5. *Id.*

6. *Id.*

7. *Id.*

8. *Id.*

9. *Id.*

10. *Id.*

11. For general material on Fitness Landscapes, see M. Gell-Mann, *The Quark and the Jaguar* (New York: Freeman, 1994); see Roger Lewin, *Life at the Edge of Chaos* (New York: MacMillan, 1992), pp. 57–59.

12. R. Pascale, *Managing on the Edge* (New York: Simon & Schuster, 1990), pp. 245–259.

13. Kevin Kelly, "New Rules for the New Economy," *Wired,* September 1997, pp. 192–194.

14. See John Sterman, "Learning in and About Complex Systems," *Systems Dynamics Review,* Vol. 10, No. 2–3, Summer-Fall 1994, pp. 291–330. Also, Peter Senge, *The Fifth Discipline* (New York: Doubleday, 1990), pp. 4–9, chapters 9–12, and J.W. Forrester, *Industrial Dynamics* (Cambridge, MA: MIT Press, 1961).

15. See S. Liebes, E. Sahtouris and B. Swimme, *A Walk Through Time* (New York: Wiley & Sons, 1998), pp. 38–64; also R. Monastersky, "The Rise of Life on Earth," *National Geographic Magazine,* March 1998, pp. 58–81.

16. Liebes, et al., *ibid.,* pp. 74–81; also, Monastersky, *ibid.,* pp. 70–75.

17. Liebes, *ibid.,* pp. 74–81.
18. *Id.*

CHAPTER 7

1. Neil Gross, "The Earth Will Don an Electric Skin," *Business Week,* August 30, 1999, p. 134.
2. Kevin Kelly, *New Rules for the New Economy* (New York: Viking-Penguin, 1998, p. 22.
3. Thomas Petzinger, *The New Pioneers* (New York: Simon & Schuster, 1999), p. 47; also, see Anonymous, "Pushing Adam Smith Past the Millennium," *The Wall Street Journal,* June 21, 1991, p. A-1.
4. See S. Liebes, E. Sahtouris and B. Swimme, *A Walk Through Time* (New York: Wiley & Sons, 1998), p. 32.
5. Ellen Licking, "Getting a Grip on Bacterial Slime," *Business Week,* September 13, 1999, p. 98.
6. Thomas Canby, "Bacteria: Teaching Old Bugs New Tricks," *National Geographic Magazine,* August 1993, pp. 36–60.
7. This description was drawn from research and interviews summarized in R. Pascale, "Tupperware" case study written for classroom discussion, Stanford University, 1984.
8. Catherine Bender, et al., "Predicting the Next Move of Flue Viruses," *Science,* Vol. 286, No. 5446, December 3, 1999, pp. 1921–1925.
9. As quoted in Petzinger, *The New Pioneers, supra* note 3, p. 18.
10. Virginia Morrell, "The Variety of Life," *National Geographic Magazine,* February 1999, pp. 25–26; also, Harriet Rubin, "Only the Pronoid Survive," *Fast Company,* November 1999, p. 331.
11. Brian O'Reilly, "From Intel to Amazon," *Fortune,* April 26,1999, p. 182.
12. Scott Killman, "Once Quick Converts, Farmers Begin to Lose Faith in Biotech Crops," *The Wall Street Journal,* November 19, 1999, pp. A1–A8; David Stipp, "Is Monsanto Worth a Hill of Beans?" *Fortune,* February 21, 2000, p. 160.
13. R. Pascale, Interviews with Richard Heimlich, V.P. Strategic Planning on Motorola's efforts to curtail Japanese dumping, Washington, DC, October 28, 1992.
14. As reported in M. Waldrop, *Complexity* (New York: Simon & Schuster, 1992), pp. 106–108.
15. *Ibid.,* p. 106.
16. *Ibid.,* pp. 110–112.
17. *Ibid.,* p. 112.
18. D. Depew and B. Weber, *Darwinism Evolving* (Cambridge, MA: MIT Press, 1996), pp. 430–432.
19. Kevin Kelly, *New Rules for the New Economy,* op. cit., p. 23; also Petzinger, *supra* note 3, pp. 34–35, 104.

20. David H. Wolpert, et al., "Adaptivity in Agent Based Routing on the Internet," *NASA*-ARC-1C, 1999, p. 122.

21. Kelly, *supra* note 2, p. 16.

CHAPTER 8

1. R. Pascale, Conversations with Dee Hock, Pescadero, California, 1997–1998; also see Dee Hock, "The One-Horned Cow," address to the American Bankers Association, July 18, 1993; also Stewart Dougherty, "Visa International: The Management of Change," case study, Harvard Business School, 1981; also, Mitchell Waldrop, "The Trillion-Dollar Idea of Dee Hock," *Fast Company,* November 1996, pp. 76–86.

2. *Ibid.,* p. 70.

3. Waldrop, *ibid.,* p. 77.

4. R. Pascale, Conversation with Anthony Athos on the Gregory Bateson study of AA, San Francisco, California, April 29, 1997; also see F. Riessman and D. Carroll, *Redefining Self Help* (San Francisco: Jossey-Bass, 1995), pp. 13–52.

5. Pascale interview with Anthony Athos, Boston, Massachusetts, Winter 1993.

6. Pascale interview with Carol Moeller on history of MADD since its founding by Candy Lightner in 1981, Kona, Hawaii, March 1999.

7. F. Riessman and D. Carroll, *supra* note 4, p. ix.

8. Stephan H. Haeckel, *Adaptive Enterprises* (Boston, MA: Harvard Business School Press, 1999), p. 42.

9. Annalee Saxenian, "Lessons From Silicon Valley," *Technology Review,* Vol. 97, No. 5, 1994, p. 42. Also Virginia Postrel, "Resilience vs. Anticipation," *Forbes ASAP,* August 25, 1997, pp. 57–94.

10. *Ibid.,* p. 61.

11. R. Pascale, Conversation with Larry Kanarek, partner McKinsey & Co., Washington, DC, Winter 2000.

12. Virginia Postrel, "How the West Kicked Butt," *Forbes ASAP,* August 25, 1997, p. 55.

13. Postrel, "Resilience vs. Anticipation," *supra* note 9, p. 59. Also, Sanexian, *supra* note 9, pp. 42–51. Also, John Chisholm, "Silicon Valley vs. Route 128," *Unix Review,* Vol. 12, No. 11, October 1999, pp. 15–23.

14. Melanie Warner, "Inside the Silicon Valley Money Machine," *Fortune,* October 26, 1998, pp. 129–138.

15. Postrel, "Resilience vs. Anticipation," *supra* note 9, quoting Paul Koontz, p. 61.

16. R. Pascale, Conversations with General Gordon Sullivan and other Army officers, The Pentagon, Virginia; also at the National Training Center, Barstow, California, April 4–5, 1994, February 13–14 and May 6–7, 1995, and October 29, 1997.

17. George S. Patton, Jr., *War As I Knew It* (Boston: Houghton Mifflin, 1949), p. 357.

18. R. Pascale, Conversations with Sullivan, *supra* note 16.

19. R. Pascale, Conversations at the National Training Center, Barstow, California April 6–7, 1994, February 13–14, 1995, May 6–7, 1995.

20. Steffon Canback, "The Logic of Management Consulting," *Journal of Management Consulting,* 1998, p. 3; also, Jennifer Bresnahan, "The Latest in Suits," *C.I.O.,* p. 174, documents a 20% growth rate per year.

21. Illustrative of the type of media coverage that precedes an emergent issue, see Joan Oreck, "Wanted for Adoptions, Worldwide Standards," *Business Week,* June 14, 1999, p. 21. For documentation of numbers of AIDS orphans in Africa, see Jeffery Barthotel, "The Plague Years," *Newsweek,* January 17, 2000, pp. 34–35.

22. Jasper Becker, "Zhou En Lai's Dark Secrets, *South China Morning Post,* May 26, 1996. Also, Mao's "Little Red Book," *Mao Tsetung, Quotations from Chairman Mao Tsetung* (Peking, China: Foreign Language Press, 1972). On the importance of structure to self organization, see Eric Beinhocker, "Strategy at the Edge of Chaos," *McKinsey Quarterly,* No. 1, 1997, pp. 30–34.

23. See for example Bill Saporito, "The Revolt Against Working Smarter," *Fortune,* July 21, 1986, pp. 58–65. This article and other academic studies trace failure of these programs at General Motors Buick City, General Foods, P&G and Boeing.

24. Reference to Goldilocks and the Three Bears. "The porridge needed to be neither too hot nor too cold." Courtesy of Murray Gell-Mann, quoting Seth Lloyd.

CHAPTER 9

1. B. Gilbert, "Coyotes Adapted to Us, Now We Have to Adapt to Them," *Smithsonian,* March 1991, pp. 68–74.

2. *Ibid.,* pp. 68–74.

3. Douglas A. Blackmon, "FedEx Pilots Trade Their Old Loyalties for a Tougher Union," *The Wall Street Journal,* October 19, 1998, p. A-1. Also see Nicole Harris, "Flying Into a Rage," *Business Week,* April 27, 1998, p. 119.

4. R. Pascale, conversation with FedEx union leadership after strike was cancelled, December 15, 1998; also Blackmon, *supra* note 3, pp. A-1, A-10.

5. See Peter Schuster, "How Does Complexity Arise in Evolution," *Complexity,* 1996, p. 27; also see M. Gell-Mann, *The Quark and the Jaguar* (New York: Freeman, 1994).

6. Thomas H. Davenport, "The Fad That Forgot People," *Fast Company,* November 1999, pp. 71–72.

7. Schuster, *supra* note 5, p. 27.

8. As quoted in Beinhocker, "Strategy at the . . .," p. 32.

9. Niccoló Machiavelli, *The Prince* (New York: Mentor Books of the New American Library, 1952), p. 49.

10. Conversations with Murray Gell-Mann, Santa Fe, New Mexico, July 16, 1999; also see Murray Gell-Mann, "What is Complexity," *Complexity,* 1995, p. 17.

11. Jay Gould, "The Meaning of Punctuated Evolution and its Role in Validating a Hierarchical approach to Macro-evolution," in *Perspectives on Evolution,* R. Milkman, Ed. (Boston: Harvard University Press, 1982) pp. 83–104.

12. This composite account was provided to Pascale by Brian Arthur and confirmed by Michael Brown, former CFO, Microsoft, Santa Fe, New Mexico, summer 1998; also published in Joel Kurtzman, "An Interview With Brian Arthur," *Thought Leaders,* Second Quarter, 1998, Issue 11, p. 99.

13. As quoted in Alex Trisoglio, "The Strategy and Complexity Seminar," unpublished, London School of Economics, July 1995, p. 34.

14. One of the most comprehensive overviews of this topic is provided by Alfie Kohn, "Why Incentive Plans Cannot Work," *Harvard Business Review,* September-October 1993, pp. 54–69; also see Alfie Kohn, *Punished by Rewards* (New York: Houghton Mifflin, 1993). Kohn quotes Deming: "Pay is not a motivator."

15. Frederick Herzberg, *Work and the Nature of Man* (Cleveland: World Publishing, 1966); also see Kohn, *Punished by Rewards, ibid.,* pp. 50–51.

16. This assertion is well defended in Kohn, "Why Incentive Plans Cannot Work," *supra* note 14, pp. 62–63.

17. This example draws extensively from Everett Rogers, *Diffusion of Innovations, Fourth Edition* (New York: The Free Press, 1995), pp. 405–408. It is based on the research of Dr. Pertti Pelto of the University of Connecticut.

18. *Ibid.,* p. 407.

19. *Id.*

20. *Id.*

21. Brian Arthur uses the analogy of a casino. See Brian Arthur, "Increasing Returns and the New World of Business," *Harvard Business Review,"* July-August 1966, p. 104.

22. Brian Arthur in conversation lists frozen accidents; see Brian Arthur, "Positive Feedback in the Economy," *Scientific American,* February 1990, pp. 95–99; also see Lee Gomes, "QWERTY Spells a Saga of Market Economics," *The Wall Street Journal,* February 25, 1998.

23. R. Pascale, conversations with Sun executives, Barcelona, Spain, November 10–11, 1999; also, David Bank, "The Java Saga," *Wired,* December 1995, p. 168.

24. Bank, *ibid.,* p. 243.

25. *Id.*

26. P. Kirkpatrick, "The New Player," *Fortune,* April 17, 2000, p. 166.

CHAPTER 10

1. Ron Winslow, "How a Breakthrough Quickly Broke Down for Johnson & Johnson," *The Wall Street Journal,* September 18, 1998, pp. A-1, A-5; also Pascale conversations with Winslow, November 16, 1998; also Pascale conversations with Robert Gussin, Corporate V.P., Science and Technology, Fontainebleau, France, May 23, 1999.

2. Winslow, *Ibid.,* p. A-5.
3. *Ibid.,* pp. A-1, A-5.
4. *Ibid.,* p. A-5.
5. *Id.*
6. *Id.*
7. *Ibid.,* p. A-5; also R. Pascale, conversation with Robert Gussin, Corporate V.P., Science and Technology, INSEAD, Fontainebleau, France, May 23, 1999.
8. R. Pascale, Conversations and field studies with Jerry and Monique Sternin, Hanoi, Vietnam, Spring 1996, and in Boston, Summer 1997, Fall 1993.
9. *Ibid.*
10. As reported in *Fast Company* interview, Katharine Mieszkowski, "Change—Barbara Waugh," *Fast Company,* December 1998, pp. 146–157.
11. *Ibid.*
12. R. Pascale, interviews with executives at Shell London and The Hague; also, Kuala Lumpur, Prague, Houston, Rouen, France, 1996–1999.
13. R. Pascale, interviews with Steve Miller, London, The Hague, Prague, Houston, October 1997 through June 1999.
14. Pascale interviews with Miller, *ibid.*
15. *Id.*
16. *Id.*
17. *Id.*
18. *Id.*
19. *Id.*
20. *Id.*
21. *Id.*
22. *Id.*
23. *Ibid.;* also Mike Katzenbaum former country chairman of Shell (Greece), London, February 12, 2000.

CHAPTER II

1. This metaphor contributed by co-author Anthony Athos. See Tracy Goss, Richard Pascale, and Anthony Athos, "The Reinvention Roller Coaster," *Harvard Business Review,* November–December 1997, p. 98.
2. Russell Ackoff as quoted in Stephen H. Haeckel, *Adaptive Enterprise* (Boston: Harvard Business School Press, 1999), p. 191.
3. Anne B. Fisher, "Making Change Stick," *Fortune,* April 17, 1995, pp. 121, 124.
4. Fisher, *Ibid.,* quoting Michael Hammer, p. 124.
5. *Ibid.,* p. 122.
6. *Id.*
7. For a general discussion of organizations as a network of conversations, see the pioneering work of Werner Ehrhardt as reported in Perry Pascarella, "Create Breakthrough Performance by Changing the Conversation," *Industry Week,*

July 15, 1987, pp. 50–51. For Lew Platt quote, see John J. Kao, "The Art and Discipline of Business Creativity," *Strategy and Leadership,* July–August 1997, p. 11.

8. As reported in R. Pascale, *Managing on the Edge* (New York: Simmon & Schuster, 1990), pp. 152–153.

9. *Ibid.,* p. 153.

10. Richard Pascale, conversation with Werner Ehrhardt, London, England, Fall 1992.

11. *Ibid.,* p. 137.

12. R. Pascale, conversations with Stuart Pimm, Santa Fe, New Mexico, July 25, 1998; also Kevin Kelly, *Out of Control* (Reading, MA: Addison-Wesley, 1994), pp. 57–64.

13. Kelly, *ibid.,* p. 61.

14. *Ibid.,* p. 62.

15. *Ibid.,* p. 61.

16. Michael A. Hiltzik, *Dealers of Lightening: Xerox PARC and the Dawn of the Computer Age* (New York: Harper Collins, 1999). Also see Xerox PARC website.

17. Everett Rogers, *Diffusion of Innovations* (New York: Free Press, 1995), pp. 357–363.

18. Block as quoted in Pat Dillon, "Failure Is Just Part of the Culture of Innovation," *Fast Company,* December 1998, p. 137.

19. R. Pascale, conversations with Steve Miller, London, The Hague, Prague, Houston, October 1997 through June 1999.

20. *Ibid.*

CHAPTER 12

1. Video interview of Benoit Mandelbrot, *Fractals, The Colors of Infinity* (New York: Newbridge Communications, 1997).

2. Margaret J. Wheatley, *Leadership and the New Science* (San Francisco: Berrett-Koehler, 1992), pp. 83, 114–115.

3. R. Pascale, *Managing on the Edge* (New York: Simon & Schuster, 1990), pp. 116–141.

4. CFI data as presented by Anthony J. Rucci, Senior V.P. Human Resources, Sears, at New York Human Resources Institutes' 25th Anniversary Conference, February 1997.

5. Earnings of Mall Stores vs. Sears' card.

6. Conversations with Anthony Rucci, V.P. Human Resources, Sears, Chicago, October 1996.

7. R. Pascale, *Managing on the Edge, supra* note 3, pp. 51–87.

8. Alan Weber, "Learning for Change," *Fast Company,* May 1999, p. 178.

9. Richard Pascale, *Patterns of Conflict Management,* Europe and U.S., unpublished 1995.

300 ENDNOTES

10. R. Pascale, field notes of Japan visit with Intel, Tokyo, Fall 1986 and 1988.

11. R. Pascale, conversation with Craig Barrett, *ibid.*, 1988.

12. R. Pascale, conversation with David Shrigley, *ibid.*, 1988.

13. Allen R. Myerson, "Marathon Man of the Atlanta Games," *The New York Times,* February 29, 1996, p. B.1.

14. Joel Kurtzman (Ed.), "Interview with Billy Payne," *The Art of Taking Charge,* September 1997, pp. 1–7.

15. *Ibid.*, p. 6.

16. David Greising, "The Virtual Olympics," *Business Week,* April 29, 1996, p. 650.

17. Kurtzman, *supra* note 14, p. 7.

18. Paul Roberts, "Group Genius," *Fast Company,* October–November 1997, p. 214.

19. Winston S. Churchill, *The History of World War II, Their Finest Hour* (Boston: Houghton Mifflin, 1949), pp. 134–135.

20. James C. Collins and Jerry I. Porras, "Building Your Company Is Vision," *Harvard Business Review,* September–October 1996, p. 60.

21. Susan Carey, "A Call to Mr. & Mrs. CEO," *Wall Street Journal,* April 28, 1999, p. A-1.

22. *Ibid.* Also see Susan Carey, "U.S. Criticizes Northwest Air's Actions During Blizzard," June 3, 1999, p. A-4.

23. Screenplay of *Five Easy Pieces.*

24. Frederick F. Reicheld, "Learning from Customer Defections," *Harvard Business Review,* March–April 1996, p. 60.

25. Pat Dillon, "Failure Is Just Part of the Culture of Innovation," *Fast Company,* December 1998, p. 136.

26. Dillon quoting Sam Walton, *ibid.*, p. 136.

27. This notion is discussed in depth in James C. Collins, "Turning Goals into Results: The Power of Catalytic Mechanisms," *The Harvard Business Review,* July-August 1999, pp. 71–83.

28. For an excellent discussion of Capital One see Philip Anderson, "Seven Levels for Guiding Enterprise" in John Henry Clippinger III (Ed.), *The Biology of Business* (San Francisco: Jossey-Bass, 1999), pp. 141–151.

29. *Ibid.* p. 142.

30. *Ibid.* p. 144.

31. *Ibid.* p. 148.

32. *Ibid.* p. 147.

33. *Id.*

CHAPTER 13

1. Anonymous, "Rewards Make Monkeys Helpful," *Washington Post,* April 1, 2000, p. A-5.

2. James C. Collins, "Built to Flip," Fast Company, March 2000, p. 139.

3. Roy Oldenberg, *The Great Good Place* (New York: Paragon House, 1991), pp. xv, 4.
4. *Ibid.*, for quote see p. xv. For characteristics of Third Place, see pp. 22–55.
5. *Ibid.*
6. Florida, April 10, 1997. Also, Peter F. Drucker, *Managing in Times of Great Change* (New York: Dutton, 1995), pp. 256–257, 275–276, 344.
7. John Seely Brown, "The People Are the Company," *Fast Company,* November 1995, p. 80.
8. Joel Kurtzman, "An Interview with Jeff Pfeffer," *Thought Leaders,* Third Quarter 1998, pp. 85–93.
9. Linda Grant, "Happy Workers' High Returns," *Fortune,* January 12, 1998, p. 8.
10. Drawing upon John Seeley Brown's quote of William H. Whyte, Jr., *The Organization Man* (New York: Simon & Schuster, 1956), pp. 129–131.
11. See David Sanger and Steve Lohr, "The Downsizing of America," *New York Times,* March 9, 1996; also Elizabeth Lesly and Larry Light, "When Layoffs Won't Turn the Tide," *Business Week,* December 7, 1992, pp. 100–101.
12. *Ibid.*, p. 101.
13. Carol J. Loomis, "AT&T Has No Clothes," *Fortune,* February 5, 1996, pp. 77–80.
14. Lesly and Light, *supra* note 11, p. 101.
15. Mike Johnson and Mark Thomas, "Getting a Grip on Tomorrow," Human Resource Management Conference, Paris, France, April 1997.
16. See Jaclyn Fierman, "The Contingency Workforce," *Fortune,* January 24, 1994, p. 306; also Daniel Pink, "Free Agent Nation," *Fast Company,* December-January 1998, pp. 132–134; also James Ally, The Temp Biz Boom: Why It's Good," *Fortune,* October 16, 1995, pp. 53–56; also James Ally, "Where the Laid-Off Workers Go," *Fortune,* October 30, 1995, pp. 45–47.
17. Fierman, *ibid.*, p. 31.
18. John A. Byrne, "Has Outsourcing Done Too Far?" *Business Week,* April 1, 1996, pp. 25–27.
19. Joe Klein, "Rob Reich's Job Market," *Newsweek,* March 7, 1994, p. 33.
20. Peter F. Drucker, *Managing in a Time of Great Change, supra* note 6, pp. 76–91.
21. *Ibid.*, p. 71.
22. For details on Nissan's philosophy at its plant in Sunderland, England, see R. Pascale, Field Notes at the Sunderland Factory, January 25, 1994; also Peter Wickens, *The Ascendant Organization* (London: Macmillan, 1995). For Toyota, see Roger Trapp, "Toyota," *Human Resources,* March-April 1996, pp. 8–10; also, Paul Adler, "Time-and-Motion Regained," *Harvard Business Review,* January–February 1993, pp. 97–108.
23. Conversation with Colonel Michael H. Harper, Executive Officer to Chief of Staff General Gordon Sullivan, The Pentagon, Virginia, March 1994.
24. Shelly Branch, "You Hired 'Em But Can You Keep 'Em," *Fortune,* March 1998, p. 248.

25. Kenneth Labich, "America's Best CEOs," *Fortune,* May 2, 1994, pp. 43–52; also see Kevin Kelly "Southwest Flying High with Uncle Herb," *Business Week,* July 3, 1998, pp. 53–55.

26. Wendy Zellner, "Southwest's New Directions," *Business Week,* February 8, 1999, pp. 58–59.

27. K. Brooker, "Can Anyone Replace Herb?" *Fortune,* April 17, 2000, pp. 186–192.

28. Susan Chandler, "United We Own," *Business Week,* March 18, 1996, pp. 96–100; also see Aaron Bernstein, "Why ESOP Deals Have Slowed to a Crawl," *Business Week,* March 18, 1999, pp. 1012.

29. Chandler, *ibid.,* p. 97.

30. *Ibid.,* p. 97.

31. *Id.*

32. *Ibid.,* pp. 98–99.

33. *Id.*

34. *Ibid.,* p. 99.

35. *Id.*

36. Thomas Stewart, "Brain Power: Who Owns It, How They Profit From It," *Fortune,* March 17, 1997, pp. 107–112.

37. Aaron Bernstein, "Working Capital: Labor's New Weapon," *Business Week,* September 29, 1997, pp. 110–112.

38. Michael S. Malone, "Killer Results Without Killing Yourself," *Fast Company,* November 1995, p. 129.

39. *Ibid.,* pp. 125–132.

40. *Ibid.,* p. 132.

41. Richard Pascale, conversations with Barbara Waugh, Palo Alto and Pescadero, California, Spring 2000; also Barbara Waugh, "Lead from Below," unpublished, May 2000.

42. Pascale, conversations with Barbara Waugh, *Ibid.*

43. *Ibid.*

44. *Id.*

45. *Id.*

46. *Id.*

47. *Id.*

48. Barbara Waugh and Kirstan Cobble, "Self Organized Transformation," unpublished, 1997, pp. 3–6.

49. Conversation with Waugh, *supra* note 41.

ACKNOWLEDGMENTS

A book of this nature tells what you have thought. It does not tell what you have lived.

As the primary writer and one of three thought-partners in the undertaking, mine is a journey in three parts. Part One began as I was delivering a keynote address in Prague in 1995. Gathered beneath the towering arches and restored Baroque decoration were three hundred representatives of business, government, and academic institutions from Asia, Europe, and the United States. As in many parallel conferences around the world, they had come in quest of insight into organizational revitalization and renewal. The agenda featured a generally upbeat array of success stories and the latest new renewal technique.

The lecture hall reeked of history, and no doubt, had borne witness to similar gatherings centuries ago when this building stood as a towering architectural feat of the Middle Ages. I asked the audience to visualize a session of physicians, patients, and healers convened in this auditorium to discuss the alleviation of illness and the improvement of human health. Without microphone and modern visual aids, perhaps there was testimony from a prominent physician on the latest breakthroughs in blood-letting as a treatment for "humours," a patient extolling the curative power of salt baths in alleviating consumption, perhaps a panel of healers describing the potions and prayers which lessened risks from childbirth. Would one voice have punctured this optimism: "Is there any hard evidence that we're making progress in extending human life?" While systematic data were not collected on human longevity, it is estimated the average lifespan for men was 42, and for women 32 (owing largely to the hazards of childbirth).

Periodic outbreaks of the plague actually worsened these averages. It would take centuries of rigorous investigation within the health sciences before significant strides could be made in altering these dire statistics. Medicine learned to demand tough-minded proof of efficacy before a cure was widely adopted.

Fast forward to our twentieth century conference. Were a similar question asked today about our track record in sustaining the vitality of healthy organizations (or restoring the vitality of those in decline), the answer would be equally troubling. Notwithstanding the proliferation of concepts and consultants, surveys have repeatedly shown that 70% to 80% of renewal attempts fail and that corporate longevity is actually decreasing. The average life of a western company today is 35 to 40 years—half that of a human life in developed societies. These statistics offer stark testimony to our woeful inadequacy. What passes for expertise in organizational renewal is often anecdotal, consulting propaganda, or just plain wrong.

The experience at the Prague Conference gave shape to a troubling question: perhaps neither the sellers of organization renewal (the authors and consultants), nor the buyers (the corporate executives) really know what they are doing to achieve successful corporate reinvention. Management fads continue to come and go. Meanwhile last year's management fads become about as appealing as yesterday's sushi. We abandon the old, gulp down the new, and the hunger remains unslacked.

The experience in Prague crystallized the quest for better maps, frameworks, and tools. This paved the way for Part Two of the journey which unfolded in collaboration with co-authors Mark Millemann and Linda Gioja. As the writer and academic member of the team, my role was to capture the ideas that arose from a sequence of meetings over the next several years. As practicing consultants, my colleagues provided fresh new ideas, grounded in failed and successful change efforts. One result was an article on organizational agility in the *Harvard Business Review* (November–December, 1998). These ideas are fully developed in Chapters 11, 12, and 13.

Part Three of the story began when co-author Linda Gioja gently but persistently advocated an important body of ideas emerging from the Santa Fe Institute. My initial reaction to these topics (an investigation into the common properties of all living things) was one of thinly veiled disdain. It is difficult to discover, let alone mine, new veins of managerial insight. Many seemingly promising leads veer off into labyrinthine tunnels. More often than not, this results in short-lived management jargon—rich in metaphor but weak in practical relevance. So, I politely ignored the Santa Fe suggestion and tilled more traditional ground.

Coincidence intervened. The sudden illness of a keynote speaker led to an invitation to lecture at the Santa Fe Institute's business network. I accepted on the condition that the topic be: "The Irrelevance of Complexity Science to Management." A provocative discussion ensued. The Santa Fe Institute invited me to join as a visiting scholar. Two years, and deep immersion into the literature on Complexity later, outlines of relevance began to take shape in the fog. These became the cornerstone principles and organizing theme of this book.

I am enormously indebted to many individuals. First among these is Nobel Laureate Murray Gell-Mann, whose patience and critique of early drafts shaped the book in a significant way. During my time at Santa Fe, Brian Arthur and Stuart Kauffman also provided encouragement and substance.

As the writing itself progressed, I benefited enormously from the editorial support of Morris Coyle (whose eye for the logical flow of ideas and redundancies is unerring), and founding partner Donna Carpenter (whose strategic sense for communicating ideas and command of English contributed to a far clearer presentation). Random House editor, John Mahaney, was involved in this work from its inception and has made a significant personal contribution. Others who have read and suggested many improvements are Andersen Consulting partners Reinhart Zeigler and Donald Chartier, Jerry Sternin, and Ann Carol Brown. I also wish to thank Dr. Constance

Sewing for her invaluable research assistance, and Barbara Kaufman for her extraordinary labors to bring this book to print.

Finally, I wish to thank several executives with whom I worked personally and whose stories form the illustrative backbone of this book. Monsanto's Robert Shapiro was an early pioneer in applying the living sciences to organizational renewal. His successful application of these ideas in transforming Monsanto's culture was an important factor in fueling my willingness to give Complexity a second look.

I also wish to thank Army Chief-of-Staff General Gordan R. Sullivan and his Executive Officer, Colonel Michael V. Harper for the invitation to observe their pioneering efforts in applying the ideas of living systems to the military context. Their hospitality went well beyond threshold courtesies extended to researchers. They supported several visits to the Army's National Training Center to observe the translation of these ideas to battlefield conditions.

I am indebted to Steve Miller, Managing Director of Royal Dutch Shell's worldwide oil products business, a courageous executive who became a true partner in exploring the relevance of these ideas to a large global corporation. I wish to thank British Petroleum CEO, Sir John Browne, and Intel's Chairman, Andy Grove, for opportunities to work with them during defining moments in the evolution of their respective companies. These were formative episodes in my thinking about the challenges of leadership and renewal. Finally, a special thanks to GE's Jack Welch who, over the several years of our work together, became one of the most influential teachers of my adult life.

Richard Pascale
The Five Star Ranch
Pescadero, California

This book has been a work in progress for over six years. As such, it represents the collective intelligence of countless people who have contributed to and influenced our thinking, and who have touched us. We realize that in singling out some, we run the risk of unintentionally overlooking others.

First and foremost, we want to thank our colleagues and kindred spirits at The DiBianca-Berkman Group—Dave Laveman, Peter Blake, Tom D'Aquanni, Anton Lahnston, and Laura Pedro. The firm's work and commitments sourced our early thinking. Colleagues empowered us to explore and develop many of the foundational concepts which underlie the authors' current thinking. It was during our association with The DiBianca-Berkman Group, that the enduring concept of operating state was developed. A very special heartfelt thanks to Bob Berkman and Vince DiBianca. As the firm's founding partners, they had the strength of conviction to free us up to work on the early formulations of this book—to make, what was for a small firm, a substantial financial commitment to underwrite our work.

The acquisition of The DiBianca-Berkman Group by CSC Index accelerated the next phase of our inquiry. Index, consistent with its tradition of innovation, provided a vital laboratory for the generation of new ideas. The concepts of "organizational agility" and the "disciplines of agility" took form. Allan Cohen and Jane Mermelstein, colleagues at CSC Index, were cohorts from the very beginning. They were instrumental in forwarding the concepts of agility—within CSC Index and in the marketplace. Special thanks to Allan, for his many contributions, particularly the concept of designing for emergence as a "design of the present"; and to Jane for her perseverance under tough circumstances. Key leaders within CSC Index (at that time) befriended and supported the exploration of agility: Tom Waite, Don Arnoudse, Bob Dantowitz, Steve Hoffman, Judy Rosen, Gary Gulden, Nick Vitalari, Jim Kennedy, and Bob Morison. And a very special thanks to Dave Robinson and Ron Christman for their executive sponsorship of the authors' inquiry and commitment to necessary investments.

Practical consulting experience grounded our thinking. Client leaders made immense contributions to our learning: John Fiedler and Geraldine Kinsella, Arthur Martinez and Tony Rucci, Steve Dorfman and Don Cromer, Jorge Tavares and Jeff Franks, Jack Gherty, Robert Sachse, Larry Haab and Dave Butts, Stan Bunn, Rich Sonstelie, and many others.

We also thank the State of the World Forum for supporting us in developing bold expressions of these ideas and for the opportunity to explore them with world leaders in a wide and deep global context.

We are indebted to colleagues—and friends—who contributed enormously, who collaborated with us, who took instrumental roles in client work: Gary Taylor, Marie Case, Jack Gilbert, Blaire Larson, Francois Austin, Philippe Declerck, Carolyn Hendrickson, Dan Miller, and Richard Howells.

A special thanks to those who have been instrumental in encouraging us—propping us up in those dark moments: Gary, Marie, Francois, Kate, Nancy, Diane, Patricia, Millie, Rachel. Thank you Donna and Glenda.

To the memory of a dear friend, Margaret Nichols, for her passion as the Superintendent of Schools in Eugene, Oregon.

While colleagues, clients, and friends made immense contributions, it is always families that allow us to pursue our dreams. We dedicate this book to them. To Patricia and Geoffrey for their selflessness, persevering encouragement and love, and their gifts of marriages that nurture the self-expression that work can be. And to Zoe, Toby, and Amber for the inspiration they are for us, Zoe's willingness to share a mother and Toby and Amber's willingness to share a father.

Linda Gioja
Mark Millemann

INDEX

ABOUT THE AUTHORS

Richard T. Pascale is the coauthor of *The Art of Japanese Management* and author of *Managing on the Edge*. He has written for *The Harvard Business Review* and for twenty years was on the faculty of the Stanford Business School. He is now an associate Fellow of Oxford University, a writer, and a consultant.

Mark Milleman was a senior advisor to CSC Index and has extensive experience working with CEOs and executive teams of companies around the world, including Sears, Hughes Space and Communications, BP Oil, Borg Warner Automotive, and the Illinois Power Company. He is the founder of Millemann and Associates, a management consulting firm based in Portland, Oregon.

Linda Gioja has consulted with CEOs and executives at such companies as Allstate, Sears, and Hughes Space and Communications. She now leads dialogues in national policy forums at the Aspen Institute and for the California Environmental Dialogue, a group of more than twenty energy companies, automakers, high-tech companies, and environmental organizations working on the state's environmental policy. She lives in Austin, Texas.